MW01106137

Empathy and the Strangeness of Fiction

Readings in French Realism

Maria C. Scott

EDINBURGH
University Press

Edinburgh University Press is one of the leading university presses in the UK. We publish academic books and journals in our selected subject areas across the humanities and social sciences, combining cutting-edge scholarship with high editorial and production values to produce academic works of lasting importance. For more information visit our website: edinburghuniversitypress.com

Edinburgh University Press Ltd
The Tun – Holyrood Road
12(2f) Jackson's Entry
Edinburgh EH8 8PJ

Typeset in 10.5/13 Adobe Sabon by
Servis Filmsetting Ltd, Stockport, Cheshire

A CIP record for this book is available from the British Library

ISBN 978 1 4744 6303 4 (hardback)
ISBN 978 1 4744 6305 8 (webready PDF)
ISBN 978 1 4744 6306 5 (epub)

Contents

Imagination [is characterised] by the feeling of strangeness and by empathy.
Edward Bradford Titchener, *A Beginner's Psychology* (1915)

Chapter 1

Does Reading Fiction Boost Empathy? Psychological Approaches

Fiction and the Empathy Question

For a long time, it has been suspected that exposure to fiction, and particularly literary fiction, has a valuable social function. This is one of the reasons why novels and short stories have featured, historically, on school curricula, why prison reading groups are considered a good thing and why student doctors can be required to read novels as part of their training.[1] Efforts to quantify the social effects of engagement with fiction – often understood narrowly as narrative fiction in prose, or even more narrowly as literary prose fiction, but also regularly understood to include film and television drama – have become intensive over the past two decades.[2] Various studies have found that people who engage frequently with fiction tend to have better social cognition or empathy than those who do not.[3] As this wording suggests, preliminary experiments only proved correlation, rather than any causal relation, between exposure to fiction and capacity for empathy; in other words, it was possible that fiction-readers performed better on empathy tests simply because empathetic people are more likely than others to be drawn to fictional stories, rather than because fiction actively nurtures empathy. From 2012 onwards, however, psychological studies began to point more forcefully towards the existence of a causal link between exposure to fiction and the development of empathy.[4]

One 2013 Dutch study, entitled 'How Does Fiction Reading Influence Empathy?', set out to ascertain whether the experience of emotional transportation while reading fiction would produce a measurable change in participants' empathy levels one week after the event.[5] This study proposed that fiction-readers who experienced emotional transportation while reading were likely to have integrated, over the following days, the fictional world into their own mental and emotional universes, thereby opening themselves up to the possibility of change. Using a standard self-reported empathy test, the degree of 'empathic concern' of each participant was measured directly before, directly after and one week after reading either a narrative fiction or a newspaper account. The study indicated that readers who had reported high levels of emotional involvement in the fictional story also reported an increase in their level of empathic concern one week later.[6] The results of this study appeared to indicate causal links between emotionally involved fiction reading and higher levels of empathy.

A second 2013 study, this time conducted by an American social psychologist and his then PhD student, sought to identify any improvements in 'understanding others' mental states' brought about by reading short passages of literary fiction.[7] Over the course of five experiments, where participants were tested, for example, for their ability to ascribe appropriate feelings to photographs of eyes or to cartoon representations, it was found that the ability to make suitable inferences about the thoughts and feelings of others was significantly higher in cases where participants had just read a passage of literary fiction, but not in cases where they had read non-literary fiction, non-fiction or nothing at all. For various reasons, the results of this second study were controversial.[8] Nevertheless, among the rash of attention-grabbing headlines that followed this latter study were 'Reading Literary Fiction Improves Empathy, Study Finds', 'For Better Social Skills, Scientists Recommend a Little Chekhov', 'Reading Literary Fiction Improves "Mind-Reading Skills"' and 'Now We Have Proof Reading Literary Fiction Makes You a Better Person'.[9] As this list of benefits suggests, there was little agreement among lay commentators about what exactly had been proven by the American study, or even about what was being measured: was it empathy, social skills, mind-reading skills or altruism?

Part of the problem is that empathy has many different facets, and can be understood in different ways. The Dutch and American studies had set out to measure different variants of empathy. The first had focused on identifying causal links between emotional involvement in fiction (which happened to be literary) and increases in self-reported empathic concern, while the second had assessed the relationship between reading (specifically literary) fiction and the ability, known as 'Theory of Mind' (ToM), to infer another person's motivations, thoughts or feelings, an ability also known as mind-reading.[10] ToM is considered crucial for successful social interaction but bears no necessary relation to altruism, or to being a 'better person'.[11] Some cognitive scholars argue that it is deployed when interpersonal situations are too complicated to be handled using simple stereotypes and norms of behaviour. If empathic concern and ToM are both aspects of empathy, how can empathy be defined?

The word 'empathy', which first appeared in English in the early years of the twentieth century, comes from the German term 'Einfühlung' (in-feeling, or feeling into), first used by the philosopher Robert Vischer in 1873 as an aesthetic concept; it described a 'projection of the self into the object of beauty'.[12] The term, in both its English and German versions, originally denoted an ability to feel oneself into an external object, person or situation. The preposition 'into' characterises many definitions of both 'Einfühlung' and 'empathy'. Edward Titchener, the individual most often credited for translating the German term into English as 'empathy', in or around 1909, explained it as follows: 'We are told of a shocking accident, and we gasp and shrink and feel nauseated as we imagine it; we are told of some new delightful fruit, and our mouth waters as if we were about to taste it. This tendency to feel oneself *into* a situation is called empathy.'[13] Despite its close links to aesthetics, *Einfühlung* or empathy was also theorised as a way of accessing other people's minds. In the 1920s, Edmund Husserl defined empathy as follows: 'The intentionality in one's own ego that leads into the foreign (*fremde*) ego is the so-called empathy.'[14] According to the psychologist Lauren Wispé, indeed, 'the hard-core meaning of *Einfühlung*/empathy has always been the process whereby one person "feels her/himself into" the consciousness of another person'.[15]

The term 'empathy' grew out of the older concept of 'sympathy', both terms implying a feeling *with* the other person; however, sympathy tends now to describe a feeling *for*, rather than the feeling *into* that characterises empathy.[16] It is worth noting, though, that the philosopher Adam Smith had, in the eighteenth century, theorised sympathy as an imaginative entry *into* another person's body. He offers by way of example the experience of watching our 'brother' undergo physical torture:

> By the imagination we place ourselves in his situation, we conceive ourselves enduring all the same torments, we enter as it were into his body, and become in some measure him, and even feel something which, though weaker in degree, is not altogether unlike them. His agonies, when they are thus brought home to ourselves, when we have thus adopted and made them our own, begin at last to affect us, and we then tremble and shudder at the thought of what he feels.[17]

Sympathy was understood by Smith to be a moral feeling, close to compassion. However, empathy has no necessary link to altruism; it is well known that sadists, interrogators and con artists use their empathy for purposes that have little to do with compassion or generosity. The moral case for empathy is also undermined, as Paul Bloom has argued, by the biases and lack of judgement that can characterise it: 'The spotlight nature of empathy renders it innumerate, favoring the one over the many and the specific over the statistical.'[18]

From its beginnings, empathy was bound up with feeling more than thinking, even while the notion that empathy is underpinned by cognitive processes is also widely accepted. Empathy tends in fact to be defined quite broadly by psychologists, often taking in not just cognitive perspective-taking (the ability to imagine another person's situation from that other person's perspective rather than from one's own perspective) but also sometimes motor mimicry, emotional contagion, sympathy and personal distress. Some scholars include, while others exclude, automatic, 'low-level' processes, those that might be considered instances of motor mimicry. Others either include or exclude mentalising or 'higher-level' processes. Some include while others exclude personal concern and compassion. In other words, there is no absolute consensus, in the psychological literature, on the question of what empathy is. In most cases, however, it is understood to involve at least the illusion[19] of a sharing, on the part of a self, in the affective experience of an other, a foreign consciousness. Frans de Waal and Stephanie Preston, for example, define empathy very broadly as 'any process where the attended perception of the object generates a state in the subject that is more applicable to the object's state or situation than to the subject's own prior state or situation'.[20]

The notion that empathy involves a form of sharing now has a grounding in neuroscience. In the 1990s, an Italian research group published their discovery of the existence of 'mirror neurons' in macaque monkeys: it appears to be the case that the same family of premotor neurons activates in the brain of the observer of an action as in the brain of the performer of the action.[21] The discovery of mirror neurons has had exciting implications for experimental work on human empathy.[22] It has now been shown, for example, that appropriate motor neurons become activated in a person not only when she observes an action but also when she reads about an action.[23] This sharing or mirroring response is not necessarily automatic because the brain appears to regulate empathic response. This cognitive regulation of empathy explains why, in the absence of any social cognitive disorder, the observer remains aware of a self/other difference despite the illusion of sharing or identification.[24]

The centrality of both identification and cognition to empathy is highlighted by the Oxford English Dictionary, which defines empathy as the 'power of mentally identifying oneself with (and so fully comprehending) a person or object of contemplation'. While it is true that, as Terry

Eagleton notes, 'identification and comprehension are not necessarily on such intimate terms with each other as this might suggest',[25] it tends to be agreed by psychologists that empathy is 'a multidimensional process' that incorporates two 'dimensions', namely 'mentalising', or 'the ability to understand what others are thinking or feeling', and 'emotional sharing', which 'includes the capacity to emotionally resonate with other people's feelings'.[26] Empathy would, according to this definition, include comprehension of other people, or what are sometimes called mind-reading skills. The literary scholar Suzanne Keen writes, in this vein, that 'human mind reading and emotion sharing abilities' are 'the mechanisms underlying empathy'.[27]

Affective sharing and mind-reading are therefore interrelated, though not identical, skills. According to one way (often called the 'simulation theory') of conceptualising mind-reading, mental states are inferred on the basis of the observer's un-theorised internal replications of the observed or imagined person's inner state. The 'theory-theory' account of mind-reading, by contrast, holds that inference, or theorising, constitutes a necessary first step towards understanding other people, including any possibility of shared affect.[28] In either case, however, close connections are understood to exist between mind-reading, on the one hand, and affective sharing, on the other. Briefly, from a 'theory-theory' perspective, affective sharing is dependent upon mind-reading to the extent that it is inspired by inferences about another person's inner state, while from a 'simulation theory' point of view mind-reading is dependent upon affective sharing insofar as inferences about another person's inner state are understood to be informed by a mental identification with his or her perspective. While it is difficult to separate affective sharing from mind-reading in any absolute way, then, scholars do tend to maintain a distinction between the two phenomena (or sets of social skills). The first tends to be understood as identificatory in character, and the latter as inferential.[29] This book will retain a terminological distinction between the illusion of affective sharing and mind-reading (or mentalising). The distinction can also be framed as that between 'mindfeeling' and mind-reading,[30] sharing and inference or identification and comprehension, and it can be found as readily in Adam Smith's description of the operation of sympathy as in the work of cognitive neuroscientists.[31] For the purposes of this book, the crucial distinction will be between a form of empathy that involves an affective sharing (or illusion thereof) between self and other, and an inferential capacity, which is also a variant of empathy, that presupposes a mental distance from the other.

The reason why this book will retain a distinction between affective sharing and mind-reading, and the reason why this distinction is being stressed here, is that it is precisely in the intersection and interplay between these two arguably different but interlinked modes of inter-subjective relation that the specificity of the encounter with narrative fiction will be located. It is true, as already suggested, that this distinction is somewhat artificial. However, distinguishing between affective sharing and mind-reading, as the two broadly constitutive components of empathy, will allow us to suggest, on the basis of our own particular approach to the question, informed by both literary theory and close textual analysis, that one of the key skills imparted by literary fiction, and possibly by all fiction to some extent, is the ability to navigate between, or combine, a (broadly) identificatory and affective relation to the other and a reflective distance from the other. Our argument will be that narrative fiction invites the reader to engage in a complex negotiation between the two mental positions, a negotiation that can play out thematically in the story itself. In fact, it is this experience of moving between absorption and distance that this book will theorise as central to the encounter with narrative fiction, and that it will analyse in relation to a small number of narrative fictions.

The remainder of this chapter will present some brief notes about the role given by psychologists and cognitive scholars to affective sharing and mind-reading, respectively, in the encounter with fiction. It will then show how scientific studies have linked the interaction of affect and reflection to modifications of the reader's subjectivity in the course of fiction-reading.

Affective Sharing and Mind-Reading in the Encounter with Fiction

Empathy has often been considered by psychologists to play a role in the experience of reading; indeed, the degree to which one is inclined to identify imaginatively with fictitious characters in books, movies and plays is one of the standard measures of empathy in the social sciences.[32] Consequently, the term 'empathy' tends to be applied by psychologists to an ability to share in the feelings or thoughts of others, even where those others are fictional. For example, Raymond Mar and Keith Oatley observe that 'in much of literature, the author challenges readers to empathise with individuals who differ drastically from the self'.[33] Indeed, it has been argued that a self-reported tendency to be drawn into a story, or 'to really empathise with fiction', is 'an independent predictor of empathy ability' in the real world.[34] The relationship between a reader's ability to share in the implied feelings of fictional others and his or her levels of empathic concern in the real world was the focus of the Bal and Veltkamp study discussed at the beginning of this chapter.

I have suggested that empathy can be understood as a form of affective sharing between self and other. This definition would appear to be borne out by psychological studies of the operation of empathy in the course of fiction-reading. One research group has described the experience of reading fiction as productive of a 'self–other merging' that renders others less easy to perceive in reductive, objectifying terms: 'a story blurs the boundary line between the self and the other'.[35] The psychologists Maja Djikic and Keith Oatley have written the following of the mental processes involved in reading: 'we set aside our own goals and concerns, somewhat as a person does who is starting a session of meditation, and we take on the concerns and intentions of [the character] [. . .] [W]e can become metaphorical. By identification we can become a literary character.'[36] One serious psychological study even found that readers laid claim to characteristics associated with either wizards or vampires after reading fictions involving one or the other.[37]

This book will suggest that while fiction does indeed produce the illusion of affective sharing, it also engages the vigilance of readers, so that any perceived blurring of the self–other boundary is temporary only. It will argue that fiction invites readers' vigilance by activating a skill that, for many scholars, constitutes a complementary component of empathy: Theory of Mind.

As already noted, psychologists have produced evidence that regular readers of fiction, and particularly literary fiction, not only tend to score higher in ToM tests, but score higher in these tests precisely because they read fiction. In support of the general argument that fiction enhances mind-reading skills, neuroscientists have recently shown that the areas of the brain that are activated by mental processes associated with story comprehension are also activated when the brain makes inferences about people in real life, which suggests that every time an individual reads, watches, or hears a story that presents intersubjective scenarios, whether or not the narrative can be characterised as literary or artistic, he is exercising parts of the brain that are necessary for social interaction.[38]

Kidd and Castano, authors of the high-profile 2013 study that appeared to show, for the first time, that individuals who are given a piece of literary fiction to read produce better results in subsequent ToM tests than their fellow test participants, attributed their finding to the peculiarly high demands that literary fiction places on its readers' cognitive skills. Literary fiction, they argue, fosters understanding of others, 'because it forces us to engage in mind-reading and character construction'.[39] In a subsequent essay, Kidd and Castano speculate that literary fiction is particularly constructive of ToM 'because the implied (rather than explicit) sociocognitive complexity, or *roundness* of characters, in literary fiction prompts readers to make, adjust, and consider multiple interpretations of characters' mental states'.[40]

Cognitive scholars have explored in a granular way how particular fictional texts engage the mentalising capacities of readers. For example, the cognitive film scholar David Bordwell has analysed the ways in which films lend themselves to be understood by viewers, who make inferences on the basis of conventional cues.[41] The cognitive literary scholar Lisa Zunshine has argued that narrative fiction is centrally concerned with Theory of Mind, observing that 'the novel, in particular, is implicated with our mind-reading ability to such a degree that [. . .] in its currently familiar shape it exists because we are creatures with ToM'.[42] Not only do fictional characters regularly interpret verbal and visual cues about the intentions and desires of other characters, but readers too are consistently obliged to make inferences about the feelings and intentions of characters. Zunshine has argued that fiction, and literary fiction in particular, habitually involves a significantly higher level of 'sociocognitive complexity' than our everyday lives, or indeed than non-fictional discourse.[43] In short, Zunshine argues that the reason we read fiction, and specifically literary fiction, is 'because it engages, in a variety of particularly focused ways, our Theory of Mind'.[44]

While the argument that reading novels exercises, and even potentially builds, mind-reading skills is a compelling one, one of the key arguments of this book will be that fiction also crucially highlights the limits of our ability to know other people. One theorist of literary narrative has noted, in response to Zunshine's idea that novels offer 'perfect access to other people's minds via observable behavior', that 'literary works also offer [. . .] the more melancholy, yet just as familiar, confrontation with characters' and our own opacity, obtuseness, inconsistency, and duplicity'.[45] It should be noted that Zunshine herself at least partially subscribes to this arguably more pessimistic understanding of why we read fiction with her contention that 'literary narrative builds on our capacity for mind-reading but also tries its limits', and particularly with her observation that literary fiction can sometimes leave us with the suspicion that other minds can 'harbor secrets'.[46] This book will suggest, indeed, that insights into the opacity of human minds are at least as central to fiction as are its lessons in mind-reading.

Fiction and Self-Change

The relation between affective sharing and mind-reading in the reception of narrative fiction has been under-explored, to date, by psychologists and cognitive scholars, who tend to treat affective sharing and mind-reading as straightforwardly complementary skill sets. It has been speculated, for example, that 'a ready capacity to project oneself into a story may assist in projecting oneself into another's mind in order to infer their mental states'.[47]

The interaction of affective sharing and mind-reading in the encounter with fiction may not have been adequately studied yet, but the way in which a combination of affect and reflection can produce self-change has been the focus of considerable attention in recent years. It has been argued that the experience of empathy with fiction can challenge pre-existing belief structures, at least to the extent that affective sharing is accompanied by reflection. The cultural scholar Kimberley Chabot Davis has proposed, for example, that fiction-reading can make readers more open to difference in others 'when empathetic connections are accompanied by critical reflection, when thought and feeling combine to result in a critique of racism and a deeper respect for cultural difference'.[48]

A number of different hypotheses relating to self-change in the context of fiction-reading have been put forward by scholars working in the field of psychology.

Richard Gerrig, for example, has explored the way in which narrative (whether fictional or not) can metaphorically, but also phenomenologically, 'transport' readers to different times and places. He has proposed that these experiences of narrative transportation can affect a person's belief structures in lasting ways.[49] Gerrig has also argued, along with David Rapp, that 'readers who report greater experiences of being transported to narrative worlds will show more of an impact of those experiences on their attitudes and beliefs'.[50] A number of empirical studies have supported this observation. For example, one found that 'individuals who were more highly transported into a narrative showed greater belief change'.[51] Fundamental to the notion of narrative transportation (closely bound up with phenomena such as 'projection', 'adhesion', 'immersion', 'engagement', 'absorption', 'experience-taking', 'identification') is the notion of affective sharing (even if the feelings shared are not those imputable to a particular fictional other but rather those provoked by the situation of that fictional other).[52] However, it has been proposed that narrative transportation needs to be accompanied by reflection if the encounter with fiction is to bring about self-change. Gerrig and Rapp suggest, for example, that the extent to which a reader's 'everyday life' will be changed by an encounter with a fictional work 'will depend in part on the effort readers expend to disbelieve the story'.[53] In a broadly similar vein, Oatley argues that narrative transportation, insofar as it implies passive absorption, is more closely associated with escapist than with transformative reading. According to him, it is only to the extent that the reading process becomes active or projective, allowing the reader to become 'the writer of his or her own version of the story', that it can actively 'change the self'.[54] It may be that literary or artistic styles of narrative fiction invite such a combination of transportation and active reflection more consistently or successfully than other types of fiction. This is the point of view adopted by Oatley and Mitra Gholamain, who propose that while genre (or non-literary) fiction encourages 'escapist reading' and a 'merging with fictional characters', literary fiction encourages an attitude of aesthetic distance by including 'something that prevents complete merging'. According to this argument, encounters with literary fiction can prompt 'useful' or 'transformative' identification by encouraging a combination of 'engagement with and detachment from literary characters' which gives rise to potentially transformative 'reflections'.[55]

Psychologists have also proposed that fiction may effect change in the reader through the estranging operation of artistic form upon the emotions and the mind. In other words, the strangeness of literary language, its habit of defamiliarising the reader through the use of unusual stylistic devices (also known as foregrounding), may produce an unusual alertness in the reader. In 1994, the psychologist Don Kuiken and the literary scholar David Miall worked together on an empirical study that supported their hypothesis, partly inspired by the work of Russian Formalists such as Viktor Shklovsky, that literary form acts upon the psyche by activating the reader's 'self-modifying feelings': 'foregrounding prompts defamiliarization, defamiliarization evokes affect, and affect guides "refamiliarizing" interpretive efforts'; in other words, their study supported the notion that 'the distinctive language of literature fosters changes in the way we understand our personal life-worlds'.[56] Other scholars too have argued that it is the degree of perceived artistry that is decisive for self-change. One team of psychologists found, for example, that a Chekhov short story produced more pronounced self-reported fluctuations in the personality traits of readers than the same content presented in a documentary style.[57] The authors deduced that something about 'artistic form' can produce 'subtle shifts' in how the psyche represents itself. Oatley and Djikic, who formed part of that team, claim that literary fiction has the potential to change those who engage with it because it involves what Kierkegaard called 'indirect communication', different from persuasive modes of communication because more ambiguous and open-ended, requiring the reader to think for him or herself, in a 'nondirective' way, along unprescribed routes.[58] One laboratory study of reflective responses to different types of narrative tentatively indicated that 'literary texts evoke a deeper kind of reflection than other texts'.[59] The author of this study argues elsewhere, with Frank Hakemulder, that literary texts, partly on account of their defamiliarising effects, elicit a 'stillness', a slowing down of reading, that is conducive to 'self-reflection', or reflection centred on the self.[60]

In sum, two broadly different arguments are regularly made by psychologists and empirical scholars of literature about how narrative fiction effects change in its readers. On the one hand, it has been argued that a reader's attitudes and beliefs might be changed because fictional narratives invite an imaginative transportation that allows the reader's (or viewer's) established personality and beliefs to become temporarily unfixed, particularly if this experience of transportation is combined with active reflection. The notion of transportation-induced self-change plays an important role in the Bal and Veltkamp study of causal links between fiction-reading and empathic concern that was discussed at the beginning of this chapter. A second overarching hypothesis is that de-familiarising artistic effects can serve to trigger the reader's (or viewer's) affects and thoughts, by inducing a 'feeling of things becoming "strange"'.[61] This idea played a supporting role in the argument presented by Kidd and Castano, in the second study discussed at the start of this chapter, on the links between literary fiction and mind-reading.

Whether self-change takes place, then, on account of a reader's involvement in a story, or alternatively because of responses triggered by artistic defamiliarisation, psychologists and empirical scholars of literature appear to agree that any self-change that occurs as a result of reading narrative fiction arises from an interaction of affect and reflection, prompted by an encounter with difference or otherness.[62] The interaction between affective and reflective processes that is prompted by an encounter with otherness will be the focus of this book's study of the dynamics of fiction-reading. On the basis of its close readings, this study will effectively propose a third model for the interaction of affective involvement and reflection in the potentially transformative experience of fiction-reading: in this version, the relationship between affect and reflection is at least provisionally antagonistic. Affective sharing, in the encounter with narrative fiction, will be metaphorically associated with seduction, and implicitly aligned with 'narrative empathy',[63] while the form of reflection privileged in this study will be mind-reading, which will often take the form of suspicion. This book will suggest that the fictions it examines bring affective sharing and mind-reading into productive conflict, both at the thematic level and at the level of reception.

One of the purposes of this book is to argue that close readings of narrative fictions can complement psychological approaches to the question of how fiction-reading engages empathy. This book is an attempt to elaborate a hermeneutic model, based on close textual analysis, that might make a useful contribution on the part of non-empirical, non-cognitive literary studies to an area of investigation that has been commanding much attention in the field of psychology. The term 'fiction' will be used throughout this book primarily to denote narrative texts, in verbal form, that have been framed as works of fiction, but it will also be understood to extend to film and television drama ('reading' will therefore be intended to imply the idea of viewing), and will even occasionally include imaginative invention and ruse more generally, in accordance with the etymological roots of the term 'fiction' (Latin *fingere*, meaning to shape, fashion or feign).[64] Fictional narratives understood to be 'literary' in style will be given privileged status as objects of study, but there is no necessary reason why any conclusions drawn about these could not also apply to non-literary and even non-verbal fictional forms, just as there is no necessary reason to perceive the privileged narratives as literary.[65]

My previous published work has often explored the identificatory dynamics of reading, but has tended to situate itself on stable disciplinary ground, sometimes invoking philosophical ideas but never venturing outside of traditional humanist frames of reference. It has almost always addressed itself to specialists and students of nineteenth-century French literature. By choosing now to engage with current research in psychology while using the methodologies and, to a certain extent, the received wisdom of my home discipline, I am running the risk that any psychologists who take up this book will find its evidence unconvincing, while literary scholars will feel irritation at being told, in an unnecessarily convoluted way, what they know and practise already. However, my hope is firstly that, by adopting a partly strange (because partly external) perspective in my analysis of three texts, I can produce some reflections that will be of interest to literary scholars, both within nineteenth-century French studies and beyond, and secondly that I might persuade psychologists interested in the fiction–empathy relationship that, as a particularly self-conscious version of the very activity that they are studying, close reading can offer insights into how, and even possibly why, narrative fiction engages our empathy.

Notes

1. For a robust recent argument in favour of the importance of literary education at secondary school for the formation of thoughtful, empathetic and ethically minded citizens, see Alsup, *A Case for Teaching Literature*. On reading narrative fiction in prisons, see Billington, '"Reading for Life"'. On the rationale for the teaching of literary fiction as part of a medical training, see McLellan and Jones, 'Why Literature and Medicine?', as well as the special issue of *Academic Medicine* (78.10 (2003)) devoted to the role of the humanities in the teaching of medicine.
2. Previous empirical studies of the social or moral effects of narrative fiction do exist, however. For an overview, see Hakemulder, *The Moral Laboratory*.
3. See for example Mar et al., 'Bookworms versus Nerds' and Mar et al., 'Exposure to Media'. For a 'meta-analysis' of the recent scientific work in this area, see Mumper and Gerrig, 'Leisure Reading'.
4. Despite its highly suggestive title, one study was careful not to conclude that a causal relationship exists between reading fiction and an increase in either affective empathy or prosocial behaviour. Johnson, 'Transportation into a Story'. Another study involving the same author argued somewhat more forcefully for a causal link between the generation of mental imagery while reading and increases in empathy and prosocial behaviour. Johnson et al., 'Potentiating Empathic Growth'. In a third study, it was found that test participants who reported low levels of the personality trait of 'Openness to Experience' went on, after reading a short story, to report higher levels of perspective-taking skills, using Mark H. Davis's Interpersonal Reactivity Index. See Djikic et al., 'Reading Other Minds'.
5. Bal and Veltkamp, 'How Does Fiction Reading Influence Empathy?'.
6. Interestingly, and perhaps worryingly, however, the experiment also showed a deterioration in empathy after one week among fiction-readers who reported low levels of emotional transportation, suggesting that 'fiction reading might have negative effects' where transportation does not occur. Bal and Veltkamp, 'How Does Fiction Reading Influence Empathy?', p. 8. This book uses the terms 'empathic' and 'empathetic' interchangeably, though the former is more current in scientific contexts.
7. Kidd and Castano, 'Reading Literary Fiction'.
8. Koopman notes that the 2013 study 'Reading Other Minds' (see note 4) found no effect of fiction-reading on the Reading the Mind in the Eyes Test (RMET), and points out that 'Kidd and Castano (2013) did not measure what features of the literary texts were responsible for effects nor whether readers' personal characteristics play a role.' 'Empathic Reactions after Reading', p. 65. A number of independent research groups, furthermore, have replicated Kidd and Castano's experiment without finding any causal link between reading a passage of literary fiction and improved RMET performance. See for example Panero et al., 'Does Reading a Single Passage'. Kidd and Castano, in response, highlighted alleged flaws in these replications ('Panero et al.'), points that Panero and others subsequently contested ('No Support for the Claim'). See also Stansfield and Bunce, 'The Relationship between Empathy and Reading Fiction', which

urges caution in 'concluding that reading fiction is the cause of changes in empathy' (p. 17). The findings of Kidd and Castano have, however, been successfully replicated by a number of subsequent studies: see Pino and Mazza, 'The Use of "Literary Fiction"'; Kidd et al., 'On Literary Fiction'; and Black and Barnes, 'The Effects of Reading'. Interestingly, Black and Barnes also found, in a separate study, that watching award-winning TV drama boosted ToM, suggesting that 'fiction in film as well as print facilitates theory of mind'. 'Fiction and Social Cognition', p. 428.

9. <https://www.theguardian.com/books/booksblog/2013/oct/08/literary-fic tion-improves-empathy-study>; <https://well.blogs.nytimes.com/2013/10/ 03/i-know-how-youre-feeling-i-read-chekhov/?_r=1>; <https://www.scien cedaily.com/releases/2013/10/131003142621.htm>; <https://www.theatlan tic.com/entertainment/archive/2013/10/now-we-have-proof-reading-liter ary-fiction-makes-you-better-person/309996/> (all last accessed 19 October 2019).

10. The narrative fictions selected by the Dutch duo were of the type recognised as literary, and this may not be an insignificant detail, given that the authors of the second study found that literary fictions produce particular social effects. A subsequent 2016 study by Kidd and Castano showed that 'famili-arity with authors of literary, but not authors of genre fiction, predicted participants' performance on the RMET, a well-validated and widely used measure of ToM'. 'Different Stories', p. 9.

11. It has been found that psychopaths show no deficiency in this skill. Richell et al., 'Theory of Mind and Psychopathy'. A recent study found that 'ToM was not involved in altruistic sharing' among children. Liu et al., 'Altruistic Sharing Behavior', p. 222.

12. Wispé, 'History of the Concept of Empathy', p. 18.

13. Titchener, *A Beginner's Psychology*, p. 198.

14. Cited in Zahavi, *Self and Other*, p. 125.

15. Wispé, 'History of the Concept of Empathy', p. 34. For a detailed history of the concept of empathy, see Lanzoni, *Empathy*.

16. A distinction between the two terms is maintained by most scholars today, and empathy is more likely than sympathy to be designated as feeling *with*. Suzanne Keen defines empathy as 'the spontaneous, responsive sharing of an appropriate feeling', and sympathy as 'the more complex, differentiated feeling for another'. Keen, *Empathy and the Novel*, p. 4. However, Kirsty Martin, in her study of sympathy, refrains from making any 'absolute distinction' between the two phenomena (*Modernism*, p. 9), and Sophie Ratcliffe observes that '"sympathy" in its common vernacular usage still includes the notion of feeling *with* another person' (*On Sympathy*, p. 19). For a useful overview of the history of sympathy and empathy, see the introduction to Hammond and Kim, *Rethinking Empathy*.

17. A. Smith, *The Theory of Moral Sentiments* [1759], pp. 2–3.

18. Bloom, 'Empathy and its Discontents', p. 25. Fritz Breithaupt too argues in *The Dark Sides of Empathy* against any close connection between empathy and morality, and instead makes a case for empathy on the basis of the aesthetic and emotional awareness it enables.

19. References in this book to 'identification' or 'affective sharing' should be

understood always to mean 'the illusion of identification' and 'the illusion of affective sharing'.

20. De Waal and Preston, 'Empathy', p. 4. For an analysis of the mechanisms involved in empathy, including reservations about any folk notion of magical fusion, see Mellmann, 'Objects of "Empathy"', pp. 431–7.
21. See Goldman, *Simulating Minds* for a brief summary of these findings.
22. See for example de Vignemont and Singer, 'The Empathic Brain' and Iacoboni, 'Within Each Other'.
23. Speer et al., 'Reading Stories'.
24. On this point, see Decety and Jackson, 'A Social-Neuroscience Perspective'. Most scholars, indeed, insist that self–other boundaries remain in place in the experience of empathy. See for example de Vignemont and Singer, 'The Empathic Brain'. The philosopher Amy Coplan, too, maintains that the self–other distinction persists in empathy as she defines it ('Understanding Empathy', pp. 15–17). On the same point, see also Coplan, 'Empathic Engagement', pp. 144–5. The philosopher Martha Nussbaum, similarly, notes that empathy 'involves a participatory enactment of the situation of the sufferer, but is always combined with the awareness that one is not oneself the sufferer'. *Upheavals of Thought*, p. 327.
25. Eagleton, *Trouble with Strangers*, p. 76.
26. Pino and Mazza, 'The Use of "Literary Fiction"', p. 1.
27. Keen, 'A Theory of Narrative Empathy', p. 207. However, Keen also describes empathy as 'a vicarious, spontaneous sharing of affect', thereby distinguishing it from mind-reading (p. 208).
28. This binary distinction has been problematised in various ways. For an overview of the debate, and a consideration of how the phenomenological tradition of philosophy offers an alternative model of social cognition, see Zahavi, 'Empathy'.
29. This distinction has sometimes been cast in terms of 'hot' and 'cold' empathy, or 'simulative-emotional' and 'distanced-analytical'. See Breithaupt, 'A Three-Person Model', p. 84.
30. M. Smith, 'Empathy', p. 114.
31. See for example Shamay-Tsoory et al., 'Two Systems for Empathy'. This study highlights the interaction of two distinct neural systems for understanding other people's mental states.
32. The Interpersonal Reactivity Index (IRI) includes 'fantasy', or 'respondents' tendencies to transpose themselves imaginatively into the feelings and actions of fictitious characters in books, movies, and plays', as one of its four scales; the others are perspective-taking, empathic concern and personal distress. Davis, 'Measuring Individual Differences', p. 114.
33. Mar and Oatley, 'The Function of Fiction', p. 181.
34. Mar et al., 'Exploring the Link', pp. 421, 422. However, another recent study appears to indicate that 'story-induced empathy [. . .] is not strongly related to tendencies to feel affective empathy in the real-world'. In other words, the ability to identify with literary characters is not necessarily related to empathic capacity in the real world. See Stansfield and Bunce, 'The Relationship Between Empathy and Reading Fiction', p. 16.
35. Johnson et al., 'Changing Race Boundary Perception', p. 83. See also Djikic et al., 'Opening the Closed Mind' and Johnson, 'Transportation into

Literary Fiction'. This latter study, like Bal and Veltkamp's the same year, found that 'empathic growth', after reading literary fiction, was linked to the degree of transportation (p. 87).

36. Djikic and Oatley, 'The Art in Fiction', p. 502. On identification and sympathy with fictional characters as two of the processes involved in encounters with narratives, see also Oatley and Gholamain, 'Emotions and Identification'. Another psychological study of the operation of 'character identification' in reading or viewing a narrative suggests, similarly, that 'we can become what we consume'. Sestir and Green, 'You Are Who You Watch'.
37. Gabriel and Young, 'Becoming a Vampire'.
38. See Mar, 'The Neural Bases' and Tamir et al., 'Reading Fiction'.
39. Kidd and Castano, 'Reading Literary Fiction', p. 377.
40. Kidd and Castano, 'Different Stories', p. 10. The authors are here citing Lisa Zunshine.
41. See for example the study of *Mildred Pierce* in Bordwell, *Poetics of Cinema*, pp. 135–50.
42. Zunshine, *Why We Read Fiction*, p. 10.
43. Zunshine, 'From the Social to the Literary', p. 178.
44. Zunshine, *Why We Read Fiction*, p. 162.
45. Korthals Altes, *Ethos and Narrative Interpretation*, p. 35. The Zunshine quotation is from *Why We Read Fiction*, p. 72. More generally, Korthals Altes contends that uncertainty and ambiguity in relation to the ethos of a narrative drive the ethical work of the interpreter.
46. *Why We Read Fiction*, pp. 27, 20. Indeed, Zunshine's *Strange Concepts* argues that narratives can subvert our cognitive tendency to essentialise and stereotype, creating a sense of uncertainty, ambiguity and strangeness.
47. Mar et al., 'Exploring the Link', pp. 421, 422.
48. Davis, 'Oprah's Book Club', p. 414.
49. Gerrig, *Experiencing Narrative Worlds*. For Gerrig, narrative transportation is 'virtually inevitable', and occurs 'with limited conscious effort' (p. 238).
50. Gerrig and Rapp, 'Psychological Processes', p. 267.
51. Green and Brock, 'In the Mind's Eye'. For the aesthetic philosopher Schaeffer, too, imaginative immersion in fictions can produce a displacement of our mental universe. *Petite écologie*, pp. 107, 111.
52. According to Stansfield and Bunce, 'the more people are transported by a story, the more affective empathy they experience while reading' ('The Relationship between Empathy and Reading Fiction', p. 16). There are subtle differences between the various phenomena listed here. For Kuiken and others, for example, empathy, identification and transportation are produced by narrative features of a text and absorption by stylistic elements; see Kuiken et al., 'Locating Self-Modifying Feelings', p. 268. However, what is implied in all cases is a high level of involvement in the reading or viewing experience, accompanied by a degree of self-forgetting. One study goes so far as to observe that 'experience-taking requires that individuals completely transcend self–other boundaries to become the other', and 'experience-taking depends on the relinquishing of the self-concept, which should facilitate the assumption of the other's thoughts, feelings, and traits'. Kaufman and Libby, 'Changing Beliefs and Behavior', pp. 2, 3.

53. Gerrig and Rapp, 'Psychological Processes', p. 269.
54. Oatley, 'Emotions', p. 43.
55. Oatley and Gholamain, 'Emotions and Identification', p. 280. See also Oatley, 'Emotions'. A similar point is made by Kuiken et al. ('Forms of Self-Implication', p. 179), who argue, after the literary theorists Wolfgang Iser and Mikhail Bakhtin, that it is in the shifts between various transient identifications with characters or narrators in the course of reading a narrative that self-change can occur. Koopman, 'Effects of "Literariness"'. Another empirical study warns, however, that readers can be trained by their schooling to respond to literary texts in an analytical way, at the expense of a more richly self-implicating reading experience that would combine cognitive and affective response. Mangen et al., 'Empathy and Literary Style'.
56. Miall and Kuiken, 'Foregrounding', p. 404; Miall and Kuiken, 'Beyond Text Theory', p. 351. On 'self-modifying feelings', see also Miall and Kuiken 'A Feeling for Fiction'; Kuiken et al., 'Forms of Self-Implication'; Kuiken et al., 'Locating Self-Modifying Feelings'.
57. Djikic et al., 'On Being Moved by Art'.
58. Djikic and Oatley, 'The Art in Fiction'. See also Oatley and Djikic, 'Psychology of Narrative Art'.
59. Koopman, 'How Texts about Suffering', p. 438.
60. Koopman and Hakemulder, 'Effects of Literature', pp. 101–2. These conclusions about links between specifically literary reading and self-change are reminiscent of the thesis of the literary theorist Kristeva in *La Révolution du langage poétique*; for her, avant-garde poetics have the potential to destabilise and renew the foundations of the reading subject. These findings are also compatible with a point made by the cultural theorist Gayatri Chakravorty Spivak: 'The literary text gives rhetorical signals to the reader, which lead to activating the readerly imagination. Literature advocates in this special way. These are not the ways of expository prose.' 'Ethics and Politics', p. 22.
61. Koopman and Hakemulder, 'Effects of Literature', p. 94. Aesthetic distance has also been associated with the inhibition of affect.
62. In one study, Koopman found that non-fictional, sentimental life-narratives tended to trigger more thoughts, in participants, than literary narratives on similar topics (though, as noted, literary narratives appeared to elicit deeper reflections). Koopman concludes that both formal and affective features of a narrative can evoke reflection. Koopman cites a range of empirical studies whose results 'imply that when we are emotionally shaken up' by a story, 'we feel a need to contextualise that experience, probing us to reflect'. 'How Texts about Suffering', p. 432. In a similar vein, Oatley suggests that reflections can be prompted by a combination of emotional response and the use of defamiliarising techniques, or 'transformational language'. Oatley, 'Emotions', p. 55.
63. The term 'narrative empathy' will be used to designate the kind of empathy invited by narrative fiction. See Keen, 'A Theory of Narrative Empathy'.
64. For reflections on the etymology of the word 'fiction', see Lang, *Délit de fiction*, pp. 27–49.
65. Contemporary theorists tend to agree that a text is designated as literary if

it is collectively held to have particular value, but that the criteria for attributing value are subject to variation. For some interesting reflections on this theme, see Jouve (ed.), *La Valeur littéraire*. My own study privileges literary fictional narratives, and gives fiction the central role, without analysing whether it is the literary, fictional or narrative dimension of the texts that is most decisive. By contrast, one empirical scholar, in her approach to the question of empathy effects, valiantly separates out narrative, fiction and literariness. Koopman, 'Does Originality Evoke Understanding?'.

Chapter 2

Literary Approaches to Empathy

Reasons for Reticence

While the idea that fictional works have ethical value dates back to Aristotle at least, the recent empirical evidence, outlined in our first chapter, that they nurture empathy and social understanding seems likely to be welcome news for the literary scholar. Teachers of literature, including teachers of literature in a foreign language, like myself, are often required by their managers, and more generally by the laws of the market, to package what they do in the language of employability and transferable skills, so scientific evidence for the quantifiable benefits of studying novels must surely be welcome. However, while it is true that various literary specialists have, in recent years, contributed meaningfully to the debate about whether engagement with literature can improve the empathy of readers,[1] there is not yet much local evidence that university departments of English and modern languages are rewriting their prospectuses or projected learning outcomes to incorporate the new evidence that engagement with literary fiction can enhance the empathic capabilities and social cognition of their students. What explains this apparent modesty?

At first glance, reticence seems an odd attitude. The novel has, after all, been closely associated with the cultivation of sympathy, a forerunner and occasional near-synonym of empathy, for a very long time. George Eliot wrote, for example, that 'the greatest benefit we owe the artist, whether painter, poet or novelist, is the extension of our sympathies'. For Eliot, art (including novels) offers 'a mode of amplifying experience and extending our contact with our fellow-men beyond the bounds of our personal lot'.[2] It is nonetheless true that literary scholars do not generally embrace the argument that reading novels makes us more empathetic. This reluctance can be caricatured as intellectual snobbery; it has been argued for example by one prominent commentator that literary scholars consider the idea of 'the reading of fiction as an empathy expander and a force toward humanitarian progress' to be 'too middlebrow, too therapeutic, too kitsch, too sentimental, too Oprah'.[3] Let us analyse this alleged phobia of the middlebrow and the sentimental on the part of literary scholars.

Firstly, every student and specialist in the field of literary studies knows that the very first rule of being a good reader is the maintenance of a degree of critical distance. This rule has tended to push to one side, in academic discussions of literature, the idea that we respond emotionally to fictional characters. In fact, it has long been assumed that the feelings aroused by literary fiction are of no interest whatsoever to the literary critic: affective responses are, as Wimsatt and Beardsley once influentially put it, 'no concern of criticism, no part of criteria'.[4] This antipathy towards emotion on the part of the literary critic, never entirely uncontested (in 1974, the literary theorist Hans Robert Jauss argued that 'only an aesthetic snob' could discount the role of emotion in aesthetic reception), is now seriously diminished.[5] Some critics have even begun to argue that critical suspicion has become hackneyed, and to advocate a return to a form of critical naivety: 'perhaps the time has come to resist the automatism of our own resistance, to risk alternate forms of aesthetic engagement'.[6] Suzanne Keen maintains that 'narrative theories of fictional character should accommodate evidence of readers' empathy (and other emotional responses to fiction reading)',[7] while Terence Cave has asserted that 'it hardly needs to be said that it is empathy that allows us to engage so deeply in the lives of fictional characters, and indeed to bring them to life in the first place. It is a precondition of immersion in stories and songs and poems, and not least, of course, in the mimesis of drama.'[8] While there is, then, evidence that the situation is changing, many literary scholars continue to be reluctant to foreground or even acknowledge their own affect-laden relationships to the texts they study and teach. Even among those recent literary scholars who engage with psychological approaches to the study of literature, naive or emotional responses to fiction can be problematic. For example, a reader who momentarily forgets that the characters on the page are not, in fact, real people is a victim of what Zunshine describes as 'cognitive slippage'.[9] While every reader knows that a really good story can draw us in and appeal to our most naive selves, it continues to be difficult for many literary scholars to attribute value to participatory or immersive modes of reading.

A second reason for resistance, on the part of traditional literary scholars, to the notion that reading or viewing fiction nurtures empathy stems from a deep-rooted (though, again, continually contested) rejection of the idea that literature should be made to serve a social or therapeutic or morally improving agenda. To highlight the cultivation of empathy as an important function of literary fiction is to suggest that a novel's value might lie in its social or moral effects rather than in its formal, intrinsic qualities. Statements by psychologists, such as 'the function of fiction is to abstract and simulate the social world', which suggest an instrumentalisation of the novel, are therefore unlikely to find acceptance among the majority of literary scholars.[10] Cave, for example, himself an advocate of cognitive approaches to literature, notes that 'it is not the business of literature to be the emissary of an ethical (or political, or ideological, or philosophical) master'.[11] To contend that literary fiction can be made to serve the useful social or moral purpose of nurturing empathy is to risk reducing it to the status of an instrument rather than treating it as an object worthy of study in its own right.[12]

Thirdly, however resistant they might be to the instrumentalisation of their object of study, most literary scholars are comfortable with the idea that the study of literature enhances linguistic and critical skills; but even the most socially engaged critics tend to worry about the particular social effect that is empathy. A critical mind is resistant to instrumentalisation, whereas empathy can be made to serve dubious social, political and commercial goals.[13] On the one hand, high levels of empathy might be understood to lower the critical resistance of individuals, making them vulnerable to the lures of advertising, emotionally persuasive political propaganda and emotional contagion, a phenomenon that can lead people to act in very inhumane ways. It was, in fact, wariness of the perverse social uses to which empathy could be put that led Bertolt Brecht to design a form of theatre that would inhibit the affective responses of spectators, through the operation of *Verfremdungseffekt*, or 'the alienation effect'. On the other hand, heightened levels of empathy might conceivably allow a person skilfully to manipulate others in the boardroom and salesroom. A business case has already begun to be made by some psychologists and cognitive scholars for the empathic benefits of reading fiction. The psychologists Bal and Veltkamp have suggested, for example, that the value of identifying causal links between fiction and empathy lies in the fact that 'high empathic persons are more prosocial which is associated for example in the workplace to [sic] higher performance, productivity, and creativity'.[14] The introduction to a book entitled *Theory of Mind and Literature* points out that 'Theory of Mind is central to such commercial endeavors as market research and product development.'[15] To sum up, then, heightened empathic capacity (or Theory of Mind) is an intrinsically problematic educational benefit, from the point of view of the humanities, because the argument that reading fiction nurtures empathy can be construed to mean that fiction-reading can make individuals either more prone to being instrumentalised or more capable of instrumentalising others.

Following on from this last point, literary scholars have tended to be particularly alert to the limitations of empathy, both in itself and as an effect of reading.[16] As noted by Meghan Marie Hammond and Sue J. Kim, themselves literary scholars, 'literary and cultural critics have long challenged the empathy-altruism hypothesis as it pertains to literature, particularly in Victorian studies, where the discourses of compassion, sympathy, and charity have long been central objects of inquiry'.[17] Hammond elsewhere argues that modernist fiction, notwithstanding its privileging of empathy, or what she calls the 'cognitive alignment between reader and character', also warns of the limits of empathy, its 'potential for danger, or even violence'.[18] Despite the fact that Fritz Breithaupt, a scholar of German literature, considers empathy to be a defining humain trait, he has devoted a recent book, *The Dark Sides of Empathy*, to its links to self-loss, divisive side-taking, sadism and narcissism. Kathryn Robson, a scholar of French literature, observes that 'the championing of empathy as unequivocally positive and transformative is troubling', while another literary scholar, Anne Whitehead, makes the point that resistance to 'affective identification' can be a mode of political critique.[19] Keen, also a literary scholar, points out that an ability to respond empathetically to a work of fiction has little to do with a propensity to take prosocial action.[20] She highlights, furthermore, the need to pay attention to the 'potentially negative effects of vicious or Machiavellian applications of narrative empathy – that is, when narrative empathy invites shared feeling with sadists, or when perspective taking is employed to better understand a victim'.[21]

There are several good reasons, therefore, why literary scholars tend *not* to argue that the study of literary fiction will enhance the empathic skills of students, even if they often contend that the study of literature equips individuals to be better ethical agents and citizens of the world. This latter kind of claim does in fact imply a form of empathy, understood as an openness to difference. The philosopher Martha Nussbaum has spelled out this link in her 2010 defence of the humanities, where she argues explicitly that literature and the arts teach a form of empathy, and that they do so by developing what she calls 'the narrative imagination':

> Citizens cannot relate well to the complex world around them by factual knowledge and logic alone. The third ability of the citizen, closely related to the first two, is what we can call the narrative imagination. This means the ability to think what it might be like to be in the shoes of a person dif-

ferent from oneself, to be an intelligent reader of that person's story, and to understand the emotions and wishes and desires that someone so placed might have.[22]

Nussbaum argues that literary fiction, in particular, has the important ethical function of developing the ability to listen attentively to others:

> Stories cultivate our ability to see and care for particulars, not as representatives of a law, but as what they themselves are: to respond vigorously with senses and emotions before the new; to care deeply about chance happenings in the world, rather than to fortify ourselves against them; to wait for the outcome, and to be bewildered – to wait and float and be actively passive.[23]

By cultivating an ability to listen, in other words, the study of literary fiction can, she argues, produce ethical agents.

As Nussbaum indicates, this attentiveness or responsiveness to the world outside the self is closely related to the imagination. The imagination has, in fact, long been considered a source, and even as the source, of ethical feeling for other people. According to Jean-Jacques Rousseau's *Discours sur l'origine et les fondements de l'inégalité* (1755), eighteenth-century man had lost contact with his primitive sense of compassion and needed to work hard to regain access to it.[24] In *Émile*, he argues that it is by way of the imagination that humans can activate their native sense of 'pitié': 'only the imagination allows us to feel the sufferings of another'.[25] Adam Smith, a contemporary of Rousseau's, similarly suggested that compassion requires a certain effort of the imagination. In the opening pages of his *Theory of Moral Sentiments* (1759), for example, Smith writes of how the distress of a person who witnesses an act of torture is a product of imaginative work:

> Though our brother is upon the rack, as long as we ourselves are at our ease, our senses will never inform us of what he suffers. They never did and never can carry us beyond our own persons, and it is by the imagination only that we can form any conception of what are his sensations.[26]

It has been argued that Smith's legacy endures in the Victorian realist novel, in the sense that imaginative labour, in works of 'sympathetic realism', is 'endowed with ethical force', inviting a sympathetic fellow-feeling that allows for an approximation of the other's feeling that stops short of replication or identification.[27] Reading or viewing fiction is, arguably, a way of exercising imaginative skills that might otherwise lie dormant. While there may be no *necessary* causal link between the exercise of the imagination and any acts of kindness in the real world, an ability to imagine other people's experience does appear to be a helpful first step in the direction of generosity towards others. As Nussbaum puts it, 'empathy is not clearly necessary for compassion' but 'it is a prominent route to it'.[28]

Empathy may not sit entirely comfortably within the domain of the literary specialist, for the various reasons given, but the imagination, intimately bound up with empathy, certainly does. This book will focus, then, on what works produced by and addressed to the imagination might themselves have to say about links between fiction and empathy, or more specifically about how and why fiction might engage readers in an activity of affective sharing and mind-reading. Its approach will be predicated on close reading rather than the empirical investigation of readers' responses. This is partly a decision dictated by pragmatic necessity: put bluntly, I am a literary scholar rather than a psychologist. A second pragmatic reason why this book will focus on texts, and the reader responses they programme, rather than on the actual responses of readers, is that the results of laboratory studies of complex affective and cognitive responses to fiction can be difficult to interpret. As one study puts it: 'A relationship of an individual psyche to a work of art is a highly complex process that cannot be easily brought into laboratory.'[29] My decision to focus on what literary fiction might be understood to say about the relationship between narrative fiction and empathy has a theoretical basis, too: I contend that fiction is the most reliable source of knowledge about the dynamics of its own reception. As one scholar working between literary studies and psychology puts it, 'literature is *already* a kind of brain-imaging, as the mind looks at verbal versions of the micro-movements of thought within it'.[30]

This book will consider a small number of literary fictions to ask what they say about what happens when we encounter alien fictional subjectivities. More specifically, it will suggest that when narrative fictions dramatise encounters with strangers, particularly where those strangers are closely associated with fiction, they are indirectly representing what happens when we encounter narrative fictions. Before turning to the figure of the stranger, in the next chapter, I would like to attempt to forge some links between the psychology of fiction-reading as outlined in the previous chapter and the way in which literary scholars traditionally account for the dynamics involved in this activity.

Affective Sharing and Seduction

For the cognitive literary scholar Patrick Colm Hogan, the empathic sharing of emotions is a key function of literature, speaking to our 'deep need to share emotionally consequential experiences'.[31] However, empathic responsiveness to narrative fiction has often been framed as a dangerous kind of openness. Wariness of identificatory reading has a long and distinguished history. In Books 2 and 3 of the *Republic*, Plato argues that drama is to be distrusted on account of what the philosopher Noël Carroll summarises as 'the emotionally infectious processes of identification that underwrite mimesis': Plato contends that emotional involvement with what Carroll calls 'bad role models' or enemies weakens leaders and warriors.[32] In Book 10, Plato argues more generally that drama's appeal to the emotions threatens to disrupt the rule of reason. In other words, fiction is dangerous because it addresses people's emotions and works against their powers of reason. Plato worried about fictional works making warriors less willing to fight, and therefore less obedient to their leaders.

Thinkers today continue to be concerned by fiction's ability to persuade readers to allow emotion to trump reason, though they are more likely to worry about excessive acquiescence than about disobedience. The cultural theorist Gayatri Spivak writes, for example, that 'literature buys your assent in an almost clandestine way and therefore it is an excellent instrument for a slow transformation of the mind. For good or for ill.'[33] The conception of fiction as manipulative applies mainly, in our own time, to popular, non-literary genres. The literary theorist Vincent Jouve suggests, for example, that 'the overt aim of these novels ("airport novels", erotic narratives, Harlequin romances, detective fiction), which can be filed under the heading "popular literature", is to seduce the reader for openly commercial ends'.[34] The kind of identificatory, immersive reading that such books invite is associated by many literary scholars with a naive and therefore suboptimal engagement with narrative fiction. And yet, as Jouve also points out, seduction has a crucial role to play in any good novel, and even the most vigilant of academic literary critics regularly fail to achieve the objectivity to which they aspire: 'Most of the time, readings of a text are not conscious of their bias: they conceive of themselves as objective readings, which reveal the truth of the work.'[35] As the aesthetic philosopher Jenefer Robinson observes, 'something has to draw us in emotionally for us to proceed with a novel at all'.[36] Is the reader's experience of being drawn in emotionally, whether by a potboiler or by a literary classic, identifiable as empathy?

Certainly, across a range of disciplines, empathy itself has been conceived as a risky kind of emotional receptiveness to others. The cultural critic Carolyn Pedwell defines it 'as a critical receptivity to being affected by ways of seeing, being and feeling that do not simply confirm what we think we already know'.[37] The art historian Jill Bennett, similarly, argues that empathy is 'a mode of thought that might be achieved when one allows the violence of an affective experience to truly inform thinking'.[38] The psychoanalyst Adam Phillips and historian Barbara Taylor note that empathy is 'always hazardous because it is based on a susceptibility to others'; it 'opens us up to the world (and worlds) of other people in ways that we long for and dread'.[39] All of these definitions convey the idea that empathy is an intrinsically unsettling and potentially transformative affective experience.[40] As such, it shares certain similarities with an amorous susceptibility that is, by definition, risky for the integrity of the self; this susceptibility was evoked by Jouve's metaphor of seduction. The definition of empathy offered by the philosopher of cognitive science Frédérique de Vignemont and the neuroscientist Tania Singer is particularly suggestive in the context of a parallel between empathy and seduction:

> There is empathy if: (i) one is in an affective state; (ii) this state is isomorphic to another person's affective state; (iii) this state is elicited by the observation or imagination of another person's affective state; (iv) one knows that the other person is the source of one's own affective state.[41]

Similarly, one is seduced, or at least open to seduction, if one has feelings that resemble and are prompted by another person's real or imagined feelings, and if one knows the other person to be the source of one's feelings. Empathy and amorous openness are in no sense identical. However, to the extent that empathy is understood as a kind of affective porousness, it does share some common ground with openness to seduction, a common ground that is perhaps more easily visible in the term 'sympathy', a forerunner and very close relative of empathy.[42]

The intersection between empathy and seduction, in the experience of reading fiction, is perceptible in Keen's use of the term 'emotional contagion' to describe the affect-sharing effects that fictional works have on us, and in her reference to what she calls 'narrative empathy' as an experience of 'intense emotional fusion with the imaginary experiences of fictional beings'.[43] However, the metaphor of seduction, as used by literary scholars in relation to the affective response to fiction, is often entirely divorced from any notion of empathy. The literary theorist Ross Chambers proposes that 'all narratives are necessarily seductive' and that what we call fiction might be defined as 'the narrative moves that, in a given narrative situation, produce authority through seduction'; he also describes seduction as the *modus operandi* of modern novels.[44] Roland Barthes famously refers to the (quasi-sexual) pleasure, and even in some cases the *jouissance*, of the reader (often exemplified, for him, by the reader of narrative fiction), while Paul de Man warns against 'the illusion of aesthetic seduction' produced by literary, or rather metaphorical, language.[45] The literary scholar Emma Wilson, who evokes 'the seductive power of fictional identifications', argues that reading is crucially 'a desiring activity', which involves an ambiguously pleasurable and painful process, akin to 'the transference-love of psychoanalysis'.[46] As this last quotation suggests, affective responsiveness to fictional narrative has sometimes been framed by literary and cultural scholars in psychoanalytic terms. Marina Warner, for example, asserts that the repetition of certain motifs and patterns within the stories of *The Arabian Nights* 'opens the book up to the listener/reader's transference and hence identification'.[47]

Approximate parallels between fiction-reading and amorous relations have also been implied by some psychologists interested in the subject of empathy. For example, Oatley and Djikic make the following observation:

> A great deal has been written about art, but only recently has research begun in earnest about what goes on in the mind and brain when reading literature. Outside the domain of love relationships and some forms of psychotherapy, the idea of communication that has effects of a nonpersuasive yet transformative kind has rarely been considered in psychology.[48]

Elsewhere, Oatley more directly compares the manner in which readers are changed by a fictional story to the way in which people can be changed by the experience of love:

> As with a love relationship in which something of the loved person continues in us even when the person dies, so when we put a work of narrative art back on the bookshelf, something of it remains as part of the self.[49]

The empirical scholar Eva Maria Koopman, in a similar vein, writes that any definitive solution to the problem of 'which effects which literary features have on empathic understanding and prosocial behavior [. . .] would be like finding out exactly why we fall in love with whom'.[50]

There is no need, however, to construe the transformative encounter with narrative fiction exclusively in terms of either empathy or seduction. Some commentators, in describing the effects of fiction upon the reader, choose instead to use metaphors suggestive of a more or less dark magic: fiction ensnares, captivates and lures. Rita Felski, for example, devotes a chapter of her book on the uses of literature to the theme of enchantment: 'Enchantment matters', she writes, 'because one reason that people turn to works of art is to be taken out of themselves, to be pulled into an altered state of consciousness.'[51] Some scholars have questioned the usefulness of framing the encounter with fiction in empathic terms: Carroll, for example, prefers the term 'vectorially converging emotions' to the term 'empathy'.[52] Certainly, it makes at least as much sense to conceptualise the dynamics of transformative fiction-reading as erotic as it does to theorise those dynamics as empathic. Erotic dynamics, moreover, are not necessarily sexual in nature; to be seduced is, above all, to be persuaded. Nevertheless, insofar as empirical approaches to the operation of empathy in the encounter with fiction can help us to reassess the traditional literary understanding of what is at stake in supposedly 'naive' experiences of fiction-reading, this book will attempt to read the traditional idea that novels seduce their readers through the lens of recent scholarship on empathy, and recent scholarship on the empathy/fiction relationship through the lens of the more traditional idea that novels seduce their readers.

Mind-Reading and Suspicion

What literary theorists and critics call 'the hermeneutics of suspicion', after Paul Ricoeur, can imply the belief that texts are complicit with conservative political structures, or it can evoke the idea that texts need to be deciphered for their hidden meanings. Either way, the job of the literary critic has long tended to involve reading 'against the grain and between the lines', in an effort 'to draw out what a text fails – or wilfully refuses – to see'.[53] Toril Moi has recently complained that 'the hermeneutics of suspicion has made us believe that to read critically is necessarily to debunk, deconstruct, take apart, and tear down, not praise and admire'.[54] The suspicious attitude, understood as a tendency to critique or decode, or simply as the adoption of a 'fundamentally semiotic sensibility' which 'pivots on the treatment of phenomena as signs',[55] can be applied not just to literary fictions but also to the kind of fictions propagated by advertising and the mass media, as Barthes demonstrated with his work on popular mythologies. This kind of suspicion is often considered to be the preserve of experts, unavailable to ordinary readers. However, if we understand suspicion as an inclination to disbelieve, it is an attitude that can characterise any reader's encounter with fiction.

The philosopher Colin Radford argues that 'we never really forget ourselves while reading a book or watching a play; we never fully suspend our disbelief either'.[56] Radford wonders how it is, given the endurance of disbelief in our encounters with fiction, that people are nevertheless moved by fiction, and concludes that there is something inconsistent and incoherent about our response to fictional works. Psychologist Victor Nell posits a similar coexistence of belief and disbelief in the mind of the fiction-reader, suggesting that, as in the case of hypnosis, the fiction-reader's 'disbelief is willingly suspended because it is not really suspended at all but, in the form of alert critical consciousness, remains aware that the fantasy world is never more than a wind-up toy', an attitude that gives the reader a welcome break from the default position of scepticism, or 'reality-testing feedback processes'. Nell refers to 'the strange duality of the entranced reader's experience', which allows one to feel what characters are feeling while knowing that one is not in their situation.[57] The cognitive scholar Richard Gerrig maintains that every time we engage with a work of fiction we need to work at disbelieving what it tells us. Gerrig persuasively argues, in *Experiencing Narrative Worlds*, that belief is the default attitude in fiction-reading, just as it is in everyday life. Disbelief is produced only by an effort of the will, or reflection. Gerrig suggests, therefore, that readers and viewers of fictional works do not willingly suspend their disbelief, as Samuel Taylor Coleridge famously had it, but rather they wilfully construct their disbelief every moment that they are aware that they are reading a work of fiction.[58] While Radford, Nell, and Gerrig disagree about the nature of the role given to disbelief in the experience of fiction-reading, all appear to agree that it plays a crucial supporting role in that experience, even if fictional works rely for their emotional impact upon disbelief remaining in the background, just active enough so that we remember that what we are reading is fictional, and just inactive enough to allow us to respond emotionally to the fiction.[59]

To be suspicious, or disbelieving, in one's engagement with fiction is to engage in an activity similar to that performed by the child participants in a classic psychological test of Theory of Mind.[60] Just as the child capable of ToM can at once know where chocolate is located and deduce that another person will have an incorrect belief about its location, a minimally competent reader will be able to inhabit the fiction while also situating herself outside it; she will be able to construe the beliefs of fictional characters, from the perspectives of those characters, without confusing those beliefs with her own. In other words, she will provisionally share a character's perspective while resisting complete imaginative merging with that perspective.[61] A strong link between ToM (or mind-reading ability) and suspicion is indicated by the authors of this original 'false belief' test, evoked above: they argue that ToM brings with it the ability to understand deception, or more specifically, the ability 'to infer a deceptive plan'.[62] Just as naivety, or openness to seduction, can be seen to share structural similarities with empathy understood as affective sharing, suspicion and mind-reading are structurally related. This book will show that fictional characters endowed with well-developed mind-reading skills tend to be more suspicious than others in relation to the motivations and desires of fictional stranger figures, figures who will serve, in this study, as proxies for fiction itself. To suspect someone of something is, after all, to make inferences about his or her possible beliefs or motivations: it is to engage in mind-reading.

One of the key arguments of this book will thus be that while the encounter with fiction crucially involves seduction, it also makes demands of the reader's suspicion. Suspicion is often the term used by literary critics to describe the ability to counteract the pleasurable affects produced by reading literary fiction, and to maintain an attitude of distrust with regard to the text's machinations. Certainly, other terms can be used to evoke the same phenomenon (terms such as 'critical distance'), but 'suspicion' will be the term privileged in this study because it can be applied as readily to texts as to people or characters. Suspicion will be closely associated, in this study, both with the activity of mind-reading, in relation to characters, and with the activity of reading texts. It will refer to a certain distrust of the illusions spun by texts, narrators and characters. Another reason why this book will privilege the idea of suspicion is that the suspicious attitude, or the state of being doubtful, uncertain, tentative, can alternate with its opposite (trust, acquiescence, seduction, belief, naivety) in a way that seems less easy in the case of a term like 'critical distance'. In other words, the term 'suspicion' has a hesitancy and instability about it that will suit the purposes of this book. A disadvantage of this term is its negative connotations: to suspect someone of something is often to impute nefarious intentions to him or her. However, this is certainly not always the case: a person can be suspected of modesty or generosity, for example. This book will use the term 'suspicion' (and its near-synonym 'scepticism') in a neutral sense.

It will be argued in these pages that fiction sets in play a dynamic inter-relation between seduction and suspicion, affective sharing and mind-reading. Indeed, according to the historian Susan Lanzoni, empathy itself has repeatedly been defined, over the course of its history, as a dynamic process: 'Empathy depends on movement between the poles of similarity and difference, of distance and closeness, of immersion and alienation. Empathy marks a relation between the self and other that draws a border but also builds a bridge.'[63] The next section will suggest that narrative fiction triggers precisely such an alternation between poles, and between attitudes to the other.

Fiction-Reading as a Dialectical Activity

Whether one frames the experience of reading fiction in terms of seduction and/or suspicion, or in terms of affective sharing (or narrative empathy) and/or mind-reading, this book argues that what is at stake is not so much a choice between participation in and detachment from the story as an interaction between two attitudes. Let us consider the two limit cases in turn: participatory reading and detached reading.

It is a truism to say that popular fiction seduces its readers and minimises the need for mental work. The literary scholar Janice A. Radway writes about how romances effectively do away with any need for deductive work on the part of readers; they 'obviate the need for self-conscious interpretation by almost never assuming that their readers are capable of inferring meaning, drawing conclusions, or supplying "frames"'.[64] However, it seems likely that even the least highbrow of stories activate interpretive processes to some degree. The cultural scholar Tania Modleski's study of popular romance fiction certainly suggests this:

> In both Harlequins and Gothics, the heroines engage in a continual deciphering of the motives for the hero's behavior. The Harlequin heroine probes for the secret underlying the masculine enigma, while the reader outwits the heroine in coming up with the 'correct' interpretation of the puzzling actions and attitudes of the man.[65]

If 'lowbrow fiction evokes empathy more reliably than treasured classics',[66] it seems to be the case that popular genres also engage, to varying degrees, those inferential, mind-reading skills that play such a central role in empathy. At least one recent empirical study supports this conclusion.[67] Very few readers, however prone to narrative empathy, and however seductive or emotionally manipulative the material at hand, ever entirely get away without making inferences, or ever completely forget that they are reading a book. In other words, it is possible that even mass-produced fiction, designed to seduce readers for profit, also imparts a habit of suspicion.

Conversely, as has already been suggested, and as both Wayne Booth and Lisa Zunshine argue in different ways, it is virtually impossible to remain entirely distanced or vigilant even when one is attempting to read fiction in a critically dispassionate way:

> For more than a century now we have been exhorted to resist identifying with art works; we are advised instead to maintain some sort of 'aesthetic distance'. What is forgotten in such warnings – though they are useful in combating certain kinds of sentimentality – is that even when we resist a

story, even when we view it dispassionately, it immerses us in 'the thoughts of another', unless we simply stop listening.[68]

> The trouble with th[e] ideal stance of readerly vigilance is that it presupposes a constant state of suspicion that is difficult to maintain both in real life and in our engagement with the literary narrative. [. . .] Although source-monitoring is an integral part of our information management, *exaggerated and unrelentingly strong* source-monitoring can be rather cognitively expensive and [is] thus not our default state of mind.[69]

Just as total participation or immersion is an unattainable attitude, absolute critical detachment is impossible.

Neither the entirely critically detached reading of fiction nor the wholly naive reading exists in reality. Even if a reader capable of one or the other were to exist, he would not be worthy of emulation. As the French critic Georges Poulet notes: 'Extreme closeness and extreme detachment have [. . .] the same regrettable effect of making me fall short of the total critical act.'[70] Fiction, whether literary or not, urges us to navigate between closeness and detachment, or somehow to find a way of occupying both positions. On the subject of academic criticism, Felski observes that 'there is no reason why our readings cannot blend analysis and attachment, criticism and love'; and on the theme of immersion in a work of art, the same scholar notes that 'even as we are bewitched, possessed, emotionally overwhelmed, we know ourselves to be immersed in an imaginary spectacle: we experience art in a state of double consciousness'.[71] Arguably, 'lay' readers occupy this dual position as readily as professional critics: every time we read or watch or listen to a fiction, we are obliged to negotiate flexibly between mental states: affect and cognition, immersion and detachment, an imaginary world and a real world.

This book will suggest that engagement with fiction requires a reader to negotiate between two attitudes, one broadly identificatory and one broadly detached: he must be both suggestible and sceptical, both receptive and resistant. This is implied by the so-called paradox of fiction, already touched upon in our brief discussion of the work of Radford, Nell and Gerrig. To the extent that a fiction is overtly a fiction, as distinct from counterfeit information or reassuring myth, it places the reader or auditor in an ambiguous or dual position. As Jouve puts it, '[The] referential illusion is fragile, limited and temporary. The reader is perpetually divided: he believes and he does not believe, all at the same time, privileging one position rather than the other depending on the novels, or even on the different passages within the same novel.'[72] Some thinkers have suggested that to frame the paradox of fiction in terms of belief is incorrect: what is at stake, in a reader's response to narrative fiction, is not so much (dis)belief as thought and imagination.[73] However, following this paradigm too, the reader's experience can be considered dual, poised between adherence and non-adherence to a thought, or something imagined.

Indeed, for the phenomenological critics Jean-Pierre Richard and Georges Poulet, who championed an identificatory style of literary reading whereby the critic aims to simulate the consciousness of the author, a negotiation between immersion and distance characterises any critical encounter with literature, not just fiction:

> Ultimately, there needs to be a kind of detachment on the part of the critic, in relation to the work, but I think there is a sort of dialectic: one must begin by identifying, by plunging into the darkness of the work into with which one provisionally melts, and then, gradually, one needs to take a distance.[74]

This notion of a dialectic between two attitudes, whether they are called identification and detachment (as in this passage), sympathy and comprehension,[75] affective sharing/narrative empathy and mind-reading or seduction and suspicion, will play a fundamental role in our own study.

In the first chapter, it was shown that a number of psychologists and empirical scholars have associated the possibility of self-change, on the part of the reader of fiction, with the triggering of a dialectic between affect and reflection. Various literary theorists and critics have, similarly, presented the kind of self-change that might be wrought by fiction-reading as the result of an interplay of identification and detachment. For example, the scholar of French literature Gill Rye considers identification to be 'an important factor' in what she calls 'reading for change', and evokes the potentially transformative effects of 'the negotiations the readers have to make between seduction and alienation, between being positioned by the text and (re)positioning themselves in relation to it'.[76] The French literary theorist Dominique Rabaté suggests something similar with his argument that the experience of reading prose fiction, or even of watching a film or playing a video game, involves a process of plural and partial identifications as well as a process of partial dis-identification from one's own subjectivity; in one essay he writes of this identificatory process with reference to empathy, noting that the reader 'must remain precariously poised between a controlled identification and the reaffirmation of an irreducible subjective difference'.[77] Formulations such as these, which present reading as a kind of dialectic or negotiation, imply the transformative possibilities of exposure to fiction, possibilities that are fundamentally predicated upon an 'openness to alterity',[78] the kind of alterity that can be embodied by fictional strangers.

The authors of a recent psychological investigation, who contest Kidd and Castano's finding that reading short passages of literary fiction can boost performance on Theory of Mind tests, have made the following suggestive statement:

> We [. . .] believe that we should move from asking whether reading fiction increases theory-of-mind skills to asking under what circumstances reading may do this, and how, and for whom.[79]

This study will, accordingly, focus on the processes at least as much as on the outcomes of fiction-reading. More specifically, it will study the interaction, as it is indirectly thematised within a number of fictions, of what psychologists call empathy (in the sense of affective sharing) and Theory of Mind, of what cognitive scholars of literature are more likely to refer to as narrative empathy and mind-reading, and of what more traditional literary scholars are likely to call, instead, seduction and suspicion. This book will suggest that the relationship between these differentiated attitudes can be antagonistic, rather than straightforwardly complementary, in the experience of reading fiction, and will propose that the kind of narrative fiction we tend to recognise as literary, and possibly all fiction to a greater or lesser degree, trains readers to negotiate between these different positions. The kind of skill exercised or imparted by fiction will be considered to be close to what Pedwell theorises as 'affective translation': she proposes that we think of empathy 'not as affective access to "foreign" psychic or cultural worlds', that is, not as the achievement of emotional equivalence, 'but rather as a complex and ongoing assemblage of affective, social and political processes involving difference, conflict, negotiation and, potentially, transformation'.[80] In other words, this book will try to show that if fiction helps us to understand other people, it also reminds us how very challenging the activity of 'translating' other people can be.

The invitation to empathic translation, as embodied by real and fictional other people, is particularly aptly incarnated by the figure of the stranger: 'it is precisely because there is something untranslatable about the Stranger (it would not be strange otherwise), that infinite translations are called for'.[81] Our study will propose that fictional dramatisations of encounters with fiction-associated strangers can tell us something important about encounters with narrative fictions. It will suggest that, in their depictions of interactions with a stranger, fictional stories inscribe possible configurations of the reader's relation to fictional stories, and to the various characters that populate them. The book will ask if literary fiction can, through its depictions of naive and suspicious responses to the stranger, indirectly tell us something about how fictional stories engage our empathy and, more precisely, something about the interaction of affective sharing and mind-reading in our encounters with fiction. Fictional representations of openness to seduction by a stranger will be treated as indirect portrayals of the way in which readers allow themselves to be seduced by narrative fiction, while fictional depictions of suspicion, with regard to a stranger, will be interpreted as illustrations of the critical impulse at work. It will be argued that the reader is tacitly invited to emulate suspicious characters by engaging his or her own critical skills, thereby periodically resisting narrative seduction or, in other terms, blocking narrative empathy.[82] However, in order to resist seduction, one must first be open to it. Fictions not only invite readers to be suspicious, but also to be seduced. In other words, readers may be encouraged to view Emma Bovary through the lens of irony, but she is nevertheless a highly sympathetic character for many readers, including the most astute.[83] This study will suggest that suspicion and openness to seduction often work in a mutually antagonistic but also mutually necessary way in the reception of fiction.

My argument is not that fiction teaches us to be wary of strangers. I am proposing that while fiction may encourage us to maintain a minimal self-protective distance from the strange and the new, it also, first and foremost, encourages us to open ourselves up to the adventure of the new. It is precisely because of this imperative that I do not intend simply to apply cognitive concepts to the literary fictions selected for study in this book; my aim is to see what literary fiction might tell us, however indirectly, about these concepts. It is the job of the literary critic 'to tell the tale of an adventure';[84] my hope is that this book can tell the tale in a way that makes at least some sense to psychologists and literary scholars alike.

Notes

1. See for example Keen, *Empathy and the Novel*; Leverage et al., *Theory of Mind and Literature*; Zunshine, *Why We Read Fiction*.
2. Eliot, 'The Natural History of German Life', p. 54.
3. Pinker, *The Better Angels of Our Nature*, p. 589.
4. Wimsatt and Beardsley, 'The Affective Fallacy', p. 48. This duo, who remark sarcastically in this essay on the exciting discoveries that might be made if only laboratory animals could read poetry, would no doubt have responded witheringly to empirical approaches to the fiction–empathy link.
5. Jauss, 'Levels of Identification', p. 285.
6. Felski, *Uses of Literature*, p. 4. Felski proposes a reframing of gullibility as 'recognition' (p. 29). The critic Harry Shaw makes a similar assertion: 'I believe that we have come to a point where, in literary criticism and also in politics, the hermeneutics of suspicion has become a stumbling block.' Shaw, *Narrating Reality*, p. 266.

7. Keen, 'Readers' Temperaments', p. 296.
8. Cave, *Thinking with Literature*, p. 30.
9. 'Sometimes I get so engrossed [in my reading of Jane Austen] that I lose sight, at least to some degree, of the fact that neither do I have the lawyer uncle who lives in Cheapside nor am I in love with Mr. Darcy. Or, in a related cognitive slippage, I begin to feel that there is much more to Elizabeth Bennet than meets my eye on the page.' Zunshine, *Why We Read Fiction*, p. 18.
10. Mar and Oatley, 'The Function of Fiction', p. 185. The film specialist Murray Smith, similarly, argues that empathy is a 'primary motivation for both the creation and consumption of fiction'. 'Empathy', pp. 113–14.
11. Cave, *Thinking with Literature*, p. 137. He also observes, unfortunately quite correctly, that 'devoted readers of high-quality literature may be and remain nasty people' (p. 146).
12. For a summary of this argument, see Lee Siegel, 'Should Literature Be Useful?'. On the wariness of skills-based arguments for reading literature, see Alsup, *A Case for Teaching Literature*, pp. 53–6. Gregory Currie takes literary scholars to task for their lack of interest in social usefulness in Gregory Currie, 'Let's Pretend'. Felski comments that mistrust of the notion that literature should be useful 'can be voiced in many different registers: the language of Romantic aesthetics, the neo-Marxist critique of instrumental reason, the poststructuralist suspicion of identity thinking'. *Uses of Literature*, p. 7. It should be noted that novelists are often less reluctant than literary scholars to embrace the idea that novels can play a useful role. See Alexandre Gefen's work on the recent wave of avowedly therapeutic novels in the French language: 'Le Projet thérapeutique' and *Réparer le monde*.
13. Keen points out for example that 'empathy may be strategically employed in narrative for purposes of ideological manipulation'. Keen, 'Narrative Empathy', para. 12.
14. Bal and Veltkamp, 'How Does Fiction Reading Influence Empathy?', p. 2. The 'industrial' value of empathy has been a focus of interest since the early twentieth century. See Lanzoni, *Empathy*, pp. 181–7.
15. Leverage et al., *Theory of Mind and Literature*, p. 1.
16. They are far from the only ones, of course. The moral philosopher Martha Nussbaum points out that the torturer may use his or her empathetic skills to inflict pain; she observes that if empathy has any ethical value at all, it is only insofar as it involves 'a very basic recognition of another world of experience' and of the 'reality and humanity' of others. Nussbaum, *Upheavals of Thought*, pp. 302, 333. See also Prinz, 'Is Empathy Necessary for Morality?', pp. 211–29. The cultural scholar Carolyn Pedwell sharply critiques those 'liberal narratives of empathy' which make of empathy 'the emotional ingredient that binds us together as human subjects and communities and the affective panacea to a wide range of social, political and economic divisions and grievances'. She highlights the limitations of such narratives, and in particular the fact that empathy all too easily perpetuates existing power structures, so that the privileged subject is identified as the empathiser and the less privileged subject is reified as the object of empathy. Pedwell, 'Affect at the Margins', pp. 18–19.

17. Hammond and Kim, *Rethinking Empathy*, p. 11. They note, furthermore, that novels 'often approach empathy with scepticism and represent it as frustratingly ambiguous' (p. 8). Some of the essays in this volume make points that chime with my own arguments. For example, Rebecca N. Mitchell, in the same collection, suggests that Zola's *Thérèse Raquin* reveals 'the harm in assuming incorrectly to know what another feels or wants' (p. 130).
18. Hammond, *Empathy and the Psychology of Literary Modernism*, pp. 3–4.
19. Robson, *I Suffer, Therefore I Am*, p. 12. Whitehead, 'Reading with Empathy'. For reflections on the limitations of empathy as an effect of fiction-reading, see also Kulbaga, 'Pleasurable Pedagogies' and, from a feminist perspective, Hemmings, 'Affective Solidarity'. For a nuanced overview of the fiction-reading and empathy debate, see Jurecic, 'Empathy and the Critic', which refrains from aligning itself with 'medical humanist educators on the one side', or with 'post-humanist affect theorists on the other' (p. 11).
20. Jean-Jacques Rousseau made a similar point. For a discussion of Rousseau's critique of emotional response at the theatre, see Carroll, 'Theatre and the Emotions', pp. 316–17. However, various psychological studies have incorporated elements into their experiments that appear to indicate that causal links exist between reading narrative fiction and the performance of altruistic prosocial actions. See for example Johnson, 'Transportation into a Story', which found that 'individuals who experienced high levels of affective empathy while reading were nearly twice as likely to engage in prosocial behavior as individuals experiencing low levels of affective empathy'; see also Johnson et al., 'Potentiating Empathic Growth', and Koopman, 'Empathic Reactions after Reading'. This latter study argues that it is narrativity rather than fiction per se that is decisive. One study showed that a tendency towards emotional transportation when reading, as well as 'Story-induced Affective Empathy' with fictional characters, may cultivate 'helping tendencies' in the real world. See Stansfield and Bunce, 'The Relationship between Empathy and Reading Fiction', p. 16.
21. Keen, 'Readers' Temperaments', p. 297. Fritz Breithaupt too suggests that narrative empathy can have a sadistic dimension. 'Empathic sadism'. Keen defines narrative empathy as 'feeling with fiction' and, elsewhere, as 'the sharing of feeling and perspective-taking induced by reading, viewing, hearing, or imagining narratives of another's situation and condition'. Keen, 'Readers' Temperaments', p. 296; 'Narrative Empathy' (para. 1). Keen argues that narrative empathy, or story-led emotional sharing, may resemble real-world empathy in some ways, and may even cultivate real-world empathy, but it is not identical to it, because the other person or persons are imagined rather than real. On the possibilities and limitations of empathetic responses to fiction, see also Davis, 'Oprah's Book Club'.
22. Nussbaum, *Not for Profit*, pp. 95–6.
23. Nussbaum, *Love's Knowledge*, p. 184.
24. Interestingly, recent neuroscientific research supports Rousseau's contention: 'It is our biology that makes us social and empathic, even though only at implicit, non-propositional level, while our ideas often divide us and sometimes lead us to commit atrocities.' Iacaboni, 'Within Each Other', p. 57.

25. Rousseau, *Émile*, p. 540. All translations of French-language texts are my own unless otherwise indicated.
26. A. Smith, *Theory of Moral Sentiments*, p. 2.
27. Greiner, 'Sympathy Time', p. 294. In *Sympathetic Realism*, Greiner develops this idea, for example with regard to free indirect discourse, which 'inhibits the full collapse of self into other' (p. 40).
28. Nussbaum, *Upheavals of Thought*, p. 332.
29. Djikic et al., 'On Being Moved by Art', p. 28.
30. Davis, *Reading and the Reader*, p. 23.
31. Hogan, 'Fictions and Feelings', p. 189.
32. See Carroll, 'Theatre and the Emotions', p. 314.
33. Spivak, *An Aesthetic Education*, p. 38. Overall, Spivak is optimistic about the benefits of a literary education, even speculating about how it might impart a flexibility, in certain individuals, that could help to avert wars. 'Ethics and Politics', p. 23.
34. Jouve, *L'Effet-personnage*, p. 171.
35. Jouve, 'Lecture littéraire', p. 223. Jouve points out elsewhere, of the phenomenon of identification in reading, that 'identification is indispensable to the construction of the "I", and it is unclear what austere moral law would necessitate its prohibition'. Jouve, *L'Effet-personnage*, p. 89.
36. Robinson, *Deeper than Reason*, p. 194.
37. Pedwell, 'Affect at the Margins', p. 26; *Affective Relations*, p. 36.
38. Bennett, *Empathic Vision*, p. 55.
39. Phillips and Taylor, *On Kindness*, p. 3.
40. Dominick LaCapra coined the term 'empathic settlement' to describe a way for historians to be 'responsive to the traumatic experiences of others' without taking the place of those others. It is an 'empathy that resists full identification with, and appropriation of, the experience of the other'. *Writing History*, pp. 41, 79.
41. Vignemont and Singer, 'The Empathic Brain', p. 435. Oatley, similarly, notes that 'empathy can be thought of as having an emotion similar to that of another person, which is elicited by seeing or thinking about the person, and knowing the other is the source of the emotion'. Oatley, 'Fiction: Simulation of Social Worlds', p. 619.
42. See for example the chapter devoted to *La Religieuse* in Marshall, *The Surprising Effects of Sympathy*. Marshall, who points out that the analogy with eroticism is suggested even in the *Encyclopédie*'s definition of sympathy, argues that Diderot's novel brings seduction and sympathy into disturbingly close proximity, establishing equivalences between their effects: they both 'act like a contagious disease which touches and thereby infects someone with someone else's feelings', and can both involve 'an act of identification' or even 'overidentification' (pp. 100, 101).
43. Keen, 'A Theory of Narrative Empathy', p. 209; 'Readers' Temperaments', p. 297. Keen elsewhere observes that 'emotional contagion comes into play in our reactions to narrative, for we are also story-sharing creatures. The same drive to affiliate with others for comfort and safety that expresses itself in empathy and sympathy may also play a role in our species' enthusiasm for narrative.' Keen, *Empathy and the Novel*, pp. 5–6. Jouve also uses

the notion of 'contagion' to describe the fiction-reading process. *L'Effet-personnage*, p. 197.

44. Chambers, *Story and Situation*, pp. 218, 219, 11–12.
45. Barthes, *Le Plaisir du texte* and de Man, *The Resistance to Theory*, p. 10. See also Poulet's observation that the critic's simulation of an author's consciousness is more or less the same thing as a relationship of friendship or love. Poulet and Ricardou, *Les Chemins actuels de la critique*, p. 32.
46. Wilson, *Sexuality*, pp. 2, 9, 19. Wilson is particularly interested in the formative potential of the encounter with fiction, particularly in those cases where seduction misses its target.
47. Warner, *Stranger Magic*, p. 6. Interestingly, in view of my own argument for a metaphorical relation between stories and strangers, Warner associates the enchantment of stories with foreignness. The title of her book, she writes, 'draws attention to the foreignness of many of the enchanters' who feature in the stories of the *Arabian Nights* (p. 26).
48. Oatley and Djikic, 'How Reading Transforms Us'.
49. Oatley, 'Emotions', p. 43.
50. Koopman, 'Does Originality Evoke Understanding?', p. 175.
51. Felski, *Uses of Literature*, p. 76. The psychologist Victor Nell repeatedly refers to the pleasure of fiction-reading as the 'spell of entrancement', and compares it to the experience of hypnosis. *Lost in a Book*, p. 199.
52. See Carroll, 'On Some Affective Relations', p. 180. In the same volume, Graham McFee ('Empathy: Interpersonal vs Artistic?') too questions, from a philosophical perspective, the notion that readers or viewers feel empathy with fictional characters.
53. Felski, *The Limits of Critique*, p. 1.
54. Moi, 'The Adventure of Reading', p. 127. For a contestation of the primacy of critical suspicion, and a defence of sympathetic reading, particularly in the context of scholarly responses to realist fiction, see also Lowe, *Victorian Fiction*.
55. Felski, *The Limits of Critique*, p. 38.
56. Radford, 'How Can We Be Moved by the Fate of Anna Karenina?', pp. 70–1.
57. Nell, *Lost in a Book*, pp. 56, 212.
58. Gerrig, *Experiencing Narrative Worlds*, p. 230. One literary scholar refers to the state of 'undisbelief' induced by fiction. Holland, *The Dynamics of Literary Response*, p. 69.
59. See Yanal, *Paradoxes of Emotion and Fiction*, pp. 104–5 and Sklar, *The Art of Sympathy in Fiction*, pp. 14–15.
60. Wimmer and Perner, 'Beliefs about Beliefs'.
61. Moi writes that 'for Beauvoir, [. . .] a good novel had to have the power to absorb, to hold and bewitch, to transport the reader into its world, to make him or her not so much take the fiction for reality, as to be able to experience the fiction as deeply as reality, while full well knowing that it is fiction'. 'The Adventure of Reading', p. 134.
62. Wimmer and Perner, 'Beliefs about Beliefs', p. 126. Indeed, very many of the 'complex embedments' evoked by Zunshine, in fictional stories from *The Gruffalo* to *Tom Sawyer* to *The Golden Ass*, involve a deception of some

kind; the critic herself notes that third-level embedment or nesting of mental states is a feature of 'trickster' stories. See Zunshine, 'The Commotion of Souls' and 'What Mary Poppins Knew'.

63. Lanzoni, *Empathy*, p. 17.
64. Radway, *Reading the Romance*, p. 196.
65. Modleski, *Loving with a Vengeance*, pp. 24–5.
66. Keen, *Empathy and the Novel*, p. 84.
67. It has been demonstrated that habitual readers of romance fiction perform better on RMET tasks than readers of, for example, science fiction. Fong et al., 'What You Read Matters'. See also Barnes, 'Imaginary Engagement'.
68. Booth, *The Company We Keep*, pp. 139–40.
69. Zunshine, *Why We Read Fiction*, pp. 102–3.
70. Poulet, 'Phenomenology of Reading', p. 63.
71. Felski, *Uses of Literature*, pp. 22, 74.
72. Jouve, *L'Effet-personnage*, p. 85. Barthes, too, refers to the perverse 'clivage', or division, implied by fiction-reading, in *Le Plaisir du texte*, p. 76. Similarly, the reception theorist Wolfgang Iser notes that 'in disclosing itself fictionality signalizes that everything is only to be taken *as if* it were what it seems to be, to be taken – in other words – as play'. 'The Play of the Text', p. 327. And Peter J. Rabinowitz observes that 'in the proper reading of a novel, events that are portrayed must be treated as both true and untrue at the same time', such that disbelief is 'both suspended and not suspended at the same time'. *Before Reading*, pp. 94, 95.
73. See Yanal, *Paradoxes of Emotion and Fiction*, pp. 88–99.
74. Poulet and Ricardou, *Les Chemins actuels*, pp. 34–5.
75. Richard, *Poésie et profondeur*, p. 9.
76. Rye, *Reading for Change*, p. 20.
77. Rabaté, 'Comprendre le pire', p. 277. See also Rabaté, 'Identification du lecteur'.
78. Attridge, *The Singularity of Literature*, p. 80. Attridge himself hints elsewhere at the possibility of reflexive self-doubling with his claim that 'Coetzee's works both stage, and are, irruptions of otherness into our familiar worlds'. *J. M. Coetzee*, p. xii. He also indirectly hints, in this book, at an interplay of seduction and suspicion when he follows his claim that the numbering of paragraphs necessitates the reader's 'constant awareness' of the artificial, mediated quality of a narrative with the assertion that 'it is testimony to the power of fictional narration that it is not difficult to forget the numbering as we read' (p. 21).
79. Panero et al., 'Does Reading a Single Passage', e52.
80. Pedwell, *Affective Relations*, pp. 120–1.
81. Kearney and Semonovitch, 'At the Threshold', p. 22.
82. On the frequent necessity of blocking empathy, see Breithaupt, 'A Three-Person Model'.
83. See Charles Baudelaire's essay on Flaubert's *Madame Bovary* in his *Œuvres complètes*, vol. 2, pp. 76–86. Jauss refers, in the context of *Madame Bovary*, to its instantiation of 'a not yet canonical aesthetic procedure, the ironic form of frustrated identification'. 'Levels of Identification', p. 310. Mar and Oatley count Emma Bovary among those 'literary characters we

can experience at an ironic distance that allows us both subjective experience and external observation simultaneously'. 'The Function of Fiction',
p. 183.

84. Moi, 'The Adventure of Reading', p. 137.

Chapter 3

Fictional Strangers and the Strangeness of Fiction

What Have Strangers Got to Do with Fiction?

What is a stranger, and on what basis might a fictional stranger be understood as a figure of narrative fiction?

For the sociologist and philosopher Georg Simmel, the stranger is somebody who has come from outside the group: he brings qualities into a group 'that are not, and cannot be, indigenous to it'.[1] The *OED* defines the stranger along these lines: he is a 'foreigner; an alien', 'a newcomer' or an 'unknown person'. The French word for stranger, 'l'étranger', doubles up to mean 'foreigner', and therefore conveys more strongly than in English the sense that the stranger is an outsider from the perspective of a particular group. In the modern world, however, where individuals can belong to numerous groups, often in an ephemeral or virtual way, most of us define strangers simply as people we don't (yet) know, rather than as outsiders: most of the people that many of us see every day are strangers in this banal sense. As the social scientist Margaret Wood put it in 1934, 'everyone outside of the city-dweller's own relatively small circle of friends and acquaintances is a stranger to him', so that 'there is no distinction as between the group and the stranger or between host and guest'.[2] Anyone who is not an acquaintance of mine is therefore a stranger to me. However, in certain situations we can become keenly aware of other people as strangers in a stronger sense. For example, the friendly man at the cash register in the supermarket does not become a fully fledged stranger, to my mind, until he asks me a question that I find inappropriately personal ('Will you be sharing that chocolate cake with anyone special?'). The woman standing behind me in the post office queue is simply somebody I don't know, until she asks if she can try on my watch to see how it looks on her wrist. People I don't know have suddenly become people that I am aware I don't know: unless I am a very trusting individual, I am likely to consider their possible motivations before deciding how to respond to them. Could they have a hidden agenda? Could they be other than they seem? If I am sitting in an airport departure lounge full of people, I am not conscious of being surrounded by strangers until I suddenly find myself in need of medical attention; I am now very aware that I do not know the people around me, and I wonder whom I can ask for help. In each case, the individuals in question have gone from being people I don't know, simple objects in my field of vision, of no particular interest to me, to people *I know I don't know*, and people whose trustworthiness I need to assess.[3] Alternatively, I can be married to a person and find out one day that he is a police detective who has been employed to spy on me; he may even have another family I never knew about. This person I thought I knew is now a stranger to me; someone I now know I never knew. It is only in the weakest sense of the word, then, that strangers are people we don't know. Probing beneath this commonplace a little, strangers are people we know we don't know, or who may be other than they seem. Let us begin with this definition, then: the person I call a stranger is likely to be not just someone I don't know, but someone I am aware I don't know; someone whose quality of unknown-ness is apparent to me.[4]

To turn to the second question now, on what basis can a fictional stranger be understood as a proxy for narrative fiction? Firstly, as the examples given above suggest, strangers can be suspected of having something fictitious or duplicitous about them, at least to the extent that we think of them as strangers rather than simply as people we don't know.[5] They may be suspected of being other than they seem, impostors. When we tell children not to talk to strangers we do not generally mean that they should refuse to engage with people they don't know, because we want them to make friends with other children, and want them to talk to doctors and nurses, to the lollipop lady, the shopkeeper, the house guest and the new teacher. When we tell children not to talk to strangers, we mean that they shouldn't talk to people who may be dangerous.[6] But how are children to recognise 'stranger danger', strangers who may be threatening? There seem to be few clues, in fairy stories, as to how to distinguish bad strangers from good strangers. Good strangers (the fairy godmother and the Beast spring to mind) can look very odd and out of place, while dangerous strangers often look a lot more familiar than the wolf in the granny's bed, and can take the form of a harmless-looking old lady or a friendly piper. The bad stranger is not necessarily the one who looks different or out of place, but rather the one who is actively pretending to be what she is not. Perhaps when we tell children to distrust strangers we are warning them not to be wary of people who look strange or different, but rather to look out for people who might be pretending to be what they are not.[7] We are telling them, in other words, to be suspicious of anybody who might spin them a story, anybody who might try to pass off a fiction as fact. In other words, in telling children to beware of strangers, we are effectively asking them to be alert to the dividing line between fact and fiction, insofar as one common understanding of 'stranger' entails the suspicion of falseness.

A first reason, then, why strangers have a privileged relationship with fiction is that they can be defined, in life as in fiction, as being potentially other than they seem. A second reason is simply that they may, like fiction itself, appeal to our curiosity.[8] The novelist Honoré de Balzac spells out this link in the conclusion to the novel *Ferragus*, a companion piece to *La Fille aux yeux d'or*, which we will examine in the next chapter. The narrator writes of how, upon passing an 'unknown individual' in the street, we may find both our curiosity and our emotion aroused; upon seeing that figure a second time, 'then that creature submits himself to your memory, and stays there like the first volume of a novel whose ending eludes us'.[9] The stranger is, in other words, like a novel that we have yet to read or finish reading.

A third, and related, reason why strangers might legitimately be associated with fiction is that both real and fictional strangers tend to be associated with story-telling; they have stories to tell, precisely because they have come from elsewhere, are not yet known. If strangers, in life as in fiction, can be associated with fiction on account of the possibility of duplicitousness and their appeal to our curiosity, they also have strong links to storytelling, in that they are often required or expected to have stories to tell, or indeed can have stories invented about them. The person acting suspiciously in a neighbourhood may be asked to account for her presence there. A nanny will be asked to produce a reassuring account of past placements before being allowed to mind children. Refugees are required to tell their stories in order to secure asylum.[10] Indeed, it has been argued that we always encounter other people through the medium of stories.[11] Novels frequently associate strangers with stories that they may or may not choose to tell, and these stories may be fabricated or may be suspected of falseness. One of fiction's classic strangers is Balzac's Colonel Chabert, whose account of himself, despite being true, is repudiated by all, including his wife. If strangers in fiction are often tellers or would-be tellers of stories, they can also inspire other characters to invent stories. The realisation, in Balzac's *Ferragus*, that a woman may have a secret inspires novelistic imaginings on the part of her admirer.[12] The protagonist of Marguerite Duras's *Moderato cantabile* is fascinated by the imagined story of two strangers she sees outside a café just after one has shot the other dead. Anne Desbaresdes's desire to imagine their story becomes a pretext for her regular meetings with a man, another stranger, who tells her what he knows or invents about the tragic couple.

A fourth reason for the fiction–stranger connection is that strangers are ubiquitous in fiction, to the extent that it is difficult to think of stories that don't contain one, whether in the form of a newcomer to a place, a character who is socially unorthodox or a character who is not or may not be entirely as he seems. George Eliot's narrator in *Middlemarch* explicitly reflects on the allure of a newcomer for a young heroine prone to the construction of romantic fictions:

> Strangers, whether wrecked and clinging to a raft, or duly escorted and accompanied by portmanteaus, have always had a circumstantial fascination for the virgin mind, against which native merit has urged itself in vain. And a stranger was absolutely necessary to Rosamund's social romance.[13]

Newcomers and outsiders, it is suggested here, are the very stuff of fiction. So are characters who can be defined as strangers to the extent that they diverge from social norms; Patrick Colm Hogan, indeed, refers to 'the greater attention and elaboration commonly given' to non-normative fictional characters, and to the consequently greater likelihood that the latter will inspire empathetic responses in the reader, even where they might be considered by that reader to be 'out-group' members.[14] Finally, detective and crime novels rely particularly heavily on ambiguous or duplicitous characters, but they are everywhere in fiction, and they too can be classed as strangers. Countless novels, for example, are narrated by characters whose account of events is either dubious or dramatically revealed to be unreliable.[15]

All fictional characters are, arguably, 'relative strangers with whom we will never come into contact'.[16] The fictional characters that will be privileged in this study are all presented as strangers to some extent, whether on account of their outsider status or their marked difference from others. The selected characters are also all explicitly presented as other than they seem (all fictional characters being implicitly other than they seem, to the extent that they seem real but are not). There is, I admit, an arbitrary element to my selection. For example, one could query this book's focus on Ralph and Raymon as stranger figures in *Indiana* (particularly given that Raymon is not marked as foreign, whereas several other characters are). Ultimately, the choice of one character over another to exemplify a fictional stranger has nothing inevitable about it, all fictional characters having something of the stranger about them.

The Strange(r)ness of Fiction

I have suggested thus far that strangers have privileged connections with fiction (defined broadly) because strangers can be suspected of false-ness, because they inspire curiosity, because they are often associated with storytelling and because strangers are the very stuff of fiction. In addition, texts that present themselves as fictions can be understood to resemble strangers. We arguably engage with fictions and with strangers in similar ways, moving between credulity and scepticism, openness and defensiveness. Because all fictional narratives introduce us to simulacra of foreign consciousnesses, the literary theorist Wayne Booth suggests that all stories can be viewed as 'companions, friends – or if that seems to push the personal metaphor too far, as *gifts* from would-be friends'.[17] Booth makes it clear that the reader can and very often does reject the offers of friendship that stories make ('we accept the companionship only of those who persuade us that their offerings are the genuine "goods"').[18] The resemblance of stories to strangers is not accidental; as Booth himself points out, the intimate relationship between fiction and the stranger is one of experiential fact: to the extent that any narrative fiction is the product of at least one human mind, every time we engage with an unfamiliar work we are brought into mental contact with at least one stranger, whether that stranger is conceived as implied author(s), narrator(s) and/or character(s). The self–other relation is, moreover, one of the essential components of any story, because stories, at least as much as any other speech act or piece of writing, are always fashioned with an addressee in mind; an addressee whose curiosity will be nurtured, whose expectations will be raised, met, frustrated or disappointed. Can we trust the person telling us this story, or the person to whom we are telling our story? Will he or she lead us up the garden path? Self–other relations are also, very often, the story's theme; as one literary critic puts it, 'the province of the novel is that of intersubjectivity'.[19]

We saw in the first chapter that fictional stories can bring about changes in the reader or viewer; in this, too, they resemble strangers. The cultural scholar Sara Ahmed writes about how 'identity itself [can] become instituted through encounters with others that surprise, that shift the boundaries of the familiar, of what we assume that we know'.[20] The notion that fiction brings us into potentially transformative contact with strangers, or other people, has in fact been an explicit theme in writing about literary fiction for a long time. The philosopher Walter Benjamin observes that 'the novel is significant [. . .] not because it presents someone else's fate to us, perhaps didactically, but because this stranger's fate by virtue of the flame which consumes it yields us the warmth which we never draw from our own fate'.[21] For the literary theorist Georges Poulet, engagement with literary fiction introduces 'foreign' or 'alien' thoughts into the reader's consciousness by way of a 'strange invasion of my person by the thoughts of another'.[22] Simone de Beauvoir notes that what she calls literature is 'the only form of communication capable of giving me the incommunicable, capable of giving me the taste of another life'.[23] Such observations echo the words of Proust's narrator in *À la recherche du temps perdu*: 'Through art alone can we get outside ourselves, know what another person sees of that universe which is not the same as ours, and whose landscapes would otherwise remain as unknown to us as those that may be found on the moon.'[24]

If encounters with foreign subjectivities are as fundamental to our engagement with art and literature as many philosophers, literary specialists and novelists suggest, it seems intuitively logical that novelistic representations of encounters with fictional strangers might help us to understand what is at stake in our encounters with fiction. The decision to consider fictional strangers as figures of fiction can be justified by reference to the post-structuralist idea that literary texts systematically though indirectly represent the processes of their own writing and reading. For Jacques Derrida, for example, texts always fold back upon themselves, striving to represent their own internal dynamics. As a result, the context or scene of writing is always placed 'en abyme', or in relief, in a given text.[25] Schor makes an analogical case for the scene of reading, arguing that, as well as indirectly representing the act of writing, novels 'represent and reflect upon interpretation as performance'.[26] Ross Chambers contends that 'readerly' fictional narratives that present themselves as literary tend to be characterised by what he calls 'situational self-reflexivity', whereby the scene of literary seduction and interpretation is staged within the narrative itself.[27] Philippe Hamon has proposed that responses provoked in an insider character by an outsider character can metaphorically represent the expansion of the reader's own horizon of expectation as he reads a work of fiction.[28] So widely accepted, indeed, is the notion that texts are self-reflexive that one literary scholar has lamented 'a stream of critical readings proving that every conceivable text, from *The Wife of Bath* to *The Wizard of Oz*, was an auto-referential commentary on its own fictional status'.[29] Assuming then that fictions are at least often, if not always, partly self-reflexive, it makes sense to interpret fictional representations of encounters with strangers as indirect representations of encounters with fiction, particularly where those strangers are associated with fiction within the narrative itself.

The fictional stranger is not just exemplary of the various foreign subjectivities encountered in literary fiction; the effects that she produces within the fictional universe echo the estranging, disorientating effects of fiction on its readers.[30] That fiction has a special relationship with strangeness is suggested at several points in Freud's 1919 essay 'The "Uncanny"', which attempts to define the anxiety produced by 'something familiar which has been repressed'.[31] Some of Freud's key examples of the uncanny (or 'das Unheimliche', usually translated into French as 'l'inquiétante étrangeté'), come from fiction, and specifically from the fantastical tales of E. T. A. Hoffmann; indeed, Freud comments that 'the uncanny as it is depicted in literature, in stories and imaginative productions [. . .] is a much more fertile province than the uncanny in real life'.[32] Interestingly, however, Freud also claims that fictional examples of would-be uncanny events often fail to produce uncanny effects: 'This may suggest', he argues, 'a possible differentiation between the uncanny that is actually experienced, and the uncanny as we merely picture it or read about it.'[33] Oddly, then, fiction is presented by Freud both as a privileged site of the uncanny and as a place where elements that would otherwise produce uncanny effects, if experienced in reality, can be perceived as 'heimlich', or unthreatening.[34] A further aspect of Freud's association of the uncanny with fiction is his claim that the 'impression of the uncanny' in everyday life might be linked to the re-emergence of 'a time when the ego was not yet sharply differentiated from the external world and from other persons'; he notes that 'the uncanny effect is often and easily produced by effacing the distinction between imagination and reality, such as when something that we have hitherto regarded as imaginary appears before us in reality'.[35] This temporary suspension of the limit between self and other and between imagination and reality calls to mind the experience of being immersed in a fiction, but Freud does not suggest that the experience of reading fiction is in any way uncanny. The experience of being immersed in a fiction has nothing anxiety-producing about it, he claims, unless, as in the case of Hoffmann's tales, the content of the story is itself productive of anxiety. For Freud, fiction is a privileged but somehow non-anxiety-producing locus of the uncanny, and encounters with fiction offer a kind of alternative to the uncanny, a means of revisiting our infantile psyches without having to confront the anxiety that this return to origins might ordinarily evoke. I would be inclined to agree with Felski, though, that the 'pleasure of enchantment' by fiction, however anxiety-free it feels or appears, is 'thoroughly *unheimlich* at its core', the partial surrender to a story always having something latently disquieting about it.[36]

Interestingly, from the perspective of our argument, many of the examples of the uncanny cited by Freud involve a dread of unknown other people, or rather of the unknown as it is manifested in other people. In his summary of Hoffmann's *The Sandman*, a story dominated by what Freud calls a 'quite unparalleled atmosphere of uncanniness', he refers to multiple figures of the stranger, who seem mysterious to the young hero, Nathaniel, and who are all associated with strangeness: the Sand-Man who rips children's eyes out, the lawyer Coppelius, Giuseppe Coppola and Olympia; Nathaniel himself becomes a kind of stranger when he is overtaken by madness.[37] Freud also refers, in his essay, to the uncanny sensations produced by 'doubles' or alter egos, including in cases where a 'foreign self' is substituted for oneself; by the fantasy of the evil eye, whereby another person's envy can be made dangerous through his or her look; by the idea that the dead might return to life; or by a living person to whom we 'ascribe evil motives' and 'special powers'.[38]

If Freud does not explicitly link his notion of the uncanny to encounters with strangers, Julia Kristeva does. Every experience of the uncanny is, according to her, a form of encounter with a stranger, and conversely every encounter with a stranger is an experience of the uncanny; these encounters leave us feeling uncertain of who we are and require us to find our bearings anew:

> Many are the variants of the uncanny: all repeat my difficulty in situating myself in relation to the other, and retrace the circuit of identification-projection that lies at the foundation of my accession to autonomy. [. . .] [The] uncanny is a *destructuration of the self* that may either remain as a psychotic *symptom* or take the form of an *opening* towards the new, in an attempted adaptation to the incongruous.[39]

For Kristeva, furthermore, the discovery of the Freudian unconscious effectively makes each of us a stranger to ourselves, and somehow uncanny to ourselves: 'Uncanny, strangeness is within us: we are our own strangers – we are divided.'[40] By contrast with Freud, who claimed that uncanny effects were rare in real life, Kristeva claims that the experience of the uncanny is an utterly everyday one, albeit one that achieves heightened expression as a theme in literature:

> The shock of the other, the identification of the self with that good or bad other who violates the fragile limits of the uncertain self, would thus be at the source of an uncanny strangeness whose excessive aspect, as it is represented in literature, could never disguise its permanence in the 'normal' psychic dynamic.[41]

As this passage suggests, the uncanny, for Kristeva, is associated with the experience of uncertainty. In his essay on the uncanny, Freud refutes the notion that 'intellectual uncertainty' has anything to do with the uncanny, though later in the same essay he expresses misgivings about his earlier intellectual certainty: 'are we in truth justified in entirely ignoring intellectual uncertainty as a factor [. . .]?'[42] For Kristeva, uncertainty is central to the everyday experience of the uncanny and to the everyday encounter with strangers. Kristeva defines the stranger as someone who is both other, different from me, and yet simultaneously part of my psyche, someone both intimately familiar and unfamiliar.[43] She thereby indirectly echoes Simmel's claim that the figure of the stranger unites two diametrically opposed qualities: detachment and attachment, 'closeness and remoteness'; the stranger is not simply someone I don't know, or have never met, but someone from outside the group, who is also within it: 'the stranger is near and far *at the same time*'; he is someone with whom I enter into an uncertain relation.[44] Even the person to whom we feel closest in life can take on a 'trace of strangeness', when we realise the contingency of our relation to him or her, according to Simmel.[45] The stranger makes me less certain of myself, forces me to reorganise the boundaries of my ego.

Encounters with fiction open us up to uncertainty in an analogous manner. Firstly, as discussed in the previous chapter, stories expose us to ambiguity in the sense that they demand to be both believed and disbelieved, both adhered to and not adhered to. In this they bring us into contact with some of the uncertainty that Kristeva associates with the stranger. Wolfgang Iser writes of how, in reading, 'there are always two levels', which 'can never be totally kept apart'; one is that of 'another person's thoughts', to which the reader partially adheres, and the other is that of the reader's own experience and orientations. Both levels interact, according to Iser, resulting in a reconstituted inner world for the reader: 'alien thoughts' awaken this inner world.[46] This is what one psychologist calls the 'strange duality' of fiction, central to what a literary scholar has recently referred to as 'this strange, uniquely human game'.[47] The ambiguity with which narrative fiction confronts its reader is also framed as strange by Zunshine, who observes that certain stories leave us 'with a *strange* feeling that the state of cognitive uncertainty that they induced in us may never be fully resolved'; she also refers to 'that *strange* mental stance of simultaneously believing and disbelieving' the unreliable narrator; and she describes the 'typical detective novel' as 'a *strange* affair', in that 'we open a detective novel with an avid anticipation that our expectations will be systematically frustrated, that we will be repeatedly made fools of'.[48]

Secondly, fictions, like strangers, are both familiar and unfamiliar to the reader who engages with them. Stories tend to follow a recognisable general order, having a beginning, middle and end, for example; and yet to the extent that no two stories are the same they bring us into contact, at least minimally, with the unfamiliar, the unknown.[49] As the psychologist Jerome Bruner remarks, 'For there to be a story, something unforeseen must happen.'[50] This does not mean that fictional stories are always disconcerting – far from it (as Bruner also notes, 'Stories render the unexpected less surprising, less uncanny: they domesticate unexpectedness, give it a sheen of ordinariness') – but insofar as they capture our attention, they are likely to bring us into contact with the unfamiliar, the alien or the strange.[51]

While the combination of familiar and unfamiliar elements is arguably as characteristic of popular fiction as it is of literary fiction,[52] the first chapter nevertheless noted that one of the features of what is often called 'literature' is that it defamiliarises readers, estranging us from our usual relation to the world and to language. This is a key tenet of Russian formalism; it was Viktor Shklovsky who in 1917 coined the term *ostranenie*, translated as defamiliarisation. However, if literary form has a tendency to disorient or estrange its readers, it is also credited with an ability to reorient and console, enabling the reader to take a distance from, and thereby cope with, the emotional content of a text.[53] Formal devices therefore provoke heightened affect while also enabling readers to manage this affect. This dual effect of aesthetic form, both estranging and consoling, may itself contribute to the strangeness that, for the post-structuralist theorist Derek Attridge, characterises literature:

> It is the case, I believe, that some sense of strangeness, mystery, or unfathom-ability is involved in every encounter with the literary. Even a work one knows well, if it retains its inventiveness, possesses an enigmatic quality; one cannot put one's finger on the sources of its power, one does not know where its meanings end.[54]

The idea that literature has something inherently strange about it is not, therefore, specific to Russian formalist approaches; it is also a feature of post-structuralist literary theory. According to the argument I am elaborating here, literary fiction is doubly estranging, firstly because it is fiction (ambiguous insofar as it demands adherence and distance at the same time, and is always at least partly unfamiliar), and secondly because it is literary.

It is arguably because we are so used to encountering strangeness when we submerge ourselves in a fiction that we can, as Freud argues, experience the uncanny without feeling any palpable anxiety. This book will focus on strangers as self-portraits of fiction in part because fiction is strange by definition. The fact that the fictions in question are literary only adds to their strangeness, as well as to the likelihood of self-reflexivity.[55] It seems logical that if literary fiction were to place its own strangeness 'en abyme', it would do so via the figure of the stranger.

To sum up, then, if fiction offers, like art in general according to Attridge, 'the possibility of a repeated encounter with alterity',[56] that alterity can be associated both with the otherness of another consciousness and with the inherent strangeness of fiction, and particularly literary fiction. Both types of otherness (that of the other consciousness and that of fiction) can be related to the Freudian uncanny which, according to Kristeva at least, has a renovating effect on the psyche. It is worth remembering that in an early account of empathy in English, in 1915, the experimental psychologist Titchener associates it with a reading experience that is also an encounter with strangeness:

> We have a natural tendency to feel ourselves into what we perceive or imagine. As we read about the forest, we may, as it were, *become* the explorer; we feel for ourselves the gloom, the silence, the humidity, the oppression, the sense of lurking danger; everything is strange, but it is to us that the strange experience has come.[57]

Shortly afterwards, the philosopher Edith Stein defined empathy as 'the experience of foreign consciousness in general'.[58] This book will argue that literary fiction narrativises, by way of the figure of the stranger, the encounter with alterity that it offers to the reader. In other words, it will be contended that when fictional narratives tell us about encounters with mysterious others, they are telling us something important about what happens when a reader engages with a fictional story.

I have argued thus far that strangers have multiple links to fiction, and that fictions have something of the stranger about them, and I have suggested that both of these facts make of the fictional stranger a logical figure of fiction. I will now attempt to outline some of the ways in which fictional responses to stranger figures model the responses of readers to narrative fictions.

Responding to Fiction and Its Strangers: Seduction and Suspicion

One dominant response elicited in fictional characters by strangers would appear to be fascination. The fascination exercised by strangers certainly plays a prominent thematic role in twentieth-century French fiction. To name just a few well-known examples, André Gide's narrator in *L'Immoraliste* becomes intrigued by a young boy who steals his wife's scissors; the narrator of André Breton's *Nadja* becomes fascinated by a young woman who wanders the streets of Paris; the hero of Albert Camus's *L'Étranger* is an object of horrified fascination for his examining magistrate; and in Marguerite Duras's *Le Ravissement de Lol V. Stein*, the heroine, Lol, becomes fascinated by an older woman who steals her fiancé, and then ten years later by a former (estranged) friend who was present at the scene of the crime, while the friend's lover, in turn, becomes fascinated by Lol; in Amélie Nothomb's *Stupeur et tremblements*, the protagonist is infatuated with her treacherous female superior. Fictional strangers charm and intrigue other characters; they inspire curiosity, a desire to know, understand or at the very least interpret.

Just as stranger figures can provoke fascination in other characters, fictional stories, along with the stranger figures they feature, can exert a fascination over readers. Indeed, the film theorist Carl Plantinga observes that 'the ubiquity of narrative fiction (in various media) rests on the human fascination with stories about other humans'.[59] Narrative fictions are, in other words, fascinating at least partly because they appeal to our curiosity about, and attraction to, other human beings. As Jouve puts it, 'it is curiosity that founds the desire to read, an intellectual, affective, or instinctual curiosity'.[60] For the conditions of curiosity to be in place, something must resist our knowledge or understanding: that something often, though certainly not always, takes the form of an enigmatic character. The more resistant to understanding a fictional character is, or the 'rounder' he is, in E. M. Forster's terms, the more fascinating he is to readers.[61] The fictional stranger is, therefore, fascinating by structural necessity: insofar as he is a stranger, whether to other characters or to readers, he invites curiosity and resists easy reading on the part of those characters or readers.

The fascination elicited by fictional strangers, whether in other characters or in readers, tends to be affective and erotic in nature. It may not be an accident that the seduction of female characters by attractive strangers often plays an important thematic role in the kind of narratives that are accused of manipulating supposedly naive female readers.[62] In Flaubert's *Madame Bovary*, a seductive stranger even explicitly describes to the heroine (the very prototype of the naive reader) the way in which a reader can become fascinated by a fictional character: 'your thought, getting entwined in the fiction, plays in the details or follows the contour of the adventures. It mingles with the characters; it feels as though it is you who are trembling beneath their clothes.'[63] The seduction exercised by fictional characters, and most programmatically by fictional strangers, is a necessary part of how fiction acts upon us. As Booth notes, while it may be advisable at least partly to resist the seductions of fiction and its characters, 'when we lose our capacity to succumb, when we reach a point at which no other character can manage to enter our imaginative or emotional or intellectual territory and *take over*, at least for the time being, then we are dead on our feet'.[64]

A certain hesitation or vacillation between surrender and suspicion can be discerned in the responses of some fictional characters to stranger figures: they are both drawn in and vigilant, both seduced and suspicious. This is the case with many of the responses to stranger figures that will be analysed in this study. This book will argue, therefore, that fictions seduce their readers while also encouraging suspicion, and it will try to show that this dynamic can be traced even in the interaction between fictional characters. It will be argued, on the basis of the readings presented here, that fictions indirectly encourage readers to succumb to seduction while also maintaining, or at least regularly resuming, an attitude of vigilance with regard to the lures of narrative fiction. This dual positioning of the reader is related to the constitutive ambiguity of fiction, which this book has already discussed. The aesthetic philosopher Jean-Marie Schaeffer refers to 'the ambivalent attitude – a mixture of fascination and distrust – that is ours when confronted by mimetic activities [. . .]. Distrust is born when the spell is broken.'[65] This book will show that, similarly, fictional strangers often elicit, from other characters as well as from readers, a mixture of credulity and vigilance.

This duality or ambiguity of responses provoked by the fictional stranger may be more pronounced in the kind of fiction that is labelled 'literary', at least according to the argument of one recent empirically oriented article:

> Literary fiction can be said to *both* encourage and problematise empathic reading strategies, confronting readers with protagonists who – unlike the heroes of popular genres – call for ambivalent ethical judgments and evaluations. Empathy often depends on a recognition or projection of similarity [. . .], while literary texts can foreground protagonists who are distant – socially, mentally, or otherwise – from typical readers.[66]

It will be shown, in the close readings of literary novels that will form the larger part of this book, that the responses of characters to fictional strangers can indeed be complicated. The stranger figures in question pose puzzles for other characters even while engaging them emotionally, just as the fictional stories themselves appeal both to the intelligence and affect of readers. It will be suggested in each case, very simply, that the fictional strangers, and by extension the fictional stories themselves, elicit a combination of suspicion and fascination, the narratives in which they feature highlighting both the dangers of affective sharing and the limits of mind-reading in the encounter with narrative fiction.

Finally, just as characters in fiction can be changed dramatically by their encounter with a stranger figure, readers can be changed by their encounter with a narrative fiction, though these real-world changes can be difficult to perceive or quantify.[67] The transformative potential of fictional strangers plays a particularly important role in eighteenth-century French-language fiction, where imaginary cultural outsiders are conceived in such a way as to introduce uncertainty and ambiguity into the stable belief systems of readers. The reader of eighteenth-century philosophical fiction can be transformed by the imaginative voyages he undertakes in the company of stranger characters:

> From Montesquieu's *Persian Letters* (1721) to Voltaire's *Zadig* (1747) and *Candide* (1757), to name only the most famous, philosophical fiction is populated with strangers who invite the reader to embark upon a dual journey. On the one hand, it is pleasant and interesting to expatriate oneself for other climates, mentalities, systems; but on the other and in particular, this movement can only take place with the goal of coming back to oneself and to one's home, to judge or make fun of our limits, our idiosyncrasies, our mental or political tyrannies. The *stranger* becomes therefore the figure invested with the perspicacious and ironic spirit of the philosopher, becoming the latter's double and mask. He is the metaphor of the distance that we need to take from ourselves in order to trigger the dynamic of ideological and social transformation.[68]

In the imagination of the French Enlightenment, as Kristeva suggests here, the fictional stranger draws readers into a relationship of complicity, thereby enabling them to see their own cultural codes and assumptions through the eyes of an outsider. The transportation and defamiliarisation evoked in the above passage have the potential to transform or enlarge the reader's imaginative universe; we saw in the first chapter that psychologists make similar arguments.

The following chapters will ask what our chosen examples of literary fiction appear to tell us about what happens to characters who let themselves be seduced by fiction-connoted strangers. What is the relationship between suspicion and openness to seduction? Can the two attitudes co-exist? What are the potential outcomes for characters who let themselves be seduced by fictional strangers? And what are the implications for readers of these novels? How does each novel require the reader to negotiate between affective sharing and mind-reading, and to what ends? These are broad, exploratory questions, and this book does not hope to answer them in any definitive way. However, it will try to argue for the interest and possibility of reading fiction closely and reflexively in order to find answers to questions about how and why fiction engages empathy. Each of the following three chapters will explain in what sense the novel's stranger figures are marked as strangers and how they are implicitly associated, by the text, with fiction. Each chapter will also examine the responses of other characters to the stranger figures, and will deduce from these the different ways in which the novel in question models the reading encounter.

All three of the novels selected for study were published in France in the 1830s, when the outsider character was an established Romantic trope. First-person outsider narrators feature in Goethe's *Werther* (1774), Chateaubriand's *René* (1802), Senancour's *Obermann* (1804), Constant's *Adolphe* (1816) and Duras's *Ourika* (1823). The Romantic outsider figure typically elicits the sympathy of implied and represented audiences; by contrast, the third-person stranger figures that will feature in this study more characteristically invite suspicion on the part of both other characters and readers. In his *Souvenirs d'égotisme*, written in the early 1830s, Stendhal evokes the difficulty of writing in the first person at a time when people distrust each other: 'the genius of *suspicion* has come into the world'.[69] In her essay 'L'Ère du soupçon', indeed, Nathalie Sarraute took this declaration as foundational of a new approach to reading and writing novels.[70] The atmosphere of suspicion that Stendhal describes arguably extended to the fabric of social reality itself. As one scholar puts it, 'in a world of strangers', like Paris in Balzac's day, 'people must exert themselves exceedingly to evaluate each new "other" of whom they must necessarily be wary'.[71] Suspicion may also have entered the collective consciousness in an even more profound way: Sandy Petrey has argued that the July Revolution, the proliferation of pear graffiti subsequent to the 1831 trial of the caricaturist Philipon, along with the advent of realism itself, are symptoms of a newly keen collective awareness of the representational – that is, 'conventional and mutable' – quality of reality. Petrey suggests that, for this reason, the period around 1830 marked a particularly important moment in the writing produced by Balzac, Sand and Stendhal.[72]

The novels that will be the focus of the remainder of this book all define themselves against Romanticism, despite containing Romantic elements, and would eventually be recognised as early examples of French literary realism. The realist novel lends itself particularly well to a study that engages with psychological questions, and particularly those that concern mind-reading skills. Stendhal's realism, for example, is regularly characterised as psychological; he has even been described as 'a cognitivist before the letter'.[73] One critic, who acknowledges the continuation of eighteenth-century notions of sympathy in the nineteenth-century realist novel, nevertheless argues that the latter privileges instead the 'sympathetic imagination', a phenomenon close to what psychologists call perspective-taking or simulation-based mind-reading, and defined as 'an aesthetic concept which stresses the cognitive and intellectual, rather than the emotional aspect of identification'.[74] Certainly, every gesture and facial movement, in the classic realist novel, is liable to prompt inferences on the part of other characters, the omniscient narrator or the reader. As Jacques Dubois notes of the characters that populate the French realist novel, 'many of these characters, it will be observed, have the job of identifying and interpreting signs. They are always exegetists in some sense.'[75] For Leo Bersani, indeed, 'realistic fiction' insists upon 'the readability of the human personality':

> Behaviour in realistic fiction is continuously expressive of character. Apparently random incidents neatly carry messages about personality; and the world is thus at least structurally congenial to character, in the sense that it is constantly proposing to our intelligence objects and events which contain human desires, which give to them an intelligible form.[76]

While none of the fictions selected for study is unambiguously realist, all three have a strong realist component, not least because all ultimately unravel the enigma of a mysterious stranger figure, thereby fulfilling, at least at first glance, the ambition of French realism to present a world that is fully legible. All three of the selected realist novels should, on account of their drive towards psychological transparency, provide useful reference texts for a study that is entering into dialogue with psychological and cognitive approaches to literature.

The selected texts also offer a useful site of enquiry for anyone interested in how fiction engages the emotions. As Jouve observes, realist fiction produces a powerful 'effet-personne' (person-effect), whereby readers are drawn into such strong affective relations with characters that they can easily forget that the latter are not real: 'The characters of Balzac, Zola, or the Goncourt brothers are constantly concerned with disguising their linguistic nature.'[77] The same theorist suggests, moreover, that novels presented in the third person are even more effective than first-person narratives in inducing empathetic feelings in readers.[78] A number of literary critics have included Victorian realist novels among their key points of reference for insightful explorations of literary sympathy, a close relative and precursor of empathy.[79] The philosopher Jenefer Robinson privileges the realist novel in her study of literature and the emotions: 'Especially in reading the great realist novels of the Western tradition, our emotions can lead us to discover subtleties in character and plot that would escape a reader who remains emotionally uninvolved in the story.'[80] Realist novels are therefore useful sites to mine not only for scholars interested in connections between fiction and mind-reading/ToM, but also for those who choose to focus on the affective dimension of fiction-reading.

Finally, given that Barthes claims that Balzac's realist novel can be understood as the classic example of a normative or 'readerly' fictional text (which he defines against more experimental 'writerly' texts), that Sarraute treats the Balzacian realist novel as the standard against which experimental fiction defines itself and that realist novels tend to straddle the literary and the popular, realist fiction seems an obvious reference point in a study where a general case is (albeit tentatively) being constructed about fiction.[81] Indeed, the very fact that the realist novel is (rightly or wrongly) associated with formal conservatism means that if an argument centred on the strangeness integral to the fictional encounter can apply to it, then it can surely apply to other, more experimental novels also.

This study takes seriously Keen's assertion that 'further research into narrative empathy will be best served by cross-disciplinary conversation and interdisciplinary collaboration'.[82] It will ask how affective sharing (or narrative empathy) and mind-reading interact in the experience of reading fiction, taking close readings of a small number of literary fictions as an experimental point of departure. All three chapters will show how the novels in question thematise the limits of suspicious mind-reading and the dangers of affective porousness, often by playing the two attitudes off against one another.

The first of these three readings, in Chapter 4 ('Balzac: The Limits of Transparency and the Dangers of Opacity'), will argue that *La Fille aux yeux d'or* both glorifies mind-reading ability and suggests the ethical and practical limitations of the desire for transparency, a desire that is closely associated with realist poetics. The text also warns, however, of the danger of neglecting to decipher.

Chapter 5, 'Stendhal and the Two Opposing Demands', draws on Stendhal's ideas about the alternation between affect and reflection in any engagement with art and narrative fiction. Instead of warning against both seduction and suspicion as reading strategies, as *La Fille aux yeux d'or* appears to do, *Le Rouge et le Noir* tacitly advocates the combination of opposing attitudes, namely naivety and suspicion, or affective sharing and mind-reading.

The sixth chapter, 'Sand and the Necessity of Suspicion', suggests that George Sand's *Indiana* thematises and dramatises the differences and interactions between naive and suspicious modes of reading even more explicitly than either of the previous two novels do. In its depiction of the responses of naive heroines to a seductive stranger figure, *Indiana* insists upon the necessity of approaching fictions with a degree of suspicion. What complicates this explicit privileging of scepticism is the fact that the novel is also critical, like Balzac's *La Fille aux yeux d'or*, of the appropriative dimension of mind-reading.

Our Conclusion draws the various strands of our analysis together, outlining the conclusions that might be drawn from the close readings effected in the three central chapters, and showing how these conclusions relate to themes evoked in the first chapters.

It will no doubt be asked why I have not chosen to focus straightforwardly on fictional depictions and explorations of empathy, opting instead to treat fictional representations of seduction by a fiction-associated stranger as indirect representations of the dynamics of narrative empathy. I am less interested, though, in how a novelist conceptualises and writes about empathy than in how a novel may inadvertently depict the dynamics it sets in play. It seems to me that a focus on the representation of the seduction wielded by a fiction-associated stranger is more likely to reveal what texts (as distinct from their authors) know about their own workings than will an examination of what a story explicitly tells us about empathy. In addition, it is only recently that fiction-reading has been explicitly linked to the cultivation of empathy, but the notion that fiction seduces is at least as old as Scheherazade. This book will therefore reframe the experience of affective sharing in fiction-reading as textual seduction, treating fictional depictions of seduction as metaphorically representative of the operation of affective empathy in the encounter with fiction. If this approach seems excessively metaphorical or analogical, it might be remembered that the experience of narrative empathy, or empathy with narrative fiction, is itself a metaphorical approximation of the phenomenon of interpersonal empathy, which is itself a metaphorical approximation to the extent that it involves a virtual sharing or 'analogizing'[83] of affective experience. In other words, in the experience of narrative empathy, fictional characters are partially confused with human beings, just as in the experience of affective empathy other people's experience is partly confused with one's own.

Notes

1. Simmel, 'The Stranger', p. 143.
2. Wood, *The Stranger*, p. 230. On the universality of strangerhood in the postmodern world, see Bauman, *Modernity and Ambivalence*, pp. 94–8.
3. The question of how to read the stranger engages what Kearney calls a 'carnal hermeneutics', an activity of empathetic interpretation that involves both mind and body. 'What is Carnal Hermeneutics'.
4. Ahmed observes, similarly, that 'the stranger is some-body we know as not

knowing, rather than some-body we simply do not know'. Ahmed also observes that 'the figure of the "stranger" is produced, not as that which we fail to recognise, but as that which we have already recognised as "a stranger"'. *Strange Encounters*, pp. 55, 3.

5. Chambers notes that, in a broad sense, 'all narrative can be understood as duplicitous'. *Story and Situation*, p. 32. One of the senses in which literary texts are duplicitous is that 'alongside their seductive power, they have necessarily an analytic power that dismantles the elements of their "charms", their "magic"' (p. 221). This idea will be echoed in our own conclusion.

6. Warner refers to the persistent association, down through the centuries, of strangers with magical powers, often of the dark and deadly variety. *Stranger Magic*, p. 102.

7. Ahmed makes a similar point in the context of Neighbourhood Watch schemes, when she notes that strangers are individuals designated as 'suspicious', *'whose lack of purpose conceals the purpose of crime'*. *Strange Encounters*, p. 31.

8. According to one literary theorist, curiosity constitutes one of the 'three master functions of narrative', along with suspense and surprise. All three of these functions could be associated with the figure of the stranger. Sternberg, 'Telling in Time (II)', p. 534.

9. Balzac, *Histoire des Treize* (*The Thirteen*), p. 168.

10. As a writer put it in a newspaper recently, 'We are always, in this country [the United Kingdom], obliging refugees to tell their arrival stories: border officials, social workers, charity workers, housing officers all want to know, and the consequences of telling the wrong tale are dire.' Clanchy, 'The Very Quiet Foreign Girls'.

11. See the brief discussion of the work of the philosopher Wilhelm Schapp in Zahavi, *Self and Other*, pp. 188–9.

12. 'He went to bed, imagining various scenarios, using some fantastical act of generosity, in which he did not believe, to justify Madame Jules. Then he resolved to devote himself entirely, from the next day, to the pursuit of whatever causes, interests, entanglement this mystery hid. It was a novel to read, or rather a drama to act out, and in which he had his part.' Balzac, *Histoire des Treize*, pp. 61–2.

13. Eliot, *Middlemarch*, p. 109 (chapter 12).

14. Hogan, 'Characters and their Plots', p. 145.

15. Kearney and Semonovitch make a list of examples of literary classics and movies that include encounters with stranger figures, concluding that 'the challenge might actually be to find successful movies that do *not* feature some crisis of discernment between guests and enemies. This suggests to us not an arbitrary coincidence, but a historically rooted and ramifying lineage in Western *mythos*.' 'At the Threshold', p. 24. Gage McWeeny too highlights the symbiotic relationship between strangers and novels: 'The modern stranger's [. . .] emergence in the nineteenth century as a phenomenon that is both singular and everyday suggests a particular historical relationship [. . .] to the emergence of the novelistic.' *The Comfort of Strangers*, pp. 17–18.

16. Sklar, *The Art of Sympathy in Fiction*, p. 22.

17. Booth, *The Company We Keep*, p. 175.

18. Ibid. p. 177.
19. Rifelj, *Reading the Other*, p. viii.
20. Ahmed, *Strange Encounters*, p. 7. Levinas refers to 'the Stranger who disturbs the being at home with oneself [le chez soi]'. Levinas, *Totality and Infinity*, p. 39. The term 'strange(r)ness', used in the title of this section, is used by Ahmed in *Strange Encounters*, and recalls Emmanuel Levinas's 'l'étrangèreté'. See Stamelman, 'The Strangeness of the Other', p. 120, note 5. According to Stamelman, the poet Edmond Jabès, for whom the figure of the stranger is of special interest, 'attempts to reveal the hidden depths of strangeness and the decentering power of alterity found in all writing' (p. 122).
21. Benjamin, 'The Storyteller', p. 373.
22. Poulet, 'Phenomenology of Reading', p. 56.
23. Beauvoir et al., *Que peut la littérature?*, pp. 82–3. For similar points, see Murdoch, *Existentialists and Mystics*, p. 253; Rorty, *Contingency*, p. 80; Spivak, 'Ethics and Politics', p. 18; Lombardo, 'De fête en fête', p. 360; Compagnon, *La Littérature*, para. 72.
24. Proust, *À la recherche*, vol. 15, pp. 43–4.
25. Derrida claims, for example, that drawings of blind people are always indirect self-portraits on the part of drawing, drawing requiring by its nature a form of blindness to the object of perception. *Mémoires d'aveugle*. A similar argument could be made for the figure of the stranger, to the extent that the creative process involves a kind of self-estrangement. Of Freud, Derrida writes that 'like all those who know how to write, he has let the scene [of writing] double itself, repeat itself and betray itself in the scene'. Derrida, *L'Écriture et la différence*, p. 338. For the theorist of literary reflexivity Lucien Dällenbach, a text's thematic representation of the context of its production or reception is a '*mise en abyme of the enunciation*'. *The Mirror in the Text*, p. 75.
26. Schor, 'Fiction as Interpretation', p. 167. Schor continues: 'via the interpretant the author is trying to tell the interpreter something *about* interpretation and the interpreter would do well to listen and to take note' (p. 170). I would argue that it is the text, rather than the author, that is using its fictional interpreters to say something about how it might be read.
27. Chambers, *Story and Situation*. Chambers suggests, moreover, that 'the real reader can come to identify with, or at least relate to, the purely fictional "seducee" produced within a literary text as the object of its seduction' (p. 15). Wilson, too, argues in the context of Proust, Duras, Tournier and Cixous that 'the representation of erotic relations serves [. . .] to illustrate the possible desires activated in the reading encounter'. *Sexuality*, pp. 9–10. Similarly, Marshall's analysis of Diderot's *La Religieuse* suggests, at various points, that the seduction being staged in the text is also being performed upon the reader. *The Surprising Effects of Sympathy*, pp. 84–104.
28. Hamon, *Le Personnel du roman*, p. 77.
29. Felski, *Uses of Literature*, p. 82.
30. Felski notes that 'a reader surrenders to a text so as to savor the pleasures of being estranged from ordinary consciousness'. *The Limits of Critique*, p. 177. Interestingly, however, she also associates what she calls 'critique' with 'an attitude of restless scepticism, irony, or estrangement' (p. 127).

31. Freud, 'The Uncanny', p. 16.
32. Ibid. p. 18.
33. Ibid. p. 16.
34. Freud himself highlights the apparent contradiction: 'The somewhat para-doxical result is that *in the first place a great deal that is not uncanny in fiction would be so if it happened in real life; and in the second place that there are many more means of creating uncanny effects in fiction than there are in real life.*' Ibid. p. 18.
35. Freud, 'The Uncanny', pp. 10, 15.
36. Felski, *Uses of Literature*, p. 134.
37. Freud, 'The Uncanny', p. 5.
38. Ibid. pp. 9, 14.
39. Kristeva, *Étrangers à nous-mêmes*, p. 276.
40. Ibid. p. 268.
41. Ibid. p. 278.
42. 'The Uncanny', pp. 7, 16.
43. For Plato, too, the status of the stranger is ambiguous: 'accepted and excluded, all at the same time'. Joly, *Études platoniciennes*, p. 39. The stranger has also been described as 'always similar and dissimilar, in a play of unsettling ambivalence'. Kearney and Semonovitch, 'At the Threshold', p. 5. Bauman argues in *Modernity and Ambivalence* that in the modern era, in particular, with its privileging of rational order, the stranger came to represent undecidability, incongruity and ambivalence.
44. Simmel, 'The Stranger', pp. 143, 148.
45. Ibid. p. 147.
46. Iser, *The Act of Reading*, pp. 155, 158.
47. Nell, *Lost in a Book*, p. 212; J. Carroll, 'Minds and Meaning', p. 135.
48. Zunshine, *Why We Read Fiction*, pp. 79, 118, 121; my emphasis. See also p. 86.
49. Similarly, 'any encounter with literature involves on the one hand a repeti-tion of old material [. . .] and on the other hand an exposure to new mate-rial'. Alcorn and Bracher, 'Literature, Psychoanalysis', p. 343.
50. Bruner, *Making Stories*, p. 15.
51. Ibid. p. 90. As Booth puts it, 'total otherness, whatever that might be, would be unintelligible and in consequence totally uninteresting. At the other end of the scale, total familiarity would yield total boredom.' *The Company We Keep*, p. 194.
52. Daniel Couégnas notes of what he calls paraliterature that 'we pass from one text to another, and it's the same text; this creates a reassuring feeling of *easiness* – the reader is protected from others, from difference, from real problems – a feeling which, for some, is characteristic of alienation.' However, he also observes that 'the feeling of familiarity and the feeling of strangeness' can be united in the reception of lowbrow works. See Couégnas, *Introduction à la paralittérature*, pp. 92, 95. Radway argues that popular romances allow readers to avoid 'having to face the usual threat of the unknown'. *Reading the Romance*, p. 207.
53. Robinson, 'The Art of Distancing'.
54. Attridge, *The Singularity of Literature*, p. 77. Jonathan Culler too assumes strangeness to be a defining feature of literature in his reference to the

literary-critical illusion of narratorial omniscience as a means of 'naturaliz-ing the strange details and practices of narrative', and in his call for greater attention to 'the strange effects of literature'. 'Omniscience', p. 32.

55. As Chambers points out, self-designation or self-reflexivity tends to connote literary status. *Story and Situation* pp. 24–8, 220–1.

56. Attridge, *The Singularity of Literature*, p. 28.

57. Titchener, *A Beginner's Psychology*, p. 198.

58. Stein, *On the Problem of Empathy*, pp. 11, 13.

59. Plantinga, 'Facing Others', p. 296.

60. Jouve, *L'Effet-personnage*, p. 82.

61. Round characters, according to E. M. Forster, 'cannot be summed up in a single phrase. [. . .] The test of a round character is whether it is capable of surprising in a convincing way.' *Aspects of the Novel*, pp. 48, 54.

62. The seduction plot is certainly prominent in novels aimed at women from the eighteenth century to the present. See Modleski, *Loving with a Vengeance*, pp. 16–18. These novels are often considered to target naive readers. Radway argues that romance fictions encourage 'identification' with a heroine, and encourage readers' inference and interpretation only in a very limited and formulaic way. *Reading the Romance*, p. 204. While women have been associated more often than men with naive reading styles, it is worth noting that statistical evidence suggests that 'women are more likely to be readers', and that scientific studies suggest that women in general tend to be 'more empathetic'. Mar et al., 'Exploring the Link', p. 410.

63. Flaubert, *Madame Bovary*, p. 123. 'Bovarism', a pejorative term for the ability to imagine oneself as different from oneself, often associated with identificatory fiction-reading, was inspired by Flaubert's *Madame Bovary* (1857) and theorised by Jules de Gaultier (1892).

64. Booth, *The Company We Keep*, p. 257.

65. Schaeffer, *Pourquoi la fiction?*, p. 22. Cave suggests that 'narrative works induce affective and kinesic immersion on the one hand and ethical reflec-tion on the other'. *Thinking with Literature*, p. 123.

66. Van Lissa et al., 'Difficult Empathy', pp. 43–4.

67. Whether the internal changes undergone by readers in the course of reading narrative fictions are likely to have effects in the real world is a question that is beyond the scope of the approach adopted in this book. Keen, however, is sceptical: 'The contract of fictionality offers a no-strings-attached opportu-nity for emotional transactions of great intensity. A novel-reader may enjoy empathy freely without paying society back in altruism.' *Empathy and the Novel*, p. 168. The existence or absence of connections between narrative empathy and real-world altruism is a major theme in Keen's study.

68. Kristeva, *Étrangers à nous-mêmes*, p. 196. Sylvie Romanowski, in *Through Strangers' Eyes*, explores the figure of the cultural outsider as a figure of ambiguity in predominantly eighteenth-century French literature.

69. Stendhal, *Souvenirs d'égotisme*, in *Œuvres intimes*, vol. 2, p. 430.

70. Sarraute, 'L'Ère du soupçon', in *L'Ère du soupçon*, pp. 55–77. In this essay Sarraute presents suspicious alertness not as an ideal state but rather as a necessary part of the process of breaking from the laziness of habit.

71. Hart, 'Strangers to Ourselves', p. 412. On the figure of the stranger in

Victorian realist literature, and its debt to 'the newly dense social landscape of nineteenth-century Britain', which brought with it 'the steadily felt, tidal presence of those unknown', see McWeeny, *The Comfort of Strangers*, pp. 3, 4.

72. Petrey, *In the Court of the Pear King*, p. 80. Petrey treats Sand's *Indiana* and Stendhal's *Le Rouge et le Noir*, along with a number of Balzac's fictions, as illustrative of this changed relation to reality.

73. Lombardo, 'L'Esthétique de la tendresse chez Stendhal', p. 176. Dorrit Cohn, indeed, refers to the 'mutual dependence of realistic intent and imaginary psychology'. *Transparent Minds*, p. 6.

74. Paraschas, *The Realist Author*, p. 14. Nevertheless, Paraschas also presents the sympathetic imagination as a process that involves an oscillation between emotional involvement and detachment.

75. Dubois, *Les Romanciers du réel*, p. 106.

76. Bersani, *A Future for Astyanax*, pp. 69, 53. It seems little wonder, then, that 'realist representation is said to be naively *transparent* and malignantly *totalistic*'. Shaw, *Narrating Reality*, p. 9.

77. Jouve, *L'Effet-personnage*, p. 172. On the manner in which realist fiction activates the embodied knowledge of readers, creating a sense of lived experience, see Auyoung, *When Fiction Feels Real*. Auyoung draws on work in cognitive psychology in the construction of her argument.

78. Jouve, *L'Effet-personnage*, pp. 180–1.

79. See for example Lowe, *Victorian Fiction*; Jaffe, *Scenes of Sympathy*; the conclusion (or 'coda') of Greiner's *Sympathetic Realism* presents a brief analysis of the transition from (realist) sympathy to (modernist) empathy in literary history. Hammond presents a more detailed and extensive analysis of the same transition in the introduction to her *Empathy and the Psychology of Literary Modernism*.

80. Robinson, *Deeper than Reason*, p. 107.

81. Barthes, *S/Z*; Sarraute, *L'Ère du soupçon*.

82. Keen, 'Narrative Empathy', para. 19.

83. Stein, *On the Problem of Empathy*, p. 55. On the metaphorical character of interpersonal understanding, see Cohen, *Thinking of Others*.

Chapter 4

Balzac: The Limits of Transparency and the Dangers of Opacity

In one of Balzac's novels, he personifies the nineteenth century as a questing surgeon or archaeologist:

> There played out in La Baudraye one of those long and monotonous conjugal tragedies that would remain unknown for all eternity if the avid scalpel of the nineteenth century, driven by the need to find the new, did not go searching in the darkest corners of the heart or, if you prefer, those parts that the discretion of previous centuries had respected.[1]

As this passage indirectly suggests, Balzac's century was a time of accelerated scientific discovery: it saw revolutionary advances in the medical understanding of disease, for example, and in the fields of archaeology and palaeontology. It is no coincidence that hieroglyphs are referenced so frequently in Balzac's novels: the author was a contemporary of Jean-François Champollion, who in the 1820s effectively completed the decryption of the Rosetta Stone, thereby unlocking the secrets of hieroglyphic script. Indeed, Balzac considered his own role as a writer to be one of quasi-scientific exploration; he compared his novelistic project to the investigations undertaken by his older contemporary, the French zoologist Geoffroy Saint-Hilaire, and used the metaphor of the scalpel, tacitly in the above passage and more explicitly elsewhere, to describe the observational skills of the novelist.[2]

Balzac's writerly scalpel was just as avid and as lacking in discretion as the one he attributes to the nineteenth century in the passage quoted above. Not only are his novels driven by a desire for knowledge, they also appeal very shrewdly to the reader's own curiosity. Barthes has written about the operation of what he calls the hermeneutic code in the classic (and, as it happens, Balzacian) novel: this is the set of textual elements that both construct a question and then lead towards – and present obstacles to – its answer.[3] Balzac's novels characteristically present enigmas, which they then proceed to solve, thereby following the basic structure of a detective novel (not coincidentally an invention of the nineteenth century) or, as Barthes puts it, a striptease (which also, as it happens, has its origins in the nineteenth century).[4] The striptease metaphor is worth pausing over. Peter Brooks has written about how Balzac's 'epistemophilia' is subtended, in the novels, by a desire to see (scopophilia), and about how the object of this desire to see is often a female body.[5] However, while the desire to know, in Balzac, may well be complicit with erotic desire, it is arguably subtended not so much by a desire to *see* the body as by a desire to *read* the body, or to see through it, as if it were a transparent screen revelatory of the mind contained within it. Brooks himself suggests as much when he observes that: 'The legibility of the body is indeed a central Balzacian obsession: he is intent on making all bodily signs, whether natural or artificial, yield their cultural meaning.'[6]

To the extent that this obsession with reading others is satisfied, Balzac's work should logically offer plentiful illustrations of one of the ideas put forward by the cognitive literary scholar Lisa Zunshine, namely the notion that one of the reasons why fictions appeal to us is because they tend to foreground brief moments that offer 'the illusion of perfect readability', wherein a character's feelings appear to be legible in his or her body:

> Representations of embodied transparency regale us with something that we hold at a premium in our everyday lives and never get much of: perfect access to other people's minds via their observable behavior. As a result, they must be immensely flattering to our Theory of Mind adaptations, which evolved to read minds through bodies but have to constantly contend with the possibility of misreading and the resulting social failure.[7]

Whereas our attributions of states of mind to the people we meet in everyday life are usually sufficient for our everyday purposes, according to Zunshine, fiction engages us in, and rewards us for, those more strenuous acts of mind-reading, involving the decryption of embedded mental states, that allow us to flex the cognitive muscles with which evolution has endowed us. Zunshine's contention here and elsewhere is that while 'mind misreading'[8] is a feature of our everyday social interactions, narrative fiction tends to challenge and reward our mind-reading capabilities by allowing us to draw complex inferences about the implied mental states of characters. This chapter will place its emphasis instead on an aspect of fiction-reading that Zunshine certainly acknowledges,[9] but does not actively explore, her interest focusing rather on the complex 'nesting' of mental states in fiction. The aspect in question is fiction's tendency to remind us of the failures and limits of our inferential skills.

Certainly, Balzac's fiction offers plenty of opportunities for perfect access to the minds of others, whether or not it requires us as readers to engage in any very burdensome cognitive labour. The third-person omniscient narrator so characteristic of realism, and so closely associated with Balzacian realism in particular, offers an especially strong expression of the way in which the novel in general 'gives access to the worlds and minds of other people and other ways of life'.[10] Thanks to the omniscient narrator, the reader glides effortlessly into the thought processes of other (albeit virtual) people. As Meir Sternberg points out, this 'strange' and 'otherworldly' practice is presented in fiction as if it were entirely natural.[11] In the opening chapters of this book, we saw that some psychologists and cognitive and literary scholars have argued that this virtual transportation into the minds of fictional others can be transformative of the reader, insofar as it enables the latter to imagine what it feels like to be another person. Some scholars have even invested this immersion in other minds, however fictional, with ethical value.

One of the suggestions that will be made by my reading of Balzac is that the pleasure we derive, as readers, from unimpeded access to fictional brains is ethically dubious, because it appeals to a morally problematic desire to possess the secrets of other people. For Sartre, indeed, the desire to know always amounts to a desire to have:

> Built into the very notion of discovery and revelation is the idea of appropriative pleasure. Vision is pleasure, to see is to *deflower*. [. . .] Every investigation inevitably includes the idea of a nudity that we expose by removing the obstacles that cover it, like Acteon removing the branches so as better to see Diane as she bathes. And besides, knowledge is a hunt. [. . .] Curiosity in animals is always sexual or alimentary. To know is to devour with one's eyes. [. . .] In knowledge, consciousness attracts to itself its object and incorporates it into itself; knowledge is assimilation.[12]

The desire to know ends, then, with what is effectively the appropriation (and potential destruction) of the object of knowledge. Insofar as this mental appropriation involves an annihilation of all distance between subject and object, the realist narrator's omniscience recalls affective empathy understood as the illusion of emotional fusion or sharing. However, it differs from empathy, understood as affective sharing, to the extent that it is cognitive in nature, and operates to absorb the other into the self, rather than preserving its integrity as other.[13]

This chapter will argue that Balzac's *La Fille aux yeux d'or* tells a story about the desire to find out another person's secrets, and about how this desire to know can also be a desire to own. It will analyse the hero's attempts to read the heroine, as well as her attempts to read him, and will examine his response to the discovery, in a moment of embodied transparency that is also a moment of embodied opacity, that he cannot own her desire, a desire that he appears to consider entirely readable but that the text suggests is unreadable, incomprehensible. The chapter will propose that Balzac's novel appeals to the reader's desire to find out the text's secret, but also frustrates that desire. It also highlights the need to resist seduction by the fictional text.

Firstly, however, to justify the significance it gives to the relationship between the two central characters, this chapter will begin by showing that Henri de Marsay and Paquita Valdès are stranger figures who are closely connected with fiction.

Henri and Paquita as Fiction-Connoted Strangers

Both main characters of *La Fille aux yeux d'or* are associated with foreignness. The narrator tells us that De Marsay, who will become 'un des hommes politiques les plus profonds du temps actuel' (one of the most penetrating politicians of our day),[14] has both English and French parentage, and the narrator several times characterises his temperament as Eastern. Paquita, a sexual plaything for a wealthy aristocrat, was born in Cuba to a Georgian mother, herself a sex slave. Paquita is described by the narrator as 'cette belle créature qui tenait aux houris de l'Asie par sa mère, à l'Europe par son éducation, aux Tropiques par sa naissance' (this beautiful creature who was linked to the Asian houris through her mother, to Europe through her upbringing and to the Tropics through her birth) (p. 434). Paquita's outsider status is far more marked than that of Henri, because unlike him she is culturally other, uncomprehending of the rules and values that govern the place where she now lives. She speaks no French and is forbidden from having any contact with the inhabitants of the city. An exotic-looking beauty, she is almost always accompanied and guarded by at least one of three other outsider figures: an elderly Spanish lady, her Georgian mother and an African eunuch.

Henri and Paquita are strangers, too, in the sense that they are enigmatic, and other than they seem. The narrator tells us, for example, that De Marsay hides a jaded soul behind a deceptively beautiful exterior, 'les dehors les plus séduisants' (the most seductive appearances) (p. 391). Henri is frivolous and playful on the one hand, and cruel on the other: he jokes with his friend Paul de Manerville about the importance of personal grooming and the sanctity of cigars, but there is something both elusive and dangerous about him; he is possessed of what the narrator calls 'un immense pouvoir inconnu' (an immense and unknown power) (pp. 424–5). The protagonist's difference is sensed by other characters.

His supposed 'ami intime' (close friend) cannot be sure of how authentic his friendship is: 'Il le craignait, et sa crainte, quoique imperceptible, réagissait sur les autres, et servait De Marsay' (He feared him, and his fear, although imperceptible, acted in turn upon others, and served De Marsay) (p. 398). In fact, Henri takes pride in his own unreadability to others. He tells Paul that he finds it amusing to mock society by keeping his affections a secret from all, and explains that he would consider it a weakness to allow anyone to glimpse his motivations. Paquita, unlike De Marsay, is obliged to be mysterious rather than choosing to be so; she cannot share her secret, namely the identity of her lover-proprietor, with the protagonist of the story, for fear of being killed. Both the fact that her controlling lover will turn out to be female, and the ambiguity surrounding Paquita's feelings for her, are further aspects of the heroine's otherness.

La Fille aux yeux d'or presents, therefore, two striking figures of the stranger. Both characters are marked out as outsiders,[15] and both are mysteriously other than they seem. Both strangers are also closely associated with fiction, often explicitly but also less directly.

Paquita is repeatedly presented as a product of the imagination, and is therefore associated with fiction in the sense of invention. She is twice linked to the quintessentially fictional figure of the chimera, first when she is compared by Henri to the chimera-caressing woman in a portrait that has its origins in a work of fiction by Henri de Latouche, and secondly when the narrator describes Paquita's hideous mother as the fishtail of a beautiful woman. Also suggestive of Paquita's resemblance to a product of fiction is her repeated designation, by both the narrator and Henri, as a masterpiece of nature.[16] The comparison of the young heroine's boudoir to the shell from which Venus is born is doubly related to imaginary invention, in that it calls to mind both classical mythology and Botticelli's painting *The Birth of Venus*. Paquita is associated with poetic invention, too: the narrator describes her as 'une fille qui réalisait si bien les idées les plus lumineuses exprimées sur les femmes par la poésie orientale' (a girl who embodied so well the most luminous ideas about women as expressed in the poetry of the East) (p. 404); and when Henri sees her, 'il éprouva une de ces sensations délicates que donne la vraie poésie' (he felt one of those delicate sensations offered by true poetry) (p. 429). Her lovemaking with Henri is described as a particularly expressive and sensual kind of poetry, and in her company Henri seems to enter a different state, designated by the narrator as '*les espaces imaginaires*' (*imaginary spaces*) (p. 445).

Paquita is also associated with narrative fiction, specifically. The portrait of the woman caressing her chimera, to which Henri compares her, has no reality other than in a work of prose fiction, while the fishtail constituted by her mother is described by the narrator as 'un dénoûment possible' (a possible denouement) (p. 420). Not only do the young men who prowl the Tuileries gardens in pursuit of her bestow a fictional name upon her, and a name redolent of the particular type of narrative fiction that is the fairy tale, this fictional name is also the name of the prose fiction in which she features; she is thereby partly identified with the story to which she lends her name. The fairy-tale connotations of the name are also present in descriptions of the character. When Paquita appears to Henri in all her voluptuous glory, she does so in the middle of a boudoir 'éclos par la baguette d'une fée' (produced by a fairy's wand) (p. 429). At their subsequent meeting, she is compared to a 'Péri', a Persian fairy-tale figure (p. 444). She is described as appealing to a passion for the infinite as felt by fictional characters such as Goethe's Faust and Don Juan. In addition, the narrator tells us that Henri needs Paquita in order to feel something approximating love, and compares this need to that of the jaded Lovelace, with regard to Richardson's heroine. Finally, Paquita is designated by Henri as a naive and uncritical consumer of fiction, like all women in his eyes; it is only much later that she tells him that she is illiterate.

Henri, too, is associated by the text with fiction. If Paquita is compared to Venus, he is referred to as an Adonis. Henri plans to put the heroine's minder to sleep in the manner described in the 'fable' of Argus (p. 413). His pursuit of Paquita is presented repeatedly in terms of a stage plot along the lines of Beaumarchais's play *Le Barbier de Seville* (*The Barber of Seville*) or Rossini's operatic adaptation of the same work. In order to gain access to Paquita, whose residence belongs (somewhat incongruously) to one Marquis de San-Réal, Henri engages in a series of elaborate ruses that are explicitly far-fetched: Paquita is so closely guarded that Henri must penetrate obstacles worthy of a fairy-tale prince. He repeatedly describes the entire episode as 'une aventure' (an adventure) (pp. 417, 448). Henri writes a letter to Paquita, which is effectively a work of fiction, insofar as he lays claim to a false name, Adolphe (a name closely associated, at the time of the novel's publication, with a famous work of fiction by Benjamin Constant), and to a passion which he does not yet feel. Finally, when Henri does finally meet and sleep with Paquita, he refuses to tell his friend Paul about his triumph, and gives him a lesson instead about the different types of discretion that a man can deploy to disguise the secret of his affections: the negative type, which involves secrecy or denial, or the active type, preferable according to Henri, which involves the telling of lies (including truths presented as lies). Henri's talent for discretion is, he implies, an ability to spin stories.

Despite not being able to write, Paquita is, like Henri, a highly competent producer of plots, and her own story enters into competition with his. As Sara Pappas puts it, 'she has her own simple plan that replaces his very convoluted one'.[17] Instead of writing a letter in response to his, as he had dictated, Paquita sends a delegate to fetch Henri; this man, likened by the narrator to the tragic hero Othello, threatens his translator with strangulation and conveys to Henri the young woman's warning that one false move could lead to the lovers' murder. Whereas his seduction plot had fitted the mould of a stage comedy, Paquita evidently has a more tragic plot in mind. Bemused by the heroine's machinations, Henri reflects on the risibly novelistic or 'romanesque' quality of the melodramatic turn, and attributes the new tone of their romance to female fancifulness: 'Mourir? pauvre enfant! Des poignards? imagination de femmes!' (Die? poor child! Daggers? Female fancy!) (p. 417). Nevertheless, it transpires that Henri himself is a consumer of female-authored gothic fiction; upon his first visit to Paquita, he is reminded of the feeling he had while reading the novels of Ann Radcliffe. Even after his second tryst with the heroine, however, he continues to persuade himself that her dark imaginings are simply 'une de ces tromperies par lesquelles toutes les femmes essaient de se rendre intéressantes' (one of those tricks used by all women in an attempt to make themselves interesting) (p. 434). Henri ultimately finds his place in Paquita's tragic plot, though not the place that he had expected; instead of being a lover pursued by a jealous rival, he turns out to be a villain (and a secondary one at that).

The relationship between Henri and Paquita is frequently presented, therefore, in terms reminiscent of fiction. Paquita is particularly skilled in the creation of a fictional atmosphere, through her insistence for example on Henri wearing a blindfold on his way to meet her, which makes him feel as though he is in 'un rêve' (a dream) (p. 441). She creates a dreamlike atmosphere at each arranged meeting – 'Cette scène fut comme un songe pour de Marsay' (This scene was like a dream for De Marsay) (p. 424) – not only dressing Henri up, but also conjuring up, for his benefit, an entire 'sérail' (harem) (p. 444).

The day after this latter episode, Henri feels revulsion for 'son idole' (his idol); the existence of this kind of 'affection confuse' (confused feeling) is proven, for Balzac's narrator, by its description in a novel by Rousseau, a description that he claims was itself inspired by Richardson's fiction (p. 433). Continuities between life and art are further reinforced when, having discovered the sex of Paquita's lover, Henri tells Paul that 'la vie est une singulière comédie' (life is a remarkable comedy) (p. 439) and when, after referring to the relative innocuousness of Laclos's *Les*

Liaisons dangereuses and Sade's *Justine*, he declares that 'il existe un livre horrible, sale, épouvantable, corrupteur, toujours ouvert, qu'on ne fermera jamais, le grand livre du monde' (there is a horrible, dirty, terrifying, corrupting, always open book, which will never be closed, the great book of society) (p. 440). A thousand times more dangerous even than this latter book is the one that is composed of whispers among men, or among women 'sous l'éventail' (behind their fans) (p. 440); this book would take as its theme homosexual relations. Paquita's lesbian relationship is metaphorically presented here as a story that might feature in a clandestinely composed, immoral book; further suggestive of links to fiction, the narrator characterises the homosexual love to which Paquita has been exposed as 'un amour en quelque sorte artificiel' (a somewhat artificial love) (p. 444). When the heroine's butchered body lies before Henri and his half-sister, Margarita, Henri refers to Paquita using a term suggestive of fiction: he asks Margarita how she will 'enlever les traces de cette fantaisie' (erase the traces of this fantasy) in order to avoid prosecution for her crime (p. 453). The story ends with Henri's own act of erasure: when his friend Paul asks where the girl with the golden eyes has got to, he suggests that she has died of consumption. The novel closes upon this expedient fiction.

To sum up, both Paquita and Henri are strangers who are closely associated with fiction, in a range of ways. If we understand them, consequently, following the reflexive logic outlined in Chapter 3, as proxies for the fictional story in which they feature, how does the novel invite us to read them?

The Limits of Transparency

La Fille aux yeux d'or opens with a famously long passage wherein the authorial narrator describes the different social spheres that compose Paris, from the large one at the bottom, composed of the workers who support the entire system, to the tiny one at the top, where the privileged few reside. In this prologue, the city is presented as a rationally ordered system, similar to a giant brain: Paris is described as 'la tête du globe, un cerveau qui crève de génie et conduit la civilisation humaine' (the head of the globe, a mind that bursts with genius and leads human civilisation) (p. 385); a related extended metaphor is that of Paris as a giant steamship, composed of various parts: 'Paris n'est-elle pas un sublime vaisseau chargé d'intelligence?' (Is Paris not a sublime ship loaded with intelligence?) (p. 386). However, the city is also portrayed, simultaneously, as a vast, desiring female body, driven by an infernal desire for gold and pleasure: Paris is 'la plus impudique des Vénus' (the most immodest of Venuses) (p. 373) and 'une reine qui, toujours grosse, a des envies irrésistiblement furieuses' (a queen who, always pregnant, has irresistibly furious cravings) (p. 385). While these metaphors may, at first glance, seem incompatible, Balzac's narrative will show that the mind too has appetites. Another metaphor appearing in the prologue is that of the city as a huge, sickly body. The narrator promises to explain the 'causes' behind the cadaverous face of this body by looking through it to its 'âme' (soul); he will also reveal 'la cause générale' (the general cause) of the sickly complexion of the city's inhabitants (pp. 371–2). The bodies evoked in the prologue are thus legible in every detail, at least in the eyes of this all-knowing narrator.

Appearing to guarantee the readability of this vast city-body and of its hordes of smaller bodies is the fact that repeatedly, in Balzac's prologue, any element that threatens to resist assimilation into the system, or hierarchy of categories, is ultimately absorbed into it. The narrator claims that foreigners, for example, are transformed by their experience of living in Paris, so that in the end they look no different from anyone else. In describing each social sphere, Balzac's narrator several times identifies an individual whose ambition makes him simultaneously representative of his sphere and an exception within it (the thrifty worker, the petty bourgeois 'Monsieur' who receives the Legion of Honour medal, the bourgeois man who becomes a member of the peerage); and yet even these exceptional individuals simply follow the logic of the system by raising their children up into the next sphere. Any exceptions are, in other words, re-absorbed into the system, any difference converted into the easy readability of stereotypes.[18]

However, as even these examples suggest, Balzac's system does betray a certain strain on its homogenising logic. This strain is revealed too by the heterogeneous and incongruous metaphors his narrator uses to describe it (a storm-blown field, a sickly face, a plaster cage, a hive, hell, a lubricious female body, a battlefield and, within just one paragraph, a pregnant queen with furious appetites, a giant and brilliant head and a ship). Just before the end of the prologue, in a final flourish, the narrator lists all of the various individuals who might be considered exceptions to the general rule of Parisian physical ugliness. Among these can be found, occasionally, a young or middle-aged member of the clergy, a virtuous child of the bourgeoisie, a young mother, a young provincial, a young shop boy, a scientist or poet, a self-satisfied idiot or a street wanderer. As well as this eclectic collection of individuals who are, unusually, not ugly, there are entire female communities, described as 'de petites peuplades heureuses qui vivent à l'orientale' (small, happy populations who live in the oriental style) (p. 388). The strain on Balzac's system is further suggested by the 'néanmoins' (nevertheless), 'mais' (but) and 'cependant' (however) that qualify the narrator's sweeping generalisations (pp. 387–8). The omniscient narrator both asserts that his system is comprehensive and draws attention to all the exceptions to its general rule, exceptions that are accounted for only weakly, with the assertion that 'Paris est essentiellement aussi le pays des contrastes' (Paris is also essentially the land of contrasts) (p. 388). Overall, the reader is left with the impression that there are so many infinitesimally rare exceptions to the general rule that the solidity of the entire system is placed in doubt.[19] It is certainly difficult to see how some Parisians might be untouched by physical and moral decrepitude and oblivious to the pursuit of gold and pleasure, in view of the narrator's frequent generalisations in the prologue about 'le Parisien' (the Parisian) and about Parisian facial and character traits. It is hard, in other words, to know how to read statements such as the following, in view of the later revelations about the various exceptions to the rule:

> Là, tout fume, tout brûle, tout brille, tout bouillonne, tout flambe, s'évapore, s'éteint, se rallume, étincelle, pétille et se consume. (pp. 371–2)

> (Here, everything smokes, everything burns, everything shines, everything simmers, everything flames, evaporates, dies down, reignites, sparkles, crackles, and consumes itself.)

> À Paris, aucun sentiment ne résiste au jet des choses. (p. 372)

> (In Paris, no feeling resists the flux of things.)

There is something forced and excessively reductive, in other words, about the reading of Paris that is offered by Balzac's narrator, in his prologue. He erects a vast system but finds that it struggles to account for anomalies.[20] In the narrative that follows, a virtually omniscient protagonist attempts to insert the eponymous heroine into a pre-existing system of his own. However, she partially resists assimilation into the hero's system: her foreign body does not give itself up entirely to his knowledge. She regularly thwarts the interpretive grids he tries to impose on her. Unfortunately, as the protagonist's friend says of him, 'rien ne lui résiste' (nothing resists him) (p. 399); Paquita will pay the price for her resistance.

Even the title of Balzac's *La Fille aux yeux d'or* suggests that its heroine will pose a reading problem. The term 'fille' can be interpreted literally, to mean that she is a young female, or euphemistically, to mean that she is a prostitute, or at least a sexually available woman of low social standing. Golden eyes also give the reader pause, calling attention to the fantastical quality of a text whose inclusion in the 'Scènes de la vie parisienne', a section of Balzac's *Comédie humaine*, and whose first chapter title, 'Physionomies parisiennes', seem by contrast to invest the text with the status of a quasi-factual document. Is this heroine to be read as a fairy-tale figure or as realistic, as extraordinary or as banal?

Paquita certainly seems extraordinary to the cynical, sexually jaded protagonist when he spies her walking in the Tuileries. The young heroine becomes even more interesting to him when he discovers the secrecy surrounding her: he discovers that the house in which she lives is highly protected, and at their various subsequent meetings she refuses to tell him the name of his rival. We learn, at an early point in the narrative, that Henri is an expert reader of other people. He belongs, according to the narrator, to a species of young men who 'étudient secrètement les pensées d'autrui' (secretly study the thoughts of others), and who 'pèsent les hommes comme un avare pèse ses pièces d'or' (weigh men as a miser weighs his gold coins) (pp. 396–7).[21] Henri deciphers gazes, for example, with such extreme accuracy that the narrator occasionally transcribes the meaning he construes from them into words; this occurs when he and the Marquis de Ronquerolles exchange looks in passing, and when he interprets a death threat in the eyes of Paquita's minder. Henri also decodes from Paquita's style of walking her aptitude for love. It seems little wonder, then, that De Marsay is described by the narrator as being possessed of 'cette promptitude de coup d'œil et d'ouïe particulière au Parisien qui paraît, au premier aspect, ne rien voir et ne rien entendre, mais qui voit et entend tout' (that quickness of eye and ear that is peculiar to the Parisian who appears, at first, not to see or hear anything, but who sees and hears everything) (p. 394).

Indeed, as this last quotation suggests, Henri appears so capable of deciphering other people, and of placing them in general categories, that he resembles Balzac's omniscient narrator. In this, he exemplifies the 'authorial double' as theorised by Sotirios Paraschas, a fictional figure who 'can enter the minds of his fellow-characters through a process of imaginative identification, who can manipulate their actions and shape the development of the plot'.[22] Like the Balzacian narrator of the pro-logue and other novels, he will prove himself capable of detecting 'les causes cachées à d'autres yeux' (causes hidden to other eyes), and which are visible only, we are told, to the strongest of men (p. 420). Like the Balzacian narrator, too, he seems able to make sense of what is ordinar-ily indecipherable, such as the bloody hieroglyphs which the Marquise de San-Réal uses to convey her passion to Paquita. Balzac's narrator, too, is in the habit of overcoming any resistance that crosses his path.

The narrator's categorising impulse, already noted in the context of the prologue, continues throughout the story of *La Fille aux yeux d'or*. Virtually every character in this fiction appears to belong, unproblematically, to a type, as is so often the case in Balzac's fiction: the narrator says of the protagonist's friend, Paul, for example, that he 'ne pouvait se classer que dans la grande, l'illustre et puissante famille des niais qui arrivent' (could only be classed in the great, illustrious, and powerful family of the idiots who succeed) (p. 399). The hero himself belongs, according to the narrator, to one of two elegant 'classes' (classes) or 'espèces' (species) of young men (pp. 394, 395). It is often difficult to differentiate the narrator's voice from Henri's, as the two even use a similar vocabulary and share certain verbal tics, such as the use of the demonstrative adjective. Even the passive construction of the phrase 'tout cela se voyait' (all of this could be seen) (p. 402), at one point, lets it be understood that Henri's interpretation coincides perfectly with that of the omniscient narrator.

Henri, like the narrator, may repeatedly describe the young heroine as '[une] inconnue' (an unknown woman), but he is as reductive of her alterity as is the narrator who repeatedly simplifies Paquita's complex cultural origins by referring to her simply as Spanish.[23] Echoing the reductive strategies of the narrator, Henri is very quick to classify her. He can tell, for example, that she does not belong to noble circles: 'une femme qui vient le dimanche aux Tuileries n'a pas de valeur, aristocratiquement parlant' (a woman who comes to the Tuileries on a Sunday has no value, aristocratically speaking) (p. 399). For him, at least at first, she is simply another woman to fall for his very visible charms. He claims, for example, not to have been surprised by the erotic shock he produced in her on their first encounter, because he is used to producing this effect in women. However, upon realising how physically beautiful she is, Henri places Paquita in a more specific category: 'Elle appartient à cette variété féminine que les Romains nommaient *fulva*, *flava*, la femme de feu' (She belongs to that female variety that the Romans called *fulva*, *flava*, the woman of fire) (p. 400). Upon their first encounter in the Tuilerie gardens, nevertheless, the heroine's eyes are defined in exotic and potentially dangerous terms, and seem to connote a radically unfamiliar, inhuman otherness. De Marsay compares her eyes to those of a tiger: 'deux yeux jaunes comme ceux des tigres; un jaune d'or qui brille, de l'or vivant, de l'or qui pense, de l'or qui aime et veut absolument venir dans votre gousset!' (two eyes yellow like those of tigers; a yellow of gleaming gold, a living gold, a thinking gold, a loving gold determined to jump into your trouser pocket!) (p. 400). The dehumanisation conveyed by the tiger simile is continued in the comparison of the yellow colour of Paquita's eyes to shiny gold coins, but only partly, because these coins are so very friendly that they want to jump into a man's pocket. Any threat conveyed by the tiger simile is defused by the image of friendly coins: the metaphorical logic suggests a movement from a situation of danger towards one of easy appropriation and domination. Those eyes that had initially marked Paquita out as dangerously other and even inhuman suddenly connote, instead, her easy sexual availability, and ultimately her similarity to other women. The golden eyes that make such an initial impression on Henri serve only to bolster his sense that this young woman is simply a particularly desirable instance of a type. The heroine is presented, therefore, as extremely familiar despite her initial unfamiliarity, and as eminently open to being possessed, despite her initial comparison to a wild animal. Paquita is effectively an object for the taking, from Henri's point of view. Certainly, the protagonist is fascinated by Paquita's eyes, and more generally by her otherness; but he also sees this otherness as provisional. She is unknown, for him, rather than unknowable. De Marsay will later persuade himself that Paquita is not as dangerous or as different as she pretends to be, and that she is in fact just like any other woman, carried away by her imagination and trying to make herself interesting. If the obstacles that block his path to the heroine render her, temporarily at least, '[une] perle introuvable' (an elusive pearl) (p.408), for Henri, her singularity is merely a result of her rarity, her various charms being so striking only because he has never encountered them united in the one body. In other words, there is nothing intrinsically new or surprising about Paquita, from Henri's perspective. She is simply another woman to add to his collection of conquests, another woman for him to have, in all senses. The comparisons of her to treasure, be it gold coins or a rare pearl, make it utterly clear that Henri's desire for Paquita is fundamentally a desire to own her.

Paquita is not, however, as easy to classify and appropriate as Henri initially imagines. His curiosity about her, triggered by her female companion, plays a significant role in his attraction to her: 'la duègne m'a rendu plus qu'amoureux, je suis devenu curieux' (the duenna made me more than enamoured; I became curious) (p. 402). Curiosity, or the desire for knowledge, here as elsewhere in the text is complicit with a desire for sexual possession.[24] Henri tries several times to find the key to the identity of this mysterious heroine, and repeatedly produces a result that is either incorrect or only partially correct. The first time he catches sight of Paquita, for example, he reads her facial expression very accurately, but fails to understand the deeper significance of what he sees: 'Moralement parlant, sa figure semblait dire: – Quoi, te voilà, mon idéal, l'être de mes pensées, de mes rêves du soir et du matin. Comment es-tu là? pourquoi ce matin? pourquoi pas hier?' (Psychologically speaking, her face seemed to say: 'What, is that you, my ideal, the creation of my thoughts, of my night-time and morning dreams. How are you here? Why this morning? Why not yesterday?) (p. 400). Henri fails, understandably, to see that what Paquita is so struck by is in fact his uncanny resemblance to her lesbian mistress; the deficiencies of his reading are only likely to be detected on a second reading of the novel. In addition, De Marsay erroneously concludes, subsequently, on the basis of intelligence received, that Paquita is 'sans doute' (no doubt) the mistress of the Marquis de San-Réal (p. 407). After his second meeting with her, moreover, Henri wrongly deduces that the heroine's frequently expressed fear of death is simply an affectation, and a product of her cultural origins: 'Elle est de la Havane, du pays le plus espagnol qu'il y ait dans le Nouveau Monde; elle a donc [. . .] aimé jouer la terreur' (She is from Havana, the most Spanish part of the New World; so she [. . .] enjoyed feigning terror) (p. 434). In all of these assumptions, Henri is mistaken, though the text never spells this out.

There is one point in the story, however, when Henri glimpses how little he knows about this heroine. This is the moment, during the first of three amorous trysts, just after she tells him that they have only twelve days before something dreadful happens. Henri concludes, in characteristically categorising mode, that the heroine is mad, a designation that Shoshana Felman claims is typically applied in Western patriarchal culture to women's incomprehensible otherness.[25] The hero is plunged, however, despite himself, into 'des réflexions étranges' (strange reflections) (p. 421): 'Peut-être avait-elle dans le cœur un autre amour qu'elle oubliait et se rappelait tour à tour. En un moment, Henri fut assailli de mille pensées contradictoires. Pour lui cette fille devint un mystère' (Perhaps she had in her heart another love that she was alternately forgetting and remembering. In a moment, Henri was assailed by contradictory thoughts. For him this girl became a mystery) (pp. 421–2). Paquita's mysteriousness, which Henri speculatively connects, here, to her sporadic memory of another lover, is rendered all the more impenetrable to him by her revelation that the physically grotesque old lady who is present at their first assignation is actually her mother. This 'vieille momie' (old mummy) (p. 420), invested with 'cette impassibilité de la statuaire sur laquelle échoue l'observation' (that impassivity of a statue that is impenetrable to the eye) (p. 422) and compared to a fishtail attached to the heroine, is no longer just circumstantially and accidentally linked to the young woman, but is now linked to her by nature. When Henri dreams of Paquita, subsequently, 'Ce fut des images monstrueuses, des bizarreries insaisissables, pleines de lumière, et qui révèlent des mondes invisibles, mais d'une manière toujours incomplète, car un voile interposé change les conditions de l'optique' (He saw monstrous images, ungraspable oddities, full of light, and giving onto invisible worlds, but only incompletely, for an intervening veil changes the optical conditions) (pp. 425–6). At least for one night, then, Paquita is not an object that can be unproblematically possessed, or a body that can be unproblematically read.

As the references to the limits of what can be seen, and to visual confusion, in this episode suggest, Henri's surprised recognition of Paquita's elusiveness to him makes this one of those Balzacian 'limit-cases' evoked by Brooks. These are moments associated by Brooks with the discovery of the female's potential as a desiring subject, 'when looking produces not clarity and mastery but trouble, the inability to see, and the disempowerment of the observer'.[26] Even Balzac's most gifted fictional mind-readers are occasionally surprised by the actions of others, and occasionally encounter the limits of their own ability to know. These are moments akin to those described by Sartre in *L'Etre et le Néant*, when the subject experiences himself as the object of another person's gaze, an object of knowledge for someone else: when the other person is the one doing the looking, the subject provisionally abandons his mastery.[27] At the first arranged meeting between Henri and Paquita in *La Fille aux yeux d'or*, the female character's impenetrability seems to reveal itself to the fictional male interpretant;[28] Henri appears to recognise, at some deep level, Paquita's troubling resistance to his masterful reading of her, on account of the insistence of her own desire; indeed, the heroine herself admits, later, that she was attracted to him by her own 'curiosité de démon' (demonic curiosity) (p. 443). As Nicole Mozet points out, Henri may think of Paquita as an object of curiosity, but, for her, he plays this role.[29]

At their second tryst, when they sleep together for the first time, Henri remains intrigued by Paquita's strangeness, which he nevertheless once again treats, condescendingly, as provisional, a problem that can be solved: 'tu me parais une bonne fille, une nature bizarre; tu es [. . .] une charade vivante dont le mot me semble bien difficile à trouver' (you appear to me to be a good girl, a strange character; you are [. . .] a living riddle whose solution seems very hard to find) (p. 431). He is fascinated by the secret that she refuses to tell him, namely the identity of his rival, 'l'être inconnu qui planait comme une ombre au-dessus d'eux' (the unknown being who hovered like a shadow above them), and even appears to suspect that he is simply standing in for a rival: 'Pour qui me prends-tu donc?' (For whom do you take me then?) (p. 430). When he finally stops asking questions and agrees to be seduced by her, the narrator speculates that it might be in the hope of learning all her 'secrets' (p. 432). During their lovemaking, Henri becomes aware of a further mysterious aspect of Paquita:

> Chose étrange! Si la *Fille aux yeux d'or* était vierge, elle n'était certes pas innocente. L'union si bizarre du mystérieux et du réel, de l'ombre et de la lumière, de l'horrible et du beau, du plaisir et du danger, du paradis et de l'enfer, qui s'était déjà rencontrée dans cette aventure, se continuait dans l'être capricieux et sublime dont se jouait De Marsay. (p. 432)

> (What a strange thing! If the *Girl with the Golden Eyes* was a virgin, she certainly was not innocent. The very bizarre union of the mysterious and the real, shadow and light, horror and beauty, pleasure and danger, heaven and hell, which this adventure had already presented, found its continuation in the capricious and sublime being with whom De Marsay was playing.)

Henri is correct in his deduction that the heroine is far from sexually innocent. It is worth noting that 'cette aventure' (this adventure) can be understood to refer both to the fantastical chain of events that has led Henri to Paquita's boudoir and to Balzac's own narrative. To the extent that it refers to the latter, the narrator formulates, very explicitly and precisely, a central premise of our own book, namely the idea that a fictional figure can figuratively embody the fiction in which she finds herself. Henri's simultaneous fascination with and ironic detachment from – 'se jouer de' suggests a playful, mocking attitude – Paquita might even be understood to mirror the reader's own simultaneous captivation and detachment, in relation both to her character and to Balzac's narrative (and also recalls the dual attitude of the fiction-reader as discussed in earlier chapters of this study).

Upon his return to mundane reality the following day, Henri retrospectively deciphers the meaning of the heroine's behaviour, and of her merely technical innocence:

> De Marsay s'aperçut qu'il avait été joué par la *Fille aux yeux d'or*, en voyant dans son ensemble cette nuit dont les plaisirs n'avaient que graduellement ruisselé pour finir par s'épancher à torrents. Il put alors lire dans cette page si brillante d'effet, en deviner le sens caché. L'innocence purement physique de Paquita, l'étonnement de sa joie, quelques mots d'abord obscurs et maintenant clairs, échappés au milieu de la joie, tout lui prouva qu'il avait posé pour une autre personne. [. . .] Si ses présomptions étaient justes, il avait été outragé dans le vif de son être. Ce seul soupçon le mit en fureur. (pp. 438–9)

> (De Marsay saw that he had been tricked by the *Girl with the Golden Eyes*, on surveying that night in its entirety, from its trickling pleasures to its torrential surges. He was then able to read into that page, so radiant in its effect, and draw from it the hidden meaning. The purely physical innocence of Paquita, the astonishment of her joy, a few words that were initially obscure and now

clear, which had escaped in the midst of her pleasure, everything proved to
him that he had stood in for another person. [. . .] If his presumptions were
correct, he had been insulted in the core of his being. This suspicion alone
threw him into a rage)

The metaphor of reading is significant: Henri deciphers the hidden
meaning of Paquita's behaviour and of her body as though he were
reading in a book. Interestingly, it is not the heroine's possible lesbianism
that bothers Henri.[30] It is suggested here that what is intolerable for
Henri is the idea that he is not the sole object and effective owner of the
heroine's desire: he believes that she desires someone else, for whom he
is a mere stand-in.[31]

After an afternoon spent gambling in the aptly-named Salon des
Étrangers, Henri returns for a third meeting with Paquita. He is pre-
pared to turn a blind eye to the latter's lesbian past, provided that he
does not have to share her with any rival, even in her memory:

> — Suis-je le préféré? se dit en lui-même Henri qui, s'il entrevoyait la vérité,
> se trouvait alors disposé à pardonner l'offense en faveur d'un amour si naïf.
> — Je verrai bien, pensa-t-il.
> Si Paquita ne lui devait aucun compte du passé, le moindre souvenir deve-
> nait un crime à ses yeux. (p. 444)

> ('Am I the favourite?', Henri wondered to himself; he glimpsed the truth,
> but was at that moment ready to pardon the offence in favour of such a naive
> love. 'I shall see,' he thought.
> While Paquita owed no account to him for the past, the slightest recollec-
> tion became a crime in his eyes.)

The narrator thus prepares the reader for Henri's explosion of anger later
in this episode. After the heroine's fatal utterance, 'Oh! Mariquita!', the
narrator adds that that exclamation was 'd'autant plus horrible pour
lui qu'il avait été détrôné du plus doux triomphe qui eût jamais agrandi
sa vanité d'homme' (all the more horrible for him because he had been
dethroned from the sweetest triumph that had ever enlarged his male
vanity) (pp. 446, 448). The reader is encouraged, therefore, to draw the
conclusion that the hero interprets the exclamation as irrefutable proof
that he is not the primary object of Paquita's desire. It is not, crucially,
the gender of the heroine's other lover that angers Henri; it is the fact
that the latter may linger somewhere in Paquita's memory, and may even
supplant him in the present moment.

It is tempting to read the heroine's exclamation as one of those
instances of 'embodied transparency' discussed by Zunshine. Certainly,
Henri treats it as revelatory, as one of those 'epiphanic moments' evoked
by David Denby, where the body expresses a truth that had been deeply

buried.[32] In fact, however, the signifier is far more opaque than the protagonist admits. Felman has noted that 'the name "Mariquita" can be read as a composite, either of "*mar*quise" and "Pa*quita*"', on the one hand, 'or of *Mar*say (Henri) and Pa*quita*', on the other.[33] Another reason why the vocable could name Henri himself, rather than (or as well as) the Marquise/Margarita, is that, as Felman also points out, the word 'mariquita' means 'effeminate man' in Spanish, which is Paquita's first language.[34] Nevertheless, when Henri hears this exclamation, he is deaf to any potential referential or semantic ambiguity. There is no longer any doubt in his mind: '— Mariquita! cria le jeune homme en rugissant, je sais maintenant tout ce dont je voulais encore douter.' ('Mariquita!' roared the young man, 'Now I know everything that I wished to deny.') (p. 446) For Henri, the term 'Mariquita' offers certain knowledge: he knows now, beyond a shadow of a doubt, that Paquita is remembering a female lover as she makes love to him. Regardless, then, of the potential ambiguities contained in the heroine's exclamation, Henri treats the vocable as incontrovertible proof that he is not the exclusive object and master of her desire. He cannot, in other words, possess his lover completely. Apparently realising that Paquita's body has resisted his attempted appropriation of it, her desire not being entirely owned by him even in the present moment (Paquita owes him no debt with regard to the past, he says, but by implication she does owe him her present), Henri resolves to kill her. The secret that he now finally knows is not the one that Paquita contrived to keep, namely the secret of the identity and gender of the heroine's former mistress (he had deduced these prior to his epiphany), but rather the possibility that this mistress continues to be an object of the heroine's desire; De Marsay discovers, in other words, the limits of his own ownership of Paquita's desire. But even as he recognises the heroine's resistance to his mastery, he resolves to rid himself of this resistance. He absents himself from society for a whole week, 'sans que personne pût savoir ni ce qu'il fit pendant ce temps, ni dans quel endroit il demeura' (without anyone knowing either what he did during that time or in what place he stayed) (p. 449). The reader is not told what he does during that time, though it can be inferred, by the suspicious, mind-reading reader, that he makes plans to murder Paquita with impunity.

It is not, however, De Marsay who kills the heroine in the end, but rather her female lover. Like Henri, the latter makes love to Paquita with the intention of finding out her secrets. She discovers very quickly that the heroine's body has changed, after sexual intercourse with a male. Arriving too late to kill the heroine himself, Henri is very capable of reading the crime scene: he spies the messy bed, the red fingerprints on the furniture and walls of the boudoir, the bite-marks on the murderer's ankle. The heroine's body is, furthermore, just as readable, for him, as it was when it told him, during their first night of lovemaking, of her lesbian sexual experiences: 'Son corps, déchiqueté à coups de poignard par son bourreau, disait avec quel acharnement elle avait disputé une vie qu'Henri lui rendait si chère' (Her body, shredded by the dagger thrusts of her tormentor, told of the ferocity with which she had defended a life that Henri had made so dear to her) (p. 450). For the reader who believes in Henri's perspicacity, a perspicacity that is repeatedly emphasised by the narrator, the text of *La Fille aux yeux d'or* is just as readable as the body of the eponymous heroine in these final moments. And in some senses this body, like the text itself, is indeed highly readable: the text allows us to understand that an intact hymen betrays the identity of Paquita's lover to Henri, that a broken hymen betrays her infidelity to her mistress, and that an exclamation uttered during lovemaking betrays her continuing attachment to the latter.

However, both text and body also put up a certain resistance to easy reading, just as certain exceptional individuals in Balzac's prologue had resisted easy assimilation into the narrator's explanatory system. On seeing Henri and noting his physical similarity to her, the Marquise de San-Réal decides, too late, that Paquita's broken hymen does not in fact have the meaning that she had initially attributed to it: '— Elle était aussi peu coupable qu'il est possible [. . .] J'ai eu tort, pardonne-moi, Paquita!' ('She was as free of blame as it is possible to be [. . .] I was wrong, forgive me, Paquita!') (p. 452). Henri, by contrast, acknowledges no potential error in his corporeal reading of Paquita, though he does admit that 'elle est fidèle au sang' (she is faithful to the blood) (p. 452). Indeed, the claim that Paquita has been faithful to her mistress because of the blood bond between the half-siblings supports Henri's reading of the heroine's utterance as proof of her psychological unfaithfulness to him. What also supports Henri's reading is the fact that Paquita dressed him as a woman during their first full night together. On the other hand, what throws doubt on Henri's conclusions about Paquita's enduring love for her former mistress is the fact that the narrator tells us that the heroine dressed Henri as a woman 'avec une innocence d'enfant' (with a child-like innocence), and that 'elle ne voyait rien au-delà' (she saw nothing behind this) (p. 432). Secondly, when the heroine tells Henri that he is the first person she has loved ('jusqu'à présent, j'étais aimée seulement, moi je n'aimais pas' (until now, I was only loved; I didn't love) and that she will not miss her former lover, she does so 'en laissant lire dans ses yeux dont la teinte d'or resta pure et claire' (letting her eyes be read, their golden colour remaining pure and clear) (p. 443).[35] There is no hint that

Paquita is lying, and the text makes it very clear that she wishes to escape from her tyrannical mistress so that she can spend her future with Henri. Thirdly, Paquita herself is uncomprehending of Henri's reaction to her exclamation, appearing not to realise that she has said anything that could cause offence; her confusion suggests that he has at least exaggerated the significance of her utterance, if not misread it entirely. Finally, the narrator states explicitly that Paquita loves Henri in as intense a way as anyone can be loved: he is 'celui qu'elle aimait comme jamais aucune créature n'aima sur cette terre' (he whom she loved as no creature had ever loved on this earth) (p. 449). There is, in other words, abundant textual evidence to suggest that Paquita's love for Henri is, to her own knowledge at least, and apparently to the knowledge of the (reliable) omniscient narrator, as undivided as even he could wish it to be.

Balzac's narrator makes no attempt to explain why Paquita cries out a feminine-sounding name in the throes of lovemaking, despite the text's repeated insistence on the genuineness of her love for Henri. Just as puzzlingly, the text suggests that Paquita herself is unaware of what crime she has committed; the narrator tells us that 'sans connaître de quel crime elle était coupable, Paquita comprit néanmoins qu'il s'agissait pour elle de mourir' (without knowing of what crime she was guilty, Paquita understood nevertheless that her life was in the balance) (p. 446). There are various possible explanations for Paquita's ignorance of her 'crime', but only one that seems plausible, to this reader at least, and all involve a certain incoherence, be it textual or psychological, and therefore a resistance to straightforward understanding. Paquita could be a duplicitous character who merely pretends not to understand how she has offended Henri. This explanation is contradicted by the text's repeated insistence on her innocence, and would suggest, somewhat implausibly, that the narrator is unreliable. Another possibility is that Paquita is so innocent, with so little an understanding of the concept of property, that she cannot comprehend her lover's jealousy; however, this hypothesis also seems implausible given her keen awareness of both her mistress's and her current lover's desire for exclusive ownership of her body and soul, and given her certainty that Margarita will avenge any disloyalty.[36] Any explanation that rests upon the heroine's innocence about the rules of property would therefore be rendered problematic by inconsistencies in the narrative. The only plausible explanation for Paquita's ignorance of her crime is, then, that she is not aware of what she has said. To the extent that we attribute psychological coherence to the heroine, her utterance can only be understood to spring from some deeply buried memory of pleasure which bears little relation to her conscious emotions, much as the word 'adieu', in Balzac's story of that name, is spoken lightly and witlessly, stripped of all the sorrow it once expressed, by a heroine no longer in possession of her (fictional) mind.

Lending weight to the hypothesis that Paquita's exclamation betrays an affect or feeling that is inaccessible to consciousness or perception is the following passage, taken from a little earlier in the text, after the first time that Henri and Paquita make love:

> Henri se trouvait donc sous l'empire de ce sentiment confus que ne connaît pas le véritable amour. [. . .] L'amour vrai règne surtout par la mémoire. La femme qui ne s'est gravée dans l'âme ni par l'excès du plaisir, ni par la force du sentiment, celle-là peut-elle jamais être aimée? À l'insu d'Henri, Paquita s'était établie chez lui par ces deux moyens. Mais en ce moment, tout entier à la fatigue du bonheur, cette délicieuse mélancolie du corps, il ne pouvait guère s'analyser le cœur en reprenant sur ses lèvres le goût des plus vives voluptés qu'il eût encore égrappées. (pp. 433–4)

> (Henri found himself therefore dominated by that confused feeling unknown to true love. [. . .] True love reigns mainly through memory. Can the woman who has not engraved herself in the soul, either by excessive pleasure or by force of feeling, ever be loved? Unbeknownst to Henri, Paquita had established herself within him by both of these means. But at that moment, given over entirely to the satiety of happiness, that delicious melancholy of the body, he was unable to analyse his own heart while tasting again on his lips the most intense pleasures that he had yet plucked.)

The text itself, then, gives an anticipatory clue as to how Paquita's inexplicable utterance might be framed: just as she has inscribed herself into Henri's memory without his realising, Margarita has inscribed herself in the heroine's deep memory, without her realising (and despite the fact that Paquita believes, possibly correctly, that she never loved the Marquise). Similarly, the heroine may be killed, and all trace of her body effaced, at the end of the story, but her trace will nevertheless endure, as intimated in this passage. What is suggested in the quoted passage is that there is a lack of communication between Henri's 'mémoire' (memory) or 'âme' (soul), on the one hand, and his mind, on the other. Balzac's novel appears to gesture towards the existence of a corporeal memory that acts independently of the mind; in this, it recalls René Descartes' early theorisation of 'a mechanistically explicable sensory and motor psychology', as well as the prize-winning thesis, 'Influence de l'habitude sur la faculté de penser' ('The Influence of Habit on the Faculty of Thinking'), published in 1803 by the French philosopher Maine de Biran.[37] The heroine is not consciously duplicitous in her denial of any feelings for her mistress. Like Henri as described in the above passage, she does not possess full knowledge of her feelings. Paquita and Henri are therefore strangers, then, in this further sense, too: they are other to themselves.

Felman points out that Paquita's exclamation transgresses against propriety, the name she utters being 'a *proper* name which names *improperly*'.[38] The exclamation also transgresses against the law of property insofar as it indicates that the girl with the golden eyes resists ownership by any one lover, even the one who finally kills her.[39] Paquita, a virtual sex slave, is ultimately never entirely known, and therefore never entirely owned, by anybody, least of all by herself. Felman goes so far as to argue that the heroine's golden eyes operate to dispossess others: 'The golden eyes do not keep their fantasmatic promise: the gold is not to be possessed; all it does is *disown* the marquise, and *dispossess* Henri of the illusion of his self-identical master-masculinity.'[40] For Felman, it is, crucially, Paquita's femininity that is misread by Henri, and that threatens his sense of self. I would argue that it is Paquita's alterity more generally that resists reading and possession, an alterity that is linked to but not reducible to femininity. Denean T. Sharpley-Whiting, who highlights the racial dynamics of the novel, interprets the heroine as 'Other, a body of utter difference'.[41] The signifier 'Mariquita' can be interpreted as the emblem or synecdoche of this alterity, the symptom of a bug in the system. This symptom cannot be read as clear proof of enduring love for a brutal mistress without suppressing its indeterminacy quite brutally, as Henri does both to the utterance and to its emitter.

Paquita's body itself behaves like a symptom, in the sense that it betrays her secrets, both conscious and unconscious. Her body makes of her a '*femme-écran*' (*screen-woman*) (p. 437), to borrow (or provisionally appropriate) the term that Henri applies to a woman who is compromised by a man in order to serve as a screen over the true object of his love: Paquita inadvertently compromises herself by revealing the secret of her own affections (the sex of her lovers) on the screen of her own body.[42] Unlike Henri, Paquita is not able to manipulate language in a way that allows her wittily to manipulate its ambiguities. She is capable of what Henri calls negative discretion, or secrecy, but not of any deliberate attempt to mislead. She tells him: 'Si j'obtiens ma grâce, ce sera peut-être à cause de ma discrétion' (If I win my pardon, it will perhaps be because of my discretion) (p. 442). Paquita attempts to keep one secret from Henri, namely the identity of her tyrannical lover, but her physical 'innocence' inadvertently reveals that identity; this secret is not a troubling one, for the protagonist. The secret of which he ultimately finds her guilty, and which her body again unwittingly betrays, is of a different order, because she is not aware of it. Whatever 'crime' we infer that Henri imputes to the heroine, the only secret that she logically betrays, with her exclamation, is that her desire is illegible even to herself.

The illegibility that is so often introduced by desire into 'realistic' texts, which privilege readability, tends to be brutally despatched, as Leo Bersani notes:

> Desire is a threat to the form of realistic fiction. Desire can subvert social order; it can also disrupt novelistic order. The nineteenth-century novel is haunted by the possibility of these subversive moments, and it suppresses them with a brutality both shocking and eminently logical.[43]

Paquita and her body are indeed suppressed, at the end of the narrative, with a savagery that is unusual even for the realistic fiction about which Bersani writes. She may well tell Henri the truth about the purity of her love for him, letting him read the candour in her eyes, but her body contradicts this truth, thereby disrupting novelistic order by resisting reading. Ironically, it is Paquita's very transparency that makes her opacity apparent, just as it is precisely her willingness to be possessed by Henri that reveals the extent to which she is resistant to possession.

I have suggested, thus far, that it is the frustration of Henri's desire to possess Paquita completely, 'de s'approprier à jamais cette créature' (to take this creature as his forever) (p. 446), that provokes his rage: the protagonist realises, on hearing her fatal exclamation, that he does not in fact own this woman, and never will.[44] Even when she is most compliant and most legible to both Henri and Margarita, something about her desire resists their possession. She is condemned to be, if not free, as Sartre would have it, then at least opaque.

But Henri, too, is opaque. His outraged response to Paquita's exclamation of 'Oh! Mariquita!' is never directly explained by the narrator. Paquita herself fails to understand the reason for Henri's murderous rage, and asks him repeatedly to explain himself:

> — Pourquoi voulais-tu me tuer, mon amour?' lui dit-elle.
> De Marsay ne répondit pas.
> — En quoi t'ai-je déplu? lui dit-elle. Parle, expliquons-nous. [. . .]
> — Mon bien-aimé, reprit Paquita, parle-moi.' (pp. 446–7)

> ('Why did you want to kill me, my love?' she said to him.
> De Marsay made no answer.
> 'How have I displeased you?' she said to him. 'Speak, let us understand each other.' [. . .]
> 'My beloved', said Paquita, 'talk to me.')

Numerous commentators have deduced that Henri's anger at Paquita's exclamation is linked to her 'emasculation' of him.[45] However, we are never told that this is the case, only that his male vanity is wounded. But what does Henri now know that he had only suspected before? We have already been told that, prior to the heroine's disastrous exclamation, Henri had guessed at his rival's identity and was ready to pardon Paquita, at least as long as he is 'le préféré' (the favourite) (p. 444). It is heavily hinted, in other words, that Henri had reconciled himself to Paquita's lesbian past, as long as it belonged firmly in the past, and that her real crime, from his point of view, is her inability to commit her entire being, including her memories, exclusively to him. But none of this is spelled out, and can only be deduced from the evidence of an ambiguous text that, like Paquita, both gives up its secret and keeps its secret.

Despite Paquita's incomprehension of Henri's anger, she is presented throughout the text as a very able reader. Contrary to Henri's claims about the heroine's gullibility, she does not in fact delude herself. She knows that she is just a plaything for Henri, telling him that he can kill her when he is finished with her. At their first tryst, when the protagonist tells her that he will kill her if he is obliged to share her with anyone else, Paquita immediately understands that the threat is a literal one. When he tries to reassure her, smilingly, that his threat was not intended in a literal sense, her response suggests not just that she recognises the close physical similarity between her two lovers, but that she guesses at their deeper bond: '—C'est la même voix! dit Paquita mélancoliquement, sans que De Marsay pût l'entendre, et . . . la même ardeur, ajouta-t-elle' ('It's the same voice!' said Paquita melancholically, without De Marsay being able to hear her, 'and . . . the same ardour', she added) (p. 423). The adverb 'mélancoliquement' suggests that Paquita is well aware of the fate that is likely to await her, because she now understands Henri's character. She makes deductions here that go unobserved by the virtually all-knowing Henri and that will also go unobserved by all but the most vigilant of readers, those for example who have already drawn the relevant conclusions from information already given in the text about the hero's half-sister. Paquita later observes that she is likely to be murdered as punishment for her infidelity, and is even more certain of this outcome after she has had sexual intercourse with Henri for the first time: 'maintenant je suis sûre de mourir pour toi' (now I am certain that I shall die for you') (p. 433). She also reads Henri's body language easily in the immediate aftermath of her exclamation:

> Sans connaître de quel crime elle était coupable, Paquita comprit néan-moins qu'il s'agissait pour elle de mourir. (p. 446)
> De Marsay lui jeta pour réponse un regard qui signifiait si bien: *tu mourras!* que Paquita se précipita sur lui.
> — Eh! bien, veux-tu me tuer? Si ma mort peut te faire plaisir, tue-moi!
> [. . .]
> Elle attendait un regard, ne l'obtint pas, et tomba demi-mort. (pp. 447–8)

(Without knowing of what crime she was guilty, Paquita understood nevertheless that her life was in the balance.

De Marsay gave her, as an answer, a look that so clearly signified: '*you
shall die!*' that Paquita threw herself upon him.

'So you wish to kill me then? If my death can give you pleasure, kill me!'
[. . .]

She waited for a look, did not get it, and fell down, half-dead.)

Paquita's only failure as a mind-reader resides, in fact, in her incomprehension of Henri's rage after she utters the word 'Mariquita' when they
make love for the second and last time.

Henri, like Paquita, poses a reading problem for others and, as in
the heroine's case, this is part of the magnetic charm that he exerts.
Unlike Paquita, however, he knows how to protect himself from
prying gazes by making himself inscrutable. Although the narrative is
often internally focalised by Henri, he remains an impenetrable character throughout the story. Even the narrator is occasionally reduced
to conjecture in relation to his intentions: 'peut-être comptait-il sur
sa puissance et sur son savoir-faire d'homme à bonnes fortunes pour
dominer quelques heures plus tard cette fille, et en apprendre tous
les secrets' (perhaps he was counting on his power and his savvy as
a ladies' man to help him to dominate, a few hours later, this girl,
and learn all her secrets) (pp. 431–2). The conclusion of the novel
is particularly interesting in this regard. When Paul de Manerville
asks Henri what has become of 'notre belle *fille aux yeux d'or*' (our
beautiful *girl with the golden eyes*), his answer both does and does
not tell the truth. She has died, Henri tells his friend, 'de la poitrine'
(of the chest) (p. 453). Henri's final answer, the last line of the novel,
is a lie to the extent that it suggests, idiomatically, that Paquita has
died of consumption, is the literal truth if it is understood to mean
that Paquita was stabbed to death, and is again close to the truth
if 'la poitrine' (the chest) is interpreted as a metonym either for the
heart (Paquita's love has been the cause of her death) or for feminine
attractions (Paquita's physical beauty has been her downfall).[46] Henri
responds in a way that draws an opaque veil (or screen) over the
heroine's death while also telling partial truths about that death and
the reasons for it.[47] While Felman suggests that Henri's answer, being
a euphemistic understatement, is an instance of what the protagonist
calls negative discretion, I would argue that his ambiguity recalls the
strategy he had previously defined as 'active discretion', namely the
attempt to mislead, even when telling the truth. Similarly, a few pages
earlier, when he releases a howl of anger and Paul asks him what
the matter is, Henri first deploys what he has designated as negative

discretion by denying that he is thinking about anything at all, and then, when Paul asks if he is planning an assassination, resorts to a more energetic deception, an active form of discretion; he opts for a phrase that tells the truth even while concealing it: 'J'exécute' (I execute) (p. 439). If the heroine loses her life on account of her unintended impenetrability, an exclamation that both does and does not tell the truth of her desire, the male protagonist, by contrast, achieves impunity on account of his calculated impenetrability, including his mastery of equivocal language.

Active discretion, or misdirection, is at the very centre of *La Fille aux yeux d'or*: Balzac's narrator reveals the key to the novel's enigma at an early point in the narrative, when he informs the reader that Henri's father also had a daughter, raised in Havana, who went on to marry the Marquis de San-Réal, and who keeps a female companion from her time in Cuba. The text therefore gives away its own secret, but most readers will fail to register the significance of this revealing passage on first reading. Misdirection is a central theme and structural device within Balzac's larger trilogy, *L'Histoire des Treize*. In *La Duchesse de Langeais*, for example, the eponymous duchess is punished for the false expectations she encourages in a man whose great heroism is attested, in the text, by his extraordinary stoicism in an episode in which he is repeatedly misled by a desert guide. In *Ferragus*, the reader is encouraged, by a misleading narrative, to believe that a wife has been unfaithful to her husband. Indeed, misdirection, or what Henri calls active discretion, is part of the very fabric of fiction, to the extent that all fictions hoodwink their readers.

Like Henri, Paquita uses ambiguous language in this novel, most notably in her fatal exclamation, but her equivocations are not designed, like Henri's, to travesty the truth. Furthermore, where Henri's calculated ambiguity secures his impunity, Paquita's unintended ambiguity ensures her punishment by death. Interestingly, Paquita's final words in the novel are just as ambiguous as Henri's final words. When she glimpses him at the doorway, just before she dies, she cries: 'Trop tard, mon bien-aimé!' (Too late, my beloved!) (p. 450). On the most literal, common-sense level, these words could mean that Henri has arrived too late to kill her, as Paquita knows he wants to; or they could prompt us to ask if she imagines that he has arrived too late to save her; or they could simply suggest that he has arrived too late for her or anyone else to know what he would have done.[48] The two principal characters, both of whom are shown to be expert mind-readers, appear, then, to represent antithetical perspectives with regard to ambiguity: Henri uses ambiguity as a self-protective device, a form of active discretion deployed against the mind-reading abilities of others, whereas Paquita is ambiguous despite herself.

It is telling that lesbianism, despite being a crucial key to understanding the text, is never actually named by it; it may be considered utterly banal by Henri, but it constitutes for Balzac's narrative an 'unspeakable' and '*unrepresentable* transgression'.[49] Proust said of *La Fille aux yeux d'or* among other Balzac novels that 'there, beneath the apparent and external action of the drama, circulate mysterious laws of flesh and feeling'.[50] The literary critic Albert Béguin made a similar observation of the text: 'Beneath this most explicit drama, a drama of passion and death, [. . .] Balzac half veils and half reveals another drama, that of a quest, a knowledge, a dive into the mystery of things.'[51] What both quotations suggest is the idea that the text gestures towards invisible mysteries, which cannot be articulated. In a different register, the critic Doris Kadish also suggests that there is something about this text that resists resolution: she observes that the entire novel is governed by what she calls 'the structure of the hybrid', or 'the presence of heterogeneous parts', which means that 'elimination or transcendence of difference is only partially achieved'.[52] She cites, in support of this argument, the mixed sexuality and origins of the main protagonists, as well as the fact that the novel itself unites a prologue and narrative which it never fully harmonises.[53]

Indeed, Paquita is arguably one of those stranger figures whom Zygmunt Bauman describes as 'the true hybrids, the monsters – not just *unclassified*, but *unclassifiable*', who 'question oppositions as such, the very principle of the opposition', and who 'unmask the brittle artificiality of division'.[54] The challenge she poses to order is strongly suggested in the passage where she begs Henri to run away with her. He protests that they would need 'de l'or' (gold) in support of this plan, and she then urges him to take gold from the house of the Marquis. Their conversation says much about their different attitudes towards property:

> — Il n'est pas à moi.
> — Qu'est-ce que cela fait? reprit-elle, si nous en avons besoin, prenons-le.
> — Il ne t'appartient pas.
> — Appartenir! répéta-t-elle. Ne m'as-tu pas prise? Quand nous l'aurons pris, il nous appartiendra.
> Il se mit à rire.
> — Pauvre innocente! tu ne sais rien des choses de ce monde. (pp. 445–6)

> ('It is not mine.'
> 'What does that matter?', she answered. 'If we need it, we shall take it.'
> 'It does not belong to you.'

'Belong!', she repeated. 'Did you not take me? When we have taken it, it will belong to us.'
He started to laugh.
'Poor innocent! You know nothing of the things of this world.')

For Paquita, property has no intrinsic legitimacy, its validity always being a simple result of taking. She thereby challenges the law of property which, as Rousseau had shown in his 1755 treatise on inequality, underpins civil society. She is herself, moreover, resistant to possession: she tells Henri in the above passage that he has taken her as his property, but just subsequent to this conversation, as the hero 'concevait le désir de s'approprier à jamais cette créature' (conceived the desire to own this creature forever) (p. 446), her exclamation reveals to him that he does not in fact own her desire. His rage drives him to an attempted murder where yet again she will elude him.

Balzac's entire novella highlights the unnameable, incomprehensible nature of human desire. Like the heroine it names, *La Fille aux yeux d'or* is a deeply ambiguous text, which both offers itself to and resists the critic as mind-reader. There is no single, unproblematic interpretation of the significance of the heroine's exclamation. The meanings suggested by the narrative, like the heroine whose improper name serves as its title, and like the improper name she utters at the moment when she is least in possession of herself, are at least partly resistant to appropriation. Paquita resists understanding – her own, Henri's and that of readers. So does the text to which she lends her name.

Henri's attempts to find out Paquita's secret reveal the ethical limitations of mind-reading: to wish to know the secret desires of the other is to wish to appropriate and even suppress the other. The interpersonal misunderstandings represented in this text also reveal the practical limits of mind-reading: even within a storyworld where others are presented as eminently readable, it is impossible to find out all the secrets of another person, because characters appear not to be entirely cognisant of their own motivations. Similarly, a narrative fiction such as Balzac's can never give up all its secrets, because it does not own all of its secrets. In the end, the mind-reader, like the reader, needs to learn to tolerate not knowing, not fully comprehending. The next section will show that if *La Fille aux yeux d'or* warns of the ethical and practical limits of suspicious mind-reading, it also alerts the reader to the risks of seduction.

The Dangers of Opacity

This chapter has suggested thus far that both Paquita and De Marsay display well-developed mind-reading skills. Henri describes, for example, the sensations that he discerns that his own extreme physical beauty produces in Paquita: 'un de ces étonnements profonds qui coupent bras et jambes, descendent le long de l'épine dorsale et s'arrêtent dans la plante des pieds pour vous attacher au sol' (one of those deep astonishments that immobilise your arms and legs, travel down the length of your spine and end in the sole of the foot to attach you to the ground) (p. 400). Henri is even capable of studying and judging Paquita's reactions during their lovemaking, looking out for any sign that she may have lingering affection for his rival. However, Henri is not always correct in his readings of others' feelings: he fails to understand, for example, that Paquita's fear for her own life, and indeed for his, is genuine, just as he fails to realise that at least part of the reason she is so surprised by his appearance, in their initial encounter, is his resemblance to her mistress.[55] Arguably, in fact, the heroine's mind-reading skills are superior to those of Henri: she is alert to the fact that he and Margarita share the same 'ardeur' (ardour) (p. 423), and correctly predicts her mistress's response to her infidelity. However, Paquita's percipience does not prevent her murder. If mind-reading skills confer social power, as psychologists and cognitive literary scholars argue, and as Balzac's narrative implies, most obviously in its explanation of the origins of Henri's authority over others – he is counted among those men who 'sont assez profonds pour avoir une pensée de plus que leurs amis qu'ils exploitent' (are penetrating enough to think a little more than do their friends, whom they exploit) (p. 397) – then why do Paquita's apparently superior skills in this area not serve her better?

What distinguishes Henri from Paquita is his ability to retain his critical skills even when he is most abandoned to his passion for her, even at the moment when he 'oubliait tout' (forgot everything) (p. 446). His ability to remain alert and watchful even in the midst of sensual pleasure is described by Balzac's narrator as '[une] triste force' (a sad strength) (p. 444). She, by contrast, lets her critical guard down, and this inability to remain self-possessed while in the grip of passion is her downfall. Paquita's incautious openness, in one crucial moment, leads directly to her death. The crucial difference between the two characters is, then, unsurprisingly, that Paquita is naive, and not just on account of her fatal ignorance of the physical consequences of heterosexual intercourse. Henri's highly developed mind-reading skills confer power upon him; meanwhile, Paquita's similarly well-developed ability to infer the feelings and intentions of others invests her with no similar power, partly because of the limitations imposed by her situation, but also partly because she allows her affect, or sensual pleasure, to dominate her critical vigilance. Her suspicion is fatally diminished, in other words, by her susceptibility to seduction.

Both Paquita and Henri are highly seductive characters, each exercising a magnetic charm over the other. He is possessed of what he himself describes, with typical modesty, as '[une] espèce de magnétisme animal' (a type of animal magnetism) (p. 400). At their first private meeting, Paquita is described by the narrator as fearlessly intoxicated by a long-dreamed-of joy ('elle s'enivrait sans crainte d'une félicité longtemps rêvée'); she is 'sous le charme' (charmed) (p. 420). She is drawn to Henri 'par une force inexplicable' (by an inexplicable force), and experiences 'un abandon de passion que rien ne saurait exprimer' (a passionate abandon that nothing could express) (p. 423). When she tells him to leave, after their first arranged meeting, her voice expresses 'combien elle était peu maîtresse d'elle-même' (how little in control of herself she was) (p. 424). Henri, for his part, is so enchanted by the heroine's beauty, at this first tryst, that their tawdry surroundings and even the strange female chaperone disappear. When they kiss, he imagines the ground opening beneath him; the narrator remarks that 'il ne fut plus lui-même, et il était assez grand cependant pour pouvoir résister aux enivrements du plaisir' (he was no longer himself, despite being big enough to be able to resist the intoxications of pleasure) (p. 424). At the beginning of their third assignation, Henri is so enchanted by Paquita that he forgets his intention to decipher her body language ('[il] oublia momentanément l'intérêt principal de ce rendez-vous' (he momentarily forgot the main reason for this meeting) (p. 441)) and eventually gives in to his passion for her: 'jeté par delà cette ligne où l'âme est maîtresse d'elle-même, il se perdit dans ces limbes délicieuses que le vulgaire nomme si niaisement *les espaces imaginaires*' (cast beyond that line where the soul is mistress of itself, he lost himself in those delicious limbo lands that vulgar people so idiotically call *imaginary spaces*) (pp. 444–5).

These episodes of imagined fusional affective attachment, for which limbo lands, as intermediate, borderline spaces, serve as an apt metaphor, are punctuated by periods of separation. Two days separate the first assignation from the second, and over the course of these two days we are told that De Marsay continues to feel love for the heroine. Between the second and third rendezvous, however, Henri feels emotionally distant from Paquita and begins to decipher the meaning of her behaviour the previous night. The story of *La Fille aux yeux d'or* therefore sees the two principal characters enjoy intimate interludes interspersed by periods of separation and, in Henri's case at least, critical distance. The narrative invites us, similarly, to enter into a relationship of attachment and detachment with both of its two principal strangers.

The narrative is predominantly focalised by Henri; it is through the lens of his desire that the narrator presents Paquita to us, and it is through his dispassionate eyes that the narrator interprets the blood-soaked scene that concludes the novel. Readers' structural complicity, or narrative empathy, with the male protagonist, established by the sharing of perspectives, is bolstered by their sympathy for him. This sympathy is elicited not only by narrative glimpses into the character's upbringing and education – we learn that 'le pauvre Henri de Marsay' (poor Henri de Marsay) (p. 390) never knew his biological father and that he was neglected by his mother and her elderly husband – but also by his presentation as a witty and likeable companion: we see him engaging, for example, in self-mocking banter with his friend Paul de Manerville as he beautifies himself at his dressing-room table. His potential for cruelty is not hidden from our view – on the contrary, it is presented hyperbolically, with the protagonist being compared repeatedly to a formidable despot[56] – but it is explained as a deliberate consequence of his education. This cruelty, furthermore, is never condemned by the narrator. Indeed, the narrator encourages us to admire both the priest who taught Henri to be callous, and the callousness that makes Henri superior to other young men. The reader who feels a complicity with the protagonist is flattered; we are told that the hero combines supreme power with extreme intelligence. He is implicitly, and highly favourably, contrasted with those mediocre, honest and virtuous young men who accuse talented people of immorality, and who are ridiculed as 'ganaches' (imbeciles) by elegant young people, and described by the narrator as 'une lymphe' (a lymph) that weighs down on and enfeebles the government of a country (p. 395). The reader is tacitly warned, therefore, against adopting a morally judgemental stance with regard to Henri. Balzac's text effectively encourages readers to suspend their moral judgement of Henri and to admire his actions uncritically.

However, this invitation to adopt an uncritical stance with regard to Henri, and by extension the narrative voice, is complicated by two structural elements.

Firstly, Henri is himself a highly distrustful, suspicious character; consequently, any reader who is uncritically admiring of him fails to resemble him. The narrator tells us that members of Henri's species 'sont armés d'une défiance continuelle des hommes qu'ils estiment à leur valeur' (are armed with a continual distrust of men, whose value they gauge) (p. 397). Henri's mind-reading abilities are presented as a route to worldly success, while credulity is very negatively connoted. The narrator himself pours scorn, for example, on those young men who are the 'dupes' of Parisian life, 'des gens médiocres' (mediocrities) who will later 'infestent' (infest) the city's administration (p. 395). An analogous scorn is reserved by Henri for Paquita, and indeed for women in general, on account of their gullibility: they believe his fictions without questioning them. Upon writing to Paquita that he would give his life for one meeting with her, he comments: 'Elles croient cela pourtant, ces pauvres creatures! se dit De Marsay; mais elles ont raison. Que penserions-nous d'une femme qui ne se laisserait pas séduire par une lettre d'amour accompagnée de circonstances si probantes?"' ('They believe it though, the poor creatures!' thought De Marsay. 'But they are right. What would we think of a woman who did not let herself be seduced by a love letter accompanied by such convincing circumstances?') (p. 414). The reader is, by implication, encouraged not to be gullible, and to adopt a sceptical approach to fictions. Paradoxically, however, this privileging of critical distance over naivety means that the reader who feels complicit with the sceptical protagonist may also remain critical of him and, by extension, critical of a narrative perspective that operates to exonerate him.

The second way in which the novel encourages readers to adopt a critical distance from Henri is, precisely, by eliciting the reader's sympathy for Paquita, who occupies the emotional heart of the story. Even the usually indulgent narrator occasionally appears to judge Henri in a lightly negative way, referring for example to his 'insouciance vraiment déshonorante' (truly dishonouring indifference) as he smokes his cigar on the boulevard after his first night of ecstasy with Paquita (p. 434). The latter is, moreover, described in affecting terms, liable to elicit pity: the narrator refers to her as 'la pauvre esclave' (the poor slave) (p. 430), while Henri calls her 'pauvre innocente' (poor innocent) (p. 446), and she describes herself as 'un pauvre animal à son piquet' (a poor animal at its stake) (p. 430). Her back-story, too, invites readers' pathos: sold into slavery by a mother who does not love her, she has become the sexual plaything of a cruel mistress. The heroine's emotions are repeatedly foregrounded: to cite just a few examples, she speaks 'd'un air triste' (sadly) (p. 421) and 'mélancoliquement' (melancholically) (p. 74); at other times she is 'heureuse d'être admirée' (happy to be admired) (p. 422), and Henri's gaze 'la combla de joie' (filled her with joy) (p. 431); at other moments again she is 'peureuse, palpitante, inquiète' (fearful, trembling, anxious) (p. 423), 'en proie à la terreur' (in prey to terror) (p. 430). The authenticity of her love for Henri may be doubted by him, but it is never doubted by the reader – her love is described by the narrator as 'naïf' (naive) (p. 444), and the narrator tells us that she feels 'cette adoration

infinie qui saisit le cœur d'une femme quand elle aime véritablement'
(this infinite adoration that grips the heart of a woman when she loves
truly) (p. 420). Her emotions, by contrast with those of Henri, then, are
presented as genuine. It is virtually impossible for the reader, for all of
these reasons, to resist feeling sympathy for Paquita.

In addition, thanks to the narrator's machinations, the reader is likely
to feel empathy with Paquita.[57] This is because most readers have something in common with this heroine from the outset: as already discussed,
the narrative is constructed in a way that ensures that we too have
been at least partly seduced or intrigued by the irresistible Henri. In
addition, if even this protagonist, so resistant to female charms, can
allow himself to be seduced by Paquita, then it is difficult to see how the
reader (particularly the reader who has been seduced into a relationship
of complicity with Henri) can resist her. There is something involuntary,
in other words, about the reader's affective response to Paquita, just as
her boudoir appeals to 'des sympathies involontaires' (involuntary sympathies), according to the narrator's description (p. 429). It is difficult,
then, not to feel an emotional attachment to the heroine, as soon as one
shares the perspective of the male protagonist and/or narrator. However,
the reader who develops an affective attachment to Paquita is very likely
to cast a critical eye on Henri, even if she has also been drawn into a
relation of complicity with him. In other words, any naive, affective
response on the part of the reader to Paquita may be at least partially
programmed by the reader's sharing of Henri's perspective, but it is also
likely to lead the reader to adopt a critical perspective with regard to
Henri. Conversely, the reader's affective attachment to Paquita is necessarily regulated by the fact that she is virtually obliged by the narrative
logic to share Henri's dispassionate perspective on events.

It is impossible, in fact, to disentangle critical and naive readerly
approaches to the two stranger protagonists of *La Fille aux yeux d'or*,
and by extension to disentangle critical and naive reading approaches
to the story itself. Even assuming that the novel's structure were to
allow the reader definitively to take the side of one character against the
other, to align oneself with the critically detached, dispassionate hero
would logically result in a naive reading of the text, if that complicit
reading were thereby to miss the text's tacit critique of the protagonist's appropriative desire, while to take the side of the gullible heroine
virtually necessitates the adoption of a critical attitude towards Henri.
This intrication of affective attachment and critical judgement that is
expressed at the novel's thematic level is, therefore, also a structural
feature of the text, which never allows the reader to settle fully into
either position. This vacillation between seduction and suspicion finds

expression, too, in the uneven tone of the novel, which combines the affective resonance of gothic melodrama and erotic romance with the detached, urbane tone of a comedy of manners.

Much of the pleasure of reading Balzac's novel depends, in fact, upon the reader's maintenance of an attitude of naivety or, in other words, upon the reader's willingness to lower her cognitive guard, allowing herself to be seduced by the fictional narrative. This is not entirely surprising, given that, as Chambers notes, 'seduction goes hand in hand with the "readerliness" or "readability" of literature – understanding these terms in the slightly technical sense given by Roland Barthes to the concept of *lisibilité*'.[58] The more the (readerly) text gives the reader the illusion of cognitive mastery, the less cognitive work she is likely to engage in, and the less vigilant she is. Balzac takes advantage of this openness to seduction on the part of the reader. As already mentioned, the identity of Paquita's lover, another biological child of Henri's English father, is effectively given away prior to the account of the protagonists' first meeting in the Tuilerie gardens:

> Pour rendre cette aventure compréhensible, il est nécessaire d'ajouter ici que Lord Dudley trouva naturellement beaucoup de femmes disposées à tirer quelques exemplaires d'un si délicieux portrait. Son second chef d'œuvre en ce genre fut une jeune fille nommée Euphémie, née d'une dame espagnole, élevée à La Havane, ramenée à Madrid avec une jeune créole des Antilles, avec les goûts ruineux des colonies; mais heureusement mariée à un vieux et puissamment riche seigneur espagnol, don Hijos, marquis de San-Réal qui, depuis l'occupation de l'Espagne par les troupes françaises, était venu habiter Paris, et demeurait rue Saint-Lazare. (p. 393)

> (To make this adventure comprehensible, it is necessary to add here that Lord Dudley naturally found many women willing to produce several copies of such a delicious portrait. His second masterpiece of this type was a young girl named Euphémie, born of a Spanish woman, brought up in Havana, brought back to Madrid with a young Creole from the Antilles and with the ruinous tastes of the colonies; but happily married to an old and powerful Spanish noble, Don Hijos, the Marquis de San-Réal who, upon the occupation of Spain by French troops, had come to live in Paris, dwelling on the Rue Saint-Lazare.)

A second key passage appears after the first accidental encounter between Paquita and Henri in the gardens, and just before the second such meeting. Paul tells Henri that the woman who occasionally accompanies the golden-eyed girl, and 'qui vaut cent mille fois mieux qu'elle' (who is worth one hundred thousand times more than she), resembles him (p. 400). The mystery that Balzac's plot so skilfully constructs depends upon both passages being treated as insignificant by most readers; the information they offer is presented in a way that encourages readers to treat it as irrelevant, just as Henri himself treats Paul's revelation as irrelevant.[59] And yet everything is here: Paquita, the young Creole from the Antilles, is the companion of Henri's beautiful but debauched half-sister and female doppelganger, who will later be named as Margarita-Euphémia, now 'heureusement' (happily/fortunately) married to the elderly Marquis de San-Réal. Just as Paris, in the prologue to the story, is presented as a perfectly rational though organic system designed to absorb any elements extraneous to it, the narrative itself will, in the end, re-integrate information that appeared superfluous. The seductions and misdirections of the text are what enable the reduction of the reader's suspicion, his effective blindfolding as he is led to a plot outcome that has already been virtually spelled out by the text, mirroring Henri's blindfolding as he is led to a house whose address he nevertheless already knows. What most readers, like Henri and Margarita, do not see until Paquita lies dying is the sibling relationship between her near-identical lovers.

This sibling relationship renders Paquita's affair virtually blameless, in Margarita's eyes, and prompts Henri to describe her as faithful to their blood. The familial relationship therefore exculpates the heroine, for Margarita. However, to the extent that Paquita confuses the brother and sister with one another, conflating them into one gender-unspecific person, as suggested by her dressing of Henri as a woman and her ambiguous exclamation, she is guilty of blurring the boundaries that crucially separate individuals from one another. As Geneviève Delattre puts it, Henri and Margarita are 'seen and loved by Paquita as one single being'.[60] Paquita is therefore guilty of something resembling the crime of incest, insofar as incest too lifts the accepted boundaries between individuals belonging to the same family. In the Balzacian universe, murders can be committed with impunity, but the incest taboo tends to be at least minimally respected. Henri may take Margarita in his arms, kiss her, and tell her she is beautiful, in an embrace that Christopher Prendergast describes as 'ambiguous', hovering between the fraternal and the sexual, but the interdiction on sexual relations between siblings is, by contrast with some other works of the time, upheld.[61] It is respected even by the sexually licentious Lord Dudley who, on learning that the handsome Henri is his son, laments his own bad luck. By contrast, Paquita's quasi-incestuous conflation of Henri and Margarita amounts to a failure of self-censorship, and to a disrespect not just of divisions between family members, but of divisions between genders and between individuals.[62] In abandoning herself to the opacity of her desire, an opacity that is expressed and represented by the ambiguous vocable 'Mariquita', Paquita effectively fails to uphold the appropriate boundaries between people, and for that she is punished by death. The reader is thereby tacitly warned to avoid succumbing to a seduction or narrative empathy that would erase boundaries between reader and character, and advised to maintain, or at least return to, a critical distance from the emotional content of the novel.

Conclusion

This chapter has argued that the logic of *La Fille aux yeux d'or* suggests that even when readers are most seduced by a fiction, they would be wise to retain a degree of critical distance from it, as Henri does even when most in thrall to Paquita's charms. The unsuspicious reader, who lowers his critical guard in reading *La Fille aux yeux d'or*, resembles Paquita, or at least one of those 'poor creatures' ridiculed by Henri for their sentimental gullibility, their openness to being duped by bogus love letters. While Henri's ability to negotiate between affective fusion and critical distance approximates the approach to reading that appears to be tacitly recommended by the text, this ability is hardly presented uncritically by Balzac's narrator, who describes it as a 'triste force' (sad strength) (p. 444). In fact, this chapter has suggested that the text presents the activity of mind-reading more generally in a negative light, showing on the one hand the dangers of naivety but also the ethical and practical limits of perspicacity. While Balzac's text appears to present a minutely legible world, where every effect has a cause that is perceptible to the astute interpreter, it also offers an indirect challenge to the idea that people can ever be fully known, either to themselves or to others. Paquita remains partly illegible even after her secret has apparently been revealed; so too does the novel that places her at its centre.

Barthes notes that the classic (or Balzacian) text often ends in what he calls 'pensiveness': 'if the classic text has nothing to say beyond what it says, at least it aims to "let it be understood" that it is not saying everything'.[63] *La Fille aux yeux d'or*, which ends on an utterance that is almost as ambiguous as the one that precipitates its bloody finale, offers no exception. The ambiguity of this text, described by one commentator as 'one of the strangest works by Balzac' on account of its combination of realism and fantasy, may account for the 'strange fascination' which the same critic ascribes to it.[64] The endurance of ambiguity, even in texts that champion legibility, means that Balzac's fiction continues to fascinate its readers.[65]

Balzac is a writer who, on the surface at least, endeavours to translate otherness into sameness, fascinating opacity into easy legibility. In this, he resembles the authors of much popular fiction, which tends towards transparency, cliché and what Barthes called 'le lisible' (the readerly).[66] But even in Balzac's fiction we find a recognition of unreadability.[67] Jacques Collin, a.k.a. Vautrin and Herrera, is the most obvious figure of the illegible stranger in Balzac's *Comédie humaine* – his dramatic unmasking in *Le Père Goriot* may restore legibility to him, but it only does so for a moment, before he resumes his mask. In later novels, Collin returns in other guises. His use of chemicals on his face and shoulder, his adoption of different personae and his suggested homosexuality are only the superficial markers of an opacity that arguably inflects all of the most interesting characters in fiction.[68] The philosopher Martha Nussbaum observes, in terms that echo those of Zunshine, that 'only in fiction is the mind of another transparent';[69] what this analysis has tried to suggest is that fiction can also remind us of the strangeness or illegibility of other people, the extent to which we are strangers to each other and to ourselves.

The next chapter, devoted to Balzac's older contemporary, Stendhal, will foreground the opacity of one of the characters in French fiction who most divides the opinions of readers: Julien Sorel. It will show that *Le Rouge et le Noir*, like *La Fille aux yeux d'or*, indirectly advocates a practice of dialectical reading, which brings into play both seduction and suspicion, naivety and detachment, affective sharing and mind-reading.

Notes

1. Balzac, *La Muse du département*, in *La Comédie humaine*, vol. 4, p. 649.
2. 'A man who was deft with the analytical scalpel would have surprised, in Nathalie, some of the difficulties that her character would present when she later found herself confronted with married or social life.' Balzac, *Le Contrat de mariage*, in *La Comédie humaine*, vol. 3, p. 548.
3. See Barthes, *S/Z*, p. 21.
4. Ibid. p. 87 (note 150); see also p. 110 (LI).
5. Brooks, *Body Work*, p. 99.
6. Ibid. p. 84.
7. Zunshine, 'Theory of Mind and Fictions of Embodied Transparency', pp. 76, 72.
8. Zunshine, 'The Secret Life of Fiction', p. 727.
9. 'Literary critics, in particular, know that the process of attributing thoughts, beliefs, and desires to other people may lead to *misinterpreting* those thoughts, beliefs, and desires. Thus, they would rightly resist any notion that we could effortlessly – that is, correctly and unambiguously, nearly telepathically – figure out what the person whose behavior we are trying to explain is thinking.' Zunshine, 'Theory of Mind and Experimental Representations', p. 274.

10. Rifelj, *Reading the Other*, p. 25.
11. Sternberg, 'Omniscience', p. 776.
12. Sartre, *L'Etre et le néant*, pp. 666–7.
13. The literary critic Rae Greiner has argued, in a similar vein, that omniscience/knowing and sympathy are fundamentally incompatible in the work of George Eliot, those characters that pride themselves on being most all-knowing also revealing a lack of sympathy for others. See 'Sympathy Time' and the chapter 'Not Getting to Know You', in *Sympathetic Realism*.
14. Balzac, *La Fille aux yeux d'or*, in *Histoire des Treize*, pp. 371–453 (p. 438). This edition will be cited, alongside my translations, henceforth in this chapter.
15. 'Exotic, abnormal, everything separates them from the group. They are defined, at first, only as impossible to define; inassimilable, they escape.' Gaubert, '*La Fille aux yeux d'or*', p. 169.
16. See pp. 417, 429, 441.
17. Pappas, 'Opening the Door', p. 174. Nicole Mozet, in a similar vein, notes that it is Paquita rather than Henri who initiates their meetings. 'Les Prolétaires', p. 94.
18. 'The pervasiveness of stereotypes has the effect of making the majority of texts *readable*, indeed *predictable*, in their content as in their form.' Dufays, *Stéréotype et lecture*, p. 35.
19. Nils Soelberg evokes 'the grotesque contradiction in which a narrative discourse that claims to embody universal knowledge gets entangled'. 'La Narration de *La Fille aux yeux d'or*', 454–65 (p. 463).
20. One is reminded of Baudelaire's refutation of systems-based thinking in his essay on the 1855 *Exposition universelle*. Baudelaire, *Œuvres complètes*, vol. 2, pp. 577–8. Oliver Bonard notes, in the context of the colour symbolism of the boudoir scene in *La Fille aux yeux d'or*, that while Balzac himself was very tempted by systematic thinking, he also maintained a certain irreverence towards systems of classification. *La Peinture dans la création balzacienne*, p. 160.
21. The association of mind-reading with ownership, a central theme of our analysis, is explicit here.
22. Paraschas, *The Realist Author*, p. 13. For Paraschas, the authorial double is invested with a 'sympathetic imagination' that allows him to treat others 'as subjects rather than as objects' (p. 13). This chapter argues, by contrast, that Henri treats others as objects.
23. See pp. 400, 401, 402, 404 and pp. 419, 420, 422.
24. Rifelj also likens desire for knowledge of others, in fiction, to a desire for (sexual) possession: she writes for example of Mérimée's *Carmen* that jealousy 'impels the relentless drive to discover everything about the thoughts and feelings of another person' and that 'Don José is desperate to empty Carmen of her secrets; the knowledge he would gain would let him possess her.' *Reading the Other*, p. 121.
25. Felman, 'Women and Madness'. Felman takes Balzac's short story *Adieu* as the focus of her analysis.
26. Brooks, *Body Work*, p. 84. On the challenge posed by female desire in this novel, and 'fear of seduction', see Czyba, 'Misogynie et gynophobie', p. 143.

27. 'With the look of the other, the "situation" escapes me or, to use a banal expression, but which conveys the idea well: *I am no longer master of the situation*.' Sartre, *L'Etre et le néant*, p. 323.
28. The term is used here in Schor's sense; see Chapter 3, note 26.
29. Mozet, 'Les Prolétaires', p. 94.
30. As Owen Heathcote notes, 'De Marsay is fascinated by Paquita not *despite* her lesbianism but *through* and *because of* her lesbianism.' 'The Engendering of Violence', p. 104.
31. Elisabeth Gerwin argues that Henri's *flâneur*-like detachment from the market economy and system of exchange means he 'cannot comprehend that he himself may have misunderstood its signs; for he becomes convinced that Paquita has been unfaithful, has gone on a shopping spree, and that he, Henri, has been exchanged'. 'Power in the City', p. 113.
32. Denby, 'Lire le monde intérieur', p. 40. According to Denby, gesture in the work of Victor Hugo is characteristically revelatory and meaningful, while in Flaubert the meaning of gestures tends to be uncertain.
33. Felman, 'Rereading Femininity', p. 30.
34. Ibid. p. 30.
35. In *Ferragus*, another of the stories of the *Histoire des treize* trilogy, the purity and transparency of the woman's gaze testifies to her fidelity, even while her husband wrongly suspects her of lying (p. 97).
36. As Soelberg puts it, 'how can Paquita remain ignorant of her crime, while Henri has never hidden his insistence on being her absolute master?'. 'La Narration de *La Fille aux yeux d'or*', p. 458.
37. See Hatfield, 'The *Passions of the Soul*', p. 1.
38. Felman, 'Rereading Femininity', p. 30.
39. Prendergast notes that Margarita's murder of Paquita is 'primarily a vengeful and compensatory act of appropriation'. *Balzac*, p. 65.
40. Felman, 'Rereading Femininity', p. 32. The wording that Henri uses to tell Paquita that he cannot leave Paris also suggests that his self-identity is illusory: 'Je ne m'appartiens pas' (I am not my own man) (p. 99).
41. Sharpley-Whiting, '"The Other Woman"', p. 45.
42. In her reading of this text, Felman highlights the 'triple function' of screens: division, concealment and protection ('Rereading Femininity', p. 30). But screens (and a hymen is a type of screen) also display.
43. Bersani, *A Future for Astyanax*, p. 66.
44. One critic refers to 'this desire for total possession of the woman in De Marsay'. Tremblay, 'Qui es-tu, Paquita?', p. 58.
45. See for example Majewski, 'Painting as Intertext', p. 378 and Sharpley-Whiting, '"The Other Woman"', p. 48.
46. All of these possible interpretations are put forward by Felman in 'Rereading Femininity'. Felman favours the idea that Paquita is 'sacrificed, repressed, because she incarnate[s] femininity as otherness, as real sexual difference' ('Rereading Femininity', p. 43). Felman draws attention to the fact that one of the names of the Marquise de San-Réal is Euphémie (pp. 43–4).
47. Nathaniel Wing refers to the closing euphemism as 'a screen for several truths that remain suspended at the end of the text'. *Between Genders*, p. 164.
48. There are further possibilities. For Heathcote, these final words confirm,

euphemistically, 'that lesbians have little or nothing to learn from hetero-sexual men'. 'The Engendering of Violence', p. 104. For Soelberg, Paquita's words mean that Henri has arrived too late to see his rival and therefore understand her innocence. 'La Narration de *La Fille aux yeux d'or*', p. 459.

49. Heathcote, 'The Engendering of Violence', p. 107. Soelberg notes of Paquita's lesbian relationship that 'the taboo truth is evoked in an extremely allusive way'. 'La Narration de *La Fille aux yeux d'or*', p. 456. A simliar point is made in Mozet, 'Les Prolétaires', p. 96.

50. Proust, *Contre Sainte-Beuve*, p. 218.

51. Béguin, *Balzac lu et relu*, pp. 81, 87.

52. Kadish, 'Hybrids in Balzac's *La Fille aux yeux d'or*', p. 270.

53. In fact, the first chapter, containing the prologue, was published in March 1834, over one year earlier than the subsequent two chapters, published in May 1835.

54. Bauman, *Modernity and Ambivalence*, pp. 58–9.

55. Wing proposes of Henri's initial interpretation of Paquita's feelings that 'the woman here speaks of desire in the voice of the male'; in other words, he projects his own desire onto her. He also refers to Henri's 'misreading' of the heroine's situation. *Between Genders*, pp. 145, 152.

56. A number of commentators have pointed to the novella's dedication to Eugène Delacroix as suggestive of a link between the text's subject matter and *Death of Sardanapalus*. See for example Majewski, 'Painting as Intertext' and Sanyal, *The Violence of Modernity*, p. 100.

57. On the distinction between feeling with (empathy) and feeling for (sympa-thy), see Keen, *Empathy and the Novel*, pp. 5–6.

58. Chambers, *Story and Situation*, p. 13.

59. As Soelberg puts it, 'the essential details are presented in such an anodyne manner that hardly any attention is paid to them'. 'La Narration de *La Fille aux yeux d'or*', p. 456.

60. Delattre, 'De *Séraphita* à *La Fille aux yeux d'or*', p. 225.

61. Prendergast, *Balzac*, p. 65. Felman considers 'narcissistic incest' to be 'the secret figure' in the novel, 'Paquita's golden eyes [being] but a mediating mirror in which the brother and the sister, each in his turn, behold their own idealised self-image, fall in love with their own reflection'. 'Rereading Femininity', p. 34.

62. Paquita's lack of socialisation is compatible with her virtual flouting of the incest taboo. As Tremblay points out with regard to Paquita, 'not knowing how to read or write, she is reduced almost to animal life and especially to the sexual function'. 'Démasquer *La Fille aux yeux d'or*', p. 77. In a similar vein, Prendergast suggests that Paquita's love for a brother and sister points towards 'the contradictoriness of primordial sexuality before the differen-tiations imposed and demanded by culture'. *Balzac*, p. 65. For Felman, by contrast, Paquita may represent transgressive otherness, but she also stands for 'the bar of censorship' ('Rereading Femininity', p. 42), to the extent that she operates as a dividing screen between Henri and Margarita.

63. Barthes, *S/Z*, pp. 204–5.

64. Delattre, 'De *Séraphita* à *La Fille aux yeux d'or*', pp. 183, 184.

65. As Lacan puts it, 'it is to the extent that a task is unfinished that the subject comes back to it'. *Le Séminaire: Livre II*, p. 109. For a cognitive approach

to the effects of unresolved questions on the processing of information, see Gerrig et al., 'Waiting for Brandon'.

66. See Couégnas, *Introduction à la paralittérature*, pp. 87, 91. For Couégnas, what distinguishes Balzac's cliché-ridden, highly readable and transparent style from paraliterature is the fact that it also subscribes to aesthetic norms that militate against banality.

67. A recent article has argued that the author's proto-modernist undermining of the legibility of the readerly text has been underestimated, and even that one particular Balzacian novel 'enacts a cognitive crisis born of the post-Revolutionary experience of history and the changes it entails in the way plots are consumed and constructed'. Sugden, 'Terre(ur)', p. 55.

68. Rifelj notes of Mérimée's Carmen that 'the very elusiveness of this character guarantees her continuing attraction'. *Reading the Other*, p. 131. Rifelj's study of a range of fictions, from those of Conan Doyle to those of Proust, suggests that even those that appear to offer the most unfettered access to the minds of characters preserve some mystery. For example, while Sherlock Holmes reads other minds easily, his own remains opaque to us, and therefore interesting: 'He is impenetrable to the reader as well as to those around him. Through his mystery and despite his detachment and his truncated emotional life, he retains his hold on our imagination. In fact, the less we know about the workings of his "finely-tuned" mind, the more he attracts us' (p. 63).

69. Nussbaum, *Upheavals of Thought*, p. 328.

Chapter 5

Stendhal and the Two Opposing Demands

Stendhal, who as well as being a novelist, literary critic and would-be playwright, wrote extensively about the visual arts and enthusiastically about music, placed emotional experience at the heart of the aesthetic encounter. On the one hand, he gave emotion a fundamental role in artistic creation. Stendhal described passion as 'the possibility and the subject of the fine arts'.[1] On the other hand, emotion played a key role in aesthetic reception for this author. In one of his autobiographical works, the author compares the novel to a bow designed to produce music by acting upon the soul of its reader.[2] When one views the work of Michelangelo, he claims, 'the soul is agitated by sensations that it is not used to receiving through the eyes'.[3] Stendhal famously believed that some people were more open than others to the experience of being moved, whether by a novel, a piece of music, a play or a painting: these sensitive souls, he suggests in various places, are 'the Happy Few'. He argues for example that 'an eye that knows how to see and a soul that knows how to feel' are necessary in order truly to see what Michelangelo achieved on the Sistine Chapel ceiling.[4] To be under forty years old was a distinct advantage in this respect, but a passionate disposition was decisive: 'A passionate man who submits to the effect of the fine arts finds everything in his heart.'[5]

For Stendhal, encounters with works of art tended to take the form of a sharing of emotion, which he associated with the phenomenon of 'sympathie', defined by him as 'the ability to identify with another person'.[6] Even the success of works that do not primarily appeal to sympathy could depend upon this faculty, to the extent that attendance at a theatre or concert could produce a 'nervous sympathy' or 'reciprocal sympathy' felt with other people in the room.[7] Novel-reading lacked this collective dimension, but could nevertheless itself be a rich source of sympathetic communication. For example, Stendhal included fictional characters, whether on the stage or on the page, among those to whom a reader's sympathy might be extended:

If the [stage] character appears in the slightest way to think about his style, mistrust emerges, sympathy flees, and pleasure in the drama disappears.[8]

I fear that Fabrice's credulity could deprive him of the reader's sympathy.[9]

Before feeling sympathy for the characters, the reader wonders: 'What are that man's political beliefs?'[10]

Stendhalian sympathy, as evoked in the above translated quotations, is close to narrative empathy, or the illusion of affective sharing; it is a form of feeling *with* a fictional entity. As the first citation above suggests, sympathy and suspicion were antithetical attitudes for Stendhal. He writes, in *Racine et Shakspeare*, of how Rousseau differs from Montesquieu and La Bruyère because while the latters' work is premised on 'a thought articulated clearly', the former's excites 'our sympathy, makes us accept many things that we would reject if we were not under the charm': 'Rousseau speaks principally to the heart.'[11] The author knew that the sympathy produced in the course of reading a fiction could be based on an illusion:

Reading the chronicles and novels of the Middle Ages, we, as sensitive people of the nineteenth century, imagine what the heroes must have felt; we lend them a sensibility that is as impossible for them as it is natural for us.[12]

As this passage suggests, for Stendhal the receiver of the aesthetic object puts at least as much into that object as she takes from it. The author's understanding of the participatory nature of aesthetic reception is highlighted by Julia Kristeva: 'In Stendhal's albeit realist universe, everything depends, indeed, and perhaps more than elsewhere, more than the naive reader believes, upon interpretation: upon the identificatory projection demanded of the reader.'[13] Indeed, in writing his own novels the author was at least as interested in provoking emotion in the reader as in producing an accurate representation of reality: he wished to 'provoke feelings, give some nuance of emotion'.[14] Ann Jefferson is consequently correct to point out that 'the reading of a text is, in Stendhal's view, only possible if the experiences that it represents are re-evoked and re-constituted within the reader. She cannot merely be a passive spectator of the representation on the page.'[15] Unlike works of non-fictional prose, novels appeal, then, according to Stendhal, to the reader's capacity for what he called sympathy and what we would refer to as narrative (or affective) empathy.

References to sympathy, which Stendhal called a 'law of nature', also feature in Stendhal's writing about love.[16] Sympathy and love were certainly distinct in his mind; for example, in *Le Rouge et le Noir* the narrator notes at one point that sympathy with the 'bonheur' (happiness) of a rival for the heroine's heart leads the hero to praise that rival, while in *Promenades dans Rome* the author writes of women's 'natural sympathy' for bright colours.[17] However, sympathy and love are nonetheless related in his writing. In one anecdote in *De l'Amour*, a woman covertly, and while retaining deniability, evokes her love for a man by speaking of her sympathy for him.[18] Elsewhere in his treatise on love he writes that where money is shared by a couple, love is increased, but where money is given by one lover to another, 'love is *killed*'; '*politics* enters into things, and the feeling of being two, and sympathy is destroyed'.[19] He observes that sympathy can mean that 'the happiness of two individuals merges', and that after 'early youth', at the stage when 'the heart becomes closed to sympathy', love can re-awaken 'the tender and generous part of the soul'.[20]

It has already been shown that aesthetic experience is linked to sympathy, for Stendhal; it is also closely associated with love. For example, the perception of beauty tends to conjure up memories of love, in his work.[21] And immediately after noting that 'a lover's daydream cannot be recorded', the author of *De l'Amour* observes that the same is true of the kind of daydreaming inspired by novels.[22] Stendhal's fictional representations of love are themselves sometimes linked to aesthetic encounters. At the same moment that Madame Grandet, in *Lucien Leuwen*, falls for the hero, she turns to novels, and Mathilde's first genuinely passionate tryst with Julien takes place just after a night at the Italian opera, when she is absorbed by the illusion of passion that she sees played out on stage, and which she assumes as her own. This book is proposing that fictional representations of amorous relations with stranger figures can say something about how fictions programme their own reception; in Stendhal's novels, this hypothesis seems particularly plausible, given the close analogical links he regularly suggests between love and encounters with works of the imagination. This chapter will examine fictional responses to a Stendhalian stranger who is closely associated with fiction, with a view to working out the kind of reading that is tacitly recommended by the novel in which he features. Despite the emphasis placed by this opening section on the role accorded by Stendhal to emotion, in the reception of art, it will be argued that *Le Rouge et le Noir*, like Balzac's *La Fille aux yeux d'or* as seen in the previous chapter, indirectly recommends that emotion be combined with reflection, and sympathy with distrust, in our relations with seductive strangers as in our reading of novels.

Julien as a Fiction-Connoted Stranger

Julien Sorel, from Stendhal's *Le Rouge et le Noir*, is a striking figure of the stranger. When we meet him first, he is something of a stranger in his own family, preferring to read than to man his father's sawmill, and choosing to study Latin in order to elevate himself in the social world. Slender and feminine, he hates and is hated by his brutish father and brothers. He describes himself as 'une sorte d'enfant trouvé, haï de mon père, de mes frères, de toute ma famille' (a sort of foundling, hated by my father, my brothers, my whole family) (p. 44). There is even village speculation that the former army surgeon, who lodged with the family 'sous prétexte qu'il était leur cousin' (on the pretext that he was their cousin) (p. 21), as Monsieur de Rênal puts it, may actually be Julien's father. Before Madame de Rênal meets her children's new tutor, she feels anxious about the threat that 'cet étranger' (this stranger) poses to her intimacy with her own children (p. 35). Julien continues, for a long time, to feel that he is viewed by Madame de Rênal as an outsider in her home. This view is mistaken, but his sense of isolation is not entirely imagined: 'Souvent Julien était inintelligible pour Mme Derville et même pour son amie, et à son tour ne comprenait qu'à demi tout ce qu'elles lui disaient' (Often Julien was incomprehensible to Madame Derville and even for her friend, and in his turn only understood half of what they said to him) (p. 71).

Julien's status as an outsider continues throughout the novel. When he arrives in the city where the seminary is located, he tells a young barmaid: 'je n'ai ni parents, ni connaissance à Besançon' (I have no relatives or acquaintances in Besançon) (p. 167). In the seminary, Julien feels 'oublié de toute la terre' (forgotten by the whole world) (p. 180) and makes no alliances among his peers, who nickname him 'Martin Luther' as a way of signalling his outsider status, as well as his perceived falseness: 'Julien se sentait de l'éloignement pour eux et eux pour lui' (Julien felt estranged from them, and they from him) (p. 179). While at the seminary, he cultivates 'la différence de [s]on extérieur et de celui d'un laïc' (the difference between his appearance and that of a layperson) (p. 184). The Abbé Pirard identifies in him '[une] nécessité d'être haï' (a need to be hated) and a quality 'qui offense le vulgaire' (which offends the vulgar) (p. 199). In Paris, too, in the Hôtel de La Mole, the hero feels 'parfaitement isolé au milieu de cette famille' (perfectly isolated amidst that family) (p. 250) and aware that 'il n'avait pas un ami' (he had not a single friend) (p. 268). It seems to him as though the nobles who surround him are speaking 'comme une langue étrangère qu'il eût comprise, mais qu'il n'eût pu parler' (something like a foreign language that he might have understood but which he could not have spoken) (p. 257). The narrator comments that a young provincial is 'toujours un étranger' (always an outsider) in Paris (p. 265). As if Julien were not already all too aware of his outsider status, Count Altamira reminds him at the ball at the Hôtel de Retz that he will always be disdained 'comme homme du peuple intrus dans la bonne compagnie' (as a commoner who has intruded upon fine company) (p. 297). In the most literal sense, then, Julien is a stranger: he is, or considers himself to be, an outsider who is never truly at home in the various social situations he inhabits. This is as true when we meet him first in the sawmill as when he walks into the church at Verrières, armed with a pistol.

In addition, Julien is a stranger in the sense that he is other than he seems. He is revealed, from a very early point in the novel, to be a 'hypocrite' (p. 28), feigning piety as a means of self-defence against his father and because he believes that feigned piety will help him to acquire social power. As suggested by his assumption of a religiously-connoted black habit despite his 'parfaite incrédulité' (perfect atheism) (p. 275), Julien is virtually always participating in a fiction, because he is almost always playing a role, whether it be that of a seducer of women, or 'son triste rôle de plébéien révolté' (his sad role as a plebeian in revolt) (p. 309), that of Madame de Fervaques's admirer, that of a spy working on behalf of the Ultras or that of a noble lieutenant.

Finally, Julien is a stranger in the sense that he is other to himself, and therefore unreadable to both himself and the reader. Julien's inscrutability is partly voluntary; he works hard at it in the seminary and when he is sent to London by the Marquis de La Mole. It is also partly involuntary, though, in the sense that he does not appear to have much purchase over his own feelings. As a result, he is prone to irrational emotional outbursts, for example when he expresses his admiration for Napoleon in the company of priests, or goes to stab Mathilde or, most famously, when he shoots his former lover in a church. Julien appears, furthermore, to misread his own emotions, failing, for example, to realise that he loves Madame de Rênal until after he shoots her. In this, he resembles Paquita, whose body seems to speak a truth different from that of her mind.

The black habit with which he is so closely identified in the novel reinforces Julien's status as a stranger: it marks him out as an outsider and is closely bound up both with his hypocritical duplicity and his resistance to reading. The black habit is, moreover, closely associated with fiction, to the extent that it not only transforms Julien, but also facilitates his dissimulations. The black habit therefore serves as a kind of metonym for Julien's fictive or duplicitous leanings, as well as for his status as a stranger. The robe has an almost magical effect when he first puts it on; it seems to elevate him, marking him out as different from other men: he is described as 'hors de lui-même' (outside himself) (p. 41), as becoming 'un autre homme' (another man) (p. 42). On the first evening he wears it, when the inhabitants of Verrières flock to the mayor's house to see Julien recite passages of the Bible from memory, 'Julien répondait à tous d'un air sombre qui tenait à distance' (answered all of them in a sombre manner that kept them at a distance) (p. 43). He deliberately maintains this aloofness, even with his employers:

> Si je veux être estimé et d'eux et de moi-même, il faut leur montrer que c'est ma pauvreté qui est en commerce avec leur richesse, mais que mon cœur est à mille lieues de leur insolence, et placé dans une sphère trop haute pour être atteint par leurs petites marques de dédain ou de faveur. (p. 76)

> (If I want to be respected both by them and by myself, I need to show them that it is only my poverty that is engaging with their wealth, and that my heart is a thousand miles away from their insolence, and placed in too high a sphere to be touched by their petty marks of disdain or favour.)

As well as transforming him into a mysterious stranger figure, the black habit helps Julien to assume a fictional identity as a would-be priest, an identity that is intended, from the moment he adopts it, to help him to achieve rank and power. He describes his gown as 'l'uniforme de [s]on siècle' (the uniform of his century) (p. 329), a means of defying social barriers as effectively as the military uniform had done in the time of Napoleon. The transformative qualities of the black habit are highlighted by the Marquis's practice of encouraging Julien to wear a blue habit whenever he wishes to be treated as a member of the family and as a noble, and to revert to the black habit whenever he is playing the role of secretary. The black habit, then, like the blue one that occasionally replaces it, helps Julien pretend to be other than he is. The habit operates in both Verrières and Paris to conceal Julien's social class; this is a large part of its purpose, for both employer and employee. It also has the advantage of screening his political leanings from view: it conceals his secret passion for Napoleon and admiration for Danton, seeming to identify him as a royalist rather than as the Bonapartist and potential revolutionary that he is, in his own mind at least. For Julien, the habit is, then, a useful fiction in that it serves him as a kind of mask.

Julien's general unreadability to other characters, his air of mystery, has the repeated effect of leading other characters to tell or imagine stories about him. Monsieur de Rênal is struck by the tutor's 'ton étrange' (strange tone) when he reacts angrily to criticism, and concludes, erroneously, that Julien has received another offer of employment (p. 68). Mathilde, impressed by Julien's quality of 'inconnu' (unknown-ness) (p. 334), imagines him as a new Danton or, somewhat contradictorily, as a possible future hero of the nobility. It is, in fact, Julien's impenetrability that interests Mathilde; when he becomes, for her, an open book, she loses interest. The possibility that Julien is the illegitimate son of a nobleman is originally proposed, apparently in earnest, by the Abbé Pirard to the Marquis de La Mole; the latter later proves himself happy to endorse and even subscribe to this aspect of Julien's story, but does worry temporarily that the Abbé may have spun him a false story about Julien's intellectual abilities: 'Tout ce que l'abbé m'a dit de sa science serait-il tout simplement un conte!' (Could it be that everything that the Abbé told me about his learning is a mere story!) (p. 243). A similar fiction about Julien's noble origins is knowingly concocted and circulated by the Chevalier de Beauvoisis and his friend, for purely self-serving reasons; subsequently, and for similar reasons, the Marquis de La Mole hears the new rumour, promotes 'ce récit' (this story) (p. 272) and even makes of the fiction a virtual reality through the protagonist's renaming, towards the end of the novel, as Monsieur de La Vernaye.

The close association of the protagonist with fiction is explicitly underscored at various points in the text. As commentators have often noted, Julien is doubly fictional, indeed, insofar as he often plays the role of a hero or fictional character. Numerous references are made, for example, to his role-playing and pretence in his relationship with Madame de Rênal.[23] At an early point in the novel, the narrator accuses his protagonist of playing the role of the fictional Don Juan, and no fewer than seven subsequent epigraphs are from Byron's *Don Juan*. Julien is, furthermore, inspired to quote the duplicitous Tartufe, hero of Molière's play, at several junctures, and the fictional priest is even described by the narrator as 'son maître' (his master) (p. 330). The protagonist likes, too, to imagine himself as a hero in the mould of Napoleon, and is regularly described as a hero by the narrator. Finally, Julien's trial for attempted murder is described as '[une] cause romanesque' (a novelistic case) for those who flock to Besançon to witness it (p. 478).

The protagonist is clearly presented as a dreamer, capable of appreciating fictions. It is because he is 'un homme à imagination' (an imaginative man) (p. 179) that he is ambitious and constitutionally incapable of accepting Fouqué's job offer: 'il se trouvait non entre le vice et la vertu, mais entre la médiocrité suivie d'un bien-être assuré et tous les rêves héroïques de sa jeunesse' (he found himself caught not between vice and virtue, but between the sustained mediocrity of a guaranteed comfort and all the heroic dreams of his youth) (p. 80). Julien's highly developed imagination is overtly associated by the narrator with his status as a social outsider: he lives '[une] vie solitaire toute d'imagination et de méfiance' (a solitary life of imagination and distrust) (p. 82). So imaginative is Julien that the narrator comments wryly at one point that he will never amount to anything more distinguished than an artist. While he appears only to be interested in books that purport to tell the truth (he prizes Rousseau's *Confessions*, Las Cases' *Mémorial de Sainte-Hélène*, and the news bulletins of Napoleon's Grande armée, and considers all other books to be 'menteurs' (dishonest) (p. 29)), and while the narrator suggests that Julien has not yet read any novels after having spent several months in the Rênal household, by the time he gets to Besançon he is quoting, to impress a barmaid, passages from Rousseau's *La Nouvelle Héloïse*, a copy of which he had found in Vergy; he deploys the same strategy later, with Mathilde. As a seminarian, he is familiar enough with imaginative literature to quote the Latin poets Horace and Virgil, 'et d[']autres auteurs profanes' (and other profane authors) (p. 201), during an examination. In Paris, subsequently, he takes full advantage of his access to the La Mole library and of opportunities to enjoy plays, ballets and operas.

Julien is, moreover, regularly presented as a producer of fictions.[24] He takes great pleasure, for example, in composing a false anonymous letter to Monsieur de Rênal, following Madame de Rênal's instructions. He is adept at fabricating stories, telling a Besançon barmaid for instance that he will pretend to be her cousin so that they can continue to see one another, and then inventing a story or 'narration' (p. 187) to explain the presence among his possessions, at the seminary, of a playing card with the barmaid's name. Upon returning to Verrières to pay a visit to Madame de Rênal, he eventually and gradually wins the latter over by telling her his story; the word 'récit' (narrative) appears five times in this episode. Indeed, Julien often thinks of his own life as a story to be told; he tells himself that if he seduces Madame de Rênal then it will be understood later, by others, that his lowly role as Latin tutor was motivated by love. He greatly enjoys story-making: we learn that during his time in the Hôtel de La Mole, he is obliged to burn a short biography that he had written about his beloved army surgeon. In addition, the narrator mockingly refers to the 'roman' (novel) (p. 78) that Julien invents about his own future, one night while alone in the mountains; there is even a suggestion that this novel acquired tentative written form when the narrator notes that Julien had to burn all his scribblings before leaving his cave. Julien later compares his correspondence with Mathilde to '[un] roman par lettres' (a novel of letters), and in one letter takes particular pleasure in leading his possible readers astray: 'Il se donna le plaisir de mystifier, pendant deux pages, les personnes qui voudraient se moquer de lui' (He gave himself the pleasure of mystifying, over the course of two pages, those who would like to mock him) (p. 335). The narrator again hints at Julien's novelistic aspirations with a reference to his composition of '[un] petit mémoire justificatif arrangé en forme de conte' (a little explanatory acccount, arranged in the form of a story) (p. 340) in case he is murdered by Mathilde's male friends; the invention of this hypothetical scenario leads the narrator to compare the protagonist to 'un auteur dramatique' (a dramatic author) who is 'ému de son propre conte' (moved by his own story) (p. 340). When Julien is made an army lieutenant and ennobled by the grace of the Marquis, he decides that '[s]on roman est fini' (his novel is finished) (p. 448).

It is true that, towards the end of the novel, the hero appears to have become wary of fictions, and particularly of the kind of public spectacles engaged in by Mathilde. He is interested in hearing the story of a fellow prisoner only if that story is true, and chastises a Jansenist priest who proposes that the hero save himself from the guillotine by means of a public religious conversion: 'Ah! je vous y prends vous aussi, mon père, jouant la comédie comme un missionnaire' (Ah! I have caught you too at it, my father, playing a part like a missionary) (p. 504). The hero even seems to overlook his own past hypocrisy, telling himself that he has always loved truth and criticising the hypocrisy of his contemporaries; though he does have enough insight subsequently to mock the hypocrisy of his own criticism. As this last point suggests, Julien's apparent rejection of duplicity at the end of the novel is, arguably, merely superficial. He continues, for example, to play a role with Mathilde ('peut-être un jour vous me verrez le sujet de quelque mélodrame, etc., etc.' (perhaps one day you will see me as the subject of some melodrama, etc., etc.) (p. 503)) and with most other visitors, and is adamant that nobody will glimpse any weakness in him as he confronts his death. The hero continues, moreover, to think of his own life as a fictional performance, playfully asking Mathilde how he looked as he spoke in court, and consoling himself that 'la fin du drame doit être bien proche' (the end of the drama must be very near) (p. 503). Quotations from plays by Rotrou and Voltaire come to him, in these last chapters, and he also tells himself stories, most notably the parable of the hunter and an anthill. Finally, there is plenty of textual evidence to suggest that the hero's claim to have always loved Madame de Rênal, and only her, is itself a fiction that Julien tells himself.[24] The protagonist may attempt to distance himself from fiction in the final chapters of *Le Rouge et le Noir*, but fiction does not distance itself from him.

The stranger hero of Stendhal's novel is, therefore, closely associated with narrative invention throughout the text. Returning now to our hypothesis that fictional responses to the figure of the stranger can tell us something about how a novel programmes readers' responses to it, how does Julien engage the mind-reading skills of other characters? In order to answer this question, we will first ask how the novel portrays mind-reading more generally.

The Powers and Limits of Mind-Reading in *Le Rouge et le Noir*

Characters are constantly divining each other's motivations in *Le Rouge et le Noir*, interpreting intentions from facial expressions and body language. We learn in an early episode that Julien's father 'avait l'air de vouloir lire jusqu'au fond de son âme' (looked as though he wanted to read deep into his soul) (p. 27), in a later one that Amanda Binet 'lut dans les regards de Julien' (read the expression in Julien's eyes) (p. 167), while Julien repeatedly reads, or attempts to read, Mathilde ('même quand ses beaux yeux bleus fixés sur moi sont ouverts avec le plus d'abandon, j'y lis toujours un fond d'examen' (even when her beautiful blue eyes stare at me with the most open abandonment, I always read in them an element of scrutiny) (p. 322)); of his fellow seminarians, the narrator tells us that 'Julien ne lisait jamais dans leur œil morne que le besoin physique satisfait après le dîner, et le plaisir physique attendu avant le repas' (Julien never read in their dreary eyes anything other than the fulfilment of physical need after dinner, and the expectation of physical pleasure before a meal) (p. 180). Madame Derville is 'désespérée de ce qu'elle croyait deviner' (in despair over what she thought she detected) (p. 96) when she sees Madame de Rênal and Julien together. Upon visiting Monsieur de Frilair and speaking about her influential social connections, Mathilde is initially 'effrayée du changement rapide de la physionomie de cet homme si puissant' (frightened by the rapid change in facial expression on the part of such a powerful man) (p. 468), but quickly understands the power she wields over him. Stendhal constructs a universe in which the ability to read others correctly is a source of significant power.

If certain talented mind-readers, such as Julien's mentor, the Abbé Chélan, do not wield their talents for social advantage, many do. Père Sorel's ability to decipher Monsieur de Rênal's reasons for wanting to hire Julien as a tutor brings him direct material advantage, while Julien himself profits in an equally concrete way from his own successful divination of the reasons for the mayor's reticence in registering at the local bookshop. Julien's ability to read others even wins him a lucrative job offer from his friend Fouqué: 'tu as compris les finesses du caractère de ces gens-là; te voilà en état de paraître aux adjudications' (you have understood the finer points of the character of those people, which means you are well placed to attend auctions) (p. 78). Later, Julien's ability to read his father, in the prison cell, enables him both to rid himself of the latter's presence, by offering him money, and to save his own posthumous reputation. It should nevertheless be noted that Julien is far from being the most gifted mind-reader in the novel. For a long time he fails, for example, to 'lire dans le cœur de Mme de Rênal' (read inside the heart of Madame de Rênal) (p. 51) to see that she is in love with him, and he repeatedly misreads both her and Mathilde, as well as secondary characters such as Pirard.[26]

The ability to read others correctly is closely associated, in Stendhal's novel, with the social power that comes from defending oneself success-fully against other people's attempted readings, and with the related power to mislead others. For example, when the sub-prefect Monsieur de Maugiron pays Julien a visit in Verrières and offers him a post as tutor on behalf of an anonymous party, the protagonist easily identifies the source and motivation of the offer, and replies in a way that leaves the visitor none the wiser as to his allegiances: 'Sa réponse [. . .] laissait tout entendre, et cependant ne disait rien nettement' (His answer [. . .] gave everything to be understood, without saying anything clearly) (p. 140). The text makes the link between mind-reading and duplicity clear in a passage which relates how Julien congratulates himself on working for the elegant Rênal family rather than the vulgar Valenods: 'À chaque instant, il n'était pas tiré de ses rêveries brillantes par la cruelle nécessité d'étudier les mouvements d'une âme basse, et encore afin de la tromper par des démarches ou des mots hypocrites' (At every moment, he was not pulled away from his brilliant daydreams by the cruel necessity of studying the movements of a base soul, and worse, in order to deceive that soul with hypocritical actions or words) (p. 157). Julien cannot, of course, avoid the necessity of mind-reading and duplicity by working for the Rênals, but he is convinced that, with the Rênals, at least, he can examine and mislead more rewardingly elegant souls.

If superior mind-reading skills confer social power on characters in Stendhal's novel, a deficit of these skills can pose a major disadvantage. Monsieur de Rênal's assumption that he understands the motivations of others, and that these motivations resemble his own, is clearly presented as a failing: the narrator tells us, for example, that the mayor's inability to deduce that his wife and Julien are having an affair can be attributed to a lack of imagination ('Si M. de Rênal eût été un homme d'imagination, il savait tout' (If Monsieur de Rênal had been an imaginative man, he would have known everything) (p. 118)). The inability to read other people accurately is presented by *Le Rouge et le Noir* as a significant social disadvantage. Unsurprisingly, then, Monsieur de Rênal is one of the great dupes of the novel, losing his wife to his former employee and the office of mayor to his rival, Valenod.

Julien and the Limits of Mind-Reading

For the less shrewd characters of *Le Rouge et le Noir*, the ambiguous hero is easy to read. For Monsieur de Rênal, for example, the fact that Julien intends to become a priest means that he could not therefore be a political liberal. When Julien explodes with anger because of a perceived offence, Monsieur de Rênal jumps to a false conclusion about the source of Julien's anger, because he assumes that Julien shares his own regard for money. Shortly afterwards, on noticing something unusual in Julien's firm tone of voice, he incorrectly assumes that 'ce petit paysan a sans doute en poche des propositions de quelqu'un' (this little peasant has no doubt secured someone's offers) (pp. 76–7). In sum, Monsieur de Rênal falls seriously short as a reader of Julien's mind.

Julien is repeatedly presented by the text as inscrutable for other characters. Much of this opacity is intentional. His studied dissimulation of his atheism, and his simulation of religious faith, make of him a consummate hypocrite.[27] During his months in the seminary, he goes so far as to attempt to disguise his intelligence, controlling his facial expression so as to give the impression of blind, unquestioning religious faith; however, he fails miserably at hiding the 'idées mondaines [. . .] qu'ils lisent sur [s]a figure, quoi qu['il] fasse' (worldly ideas [. . .] that they read in his face, whatever he does) (p. 185). The metaphorical reference to reading, here, is made literal in Julien's attempts to disguise his feelings for Napoleon: he burns any writings that could betray his loyalties to prying eyes.[28] Despite his strenuous efforts to disguise his true feelings when in the company of others, occasionally a character sees through his pretences: he feels a surge of affection for the priest Chélan when the latter recognises 'une ardeur sombre' (a dark ardour) in his character that indicates that he is not the pious young man he pretends to be: 'C'est lui surtout qu'il importe de tromper, et il me devine' (He is the one I especially need to deceive, and he sees through me) (p. 54).

Not all of Julien's interpretative resistance is deliberate, however. Some of it seems innate. During a visit to London, Julien's appearance of impassivity, his apparently natural 'mine froide et à *mille lieues de la sensation présente*' (cold demeanour, *a thousand miles from present sensation*) (p. 278) wins him the admiration of his dandy friends. The narrator's initial portrait of him presents him as 'faible en apparence' (weak-looking) (pp. 26, 34), with a face that nevertheless betrays great energy and intelligence; and the narrator suggests that nobody would guess that his gentle, feminine features hide steely courage and ambition.[29] Later, the narrator tells us that Julien is often 'inintelligible' (unintelligible) (p. 71) for Madame Derville and Madame de Rênal, on account of his social awkwardness. Julien's protector in the seminary, Monsieur Pirard, locates Julien's resistance to reading at the very heart of his character, referring to 'ce je ne sais quoi d'indéfinissable, du moins pour moi, qu'il y a dans [son] caractère' (this undefinable thing, at least for me, that is in his character) (p. 236).

Regardless of the extent to which Julien's resistance to mind-reading is deliberate or involuntary, this resistance to understanding makes him a source of fascination and curiosity for other characters. In the seminary, Julien's inscrutability makes him 'l'objet de la curiosité générale' (the object of general curiosity) (p. 178). Mathilde's father rewards Julien's 'imprévu' (unpredictability) with a distinction that he denies even to his own son (p. 283). However, upon learning that the secretary has made his daughter pregnant, this quality is less positively connoted: the Marquis de La Mole recognises 'au fond de ce caractère [. . .] quelque chose d'effrayant' (at the root of his character [. . .] something frightening) (p. 445), 'un point réel' (a real element) that terrifies his 'âme imaginative' (imaginative soul) (p. 446). He finds it extraordinarily difficult to decide whether Julien is a shrewd social player or a generous, passionate character: 'Y a-t-il eu amour véritable, imprévu? Ou bien désir vulgaire de s'élever à une belle position?' (Was there a true, unpremediated love? Or rather a vulgar desire to attain a fine position?) (p. 446). Even after ennobling Julien and preparing the ground for a possible future marriage, the Marquis de La Mole tells his daughter: 'Je ne sais pas encore ce que c'est que votre Julien' (I do not know what your Julien is) (p. 447). It is only after receiving the fatal letter from Madame de Rênal that he decides that the 'affreuse vérité' (awful truth) is that Julien is 'un homme vil' (an odious man) (p. 451).

Although Julien, then, both intentionally and unintentionally poses an interpretive problem for other characters, his secret intentions and motivations are regularly revealed to readers. The narrator lets us behind the scenes repeatedly, pointing out what other characters fail to divine in Julien: 'Ce regard étonna Mme Derville, et l'eût surprise bien davantage si elle en eût deviné la véritable expression; elle y eût lu comme un espoir vague de la plus atroce vengeance' (This gaze astonished Madame Derville, and would have surprised her even more had she guessed the true meaning of its expression; she would have read in it something like a vague hope of the most terrible vengeance) (pp. 64–5). Despite this privileged access to Julien's thought processes, the hero remains perplexingly elusive to readers of the novel; or rather, some readers consider him easy to read, but disagree with one other as to how to read him, while others emphasise his contradictory qualities. As Yves Ansel puts it, the hero is 'a fragmented, divided character, who divides critics'.[30] Julien can be interpreted as hypocritical or sincere, as prudent or imprudent, as cynical or naive. The text itself does not allow us definitively to decide one way or the other, or rather allows us to decide either way, depending on which evidence we decide to privilege. On the one hand, the narrator suggests that Julien's character is primarily scheming, his romantic sensitivity presenting itself, at first, only as an aberration: forgetting 'sa noire ambition' (his dark ambition) in Vergy one evening, he is 'perdu dans une rêverie vague et douce, si étrangère à son caractère' (lost in a vague and sweet daydream, so foreign to his character) (p. 73). His growing feelings for Madame de Rênal reveal to him 'une faculté de son âme qu'il n'avait jamais sentie' (a faculty of his soul that he had never perceived) (p. 75). Shortly after this, however, the narrator refers to a mismatch between 'l'intérieur de son âme' (the interior of his soul) and the 'langage cavalier' (cavalier language) of his thoughts (p. 86), a formula that appears to make tenderness a fundamental aspect of his character. He is repeatedly designated a hypocrite and a social climber by the narrator and other characters; and yet he is also presented as capable of intense sincerity. It is little wonder that the narrator seems undecided about the true nature of Julien's character when the hero himself is perplexed by his behaviour, pondering in the prison cell the question of whether he is, after all, 'un méchant' (a villain) (p. 470) and 'un égoïste' (a selfish man) (p. 471).

Some of the interpretative resistance posed by the hero's character can no doubt be imputed to Stendhal's characteristic hastiness and occasional negligence: for example, we read at the beginning of Chapter VII that the young man does not love the Rênal children, but a few days and pages afterwards, the narrator notes that 'il aimait beaucoup' (he greatly loved) the younger child (p. 67). It is more difficult to explain inconsistencies that affect central themes of the novel. For example, Julien is alternately presented by the narrator as prudent (pp. 80, 88, 330, 469) and imprudent (pp. 93, 469); and he quotes *La Nouvelle Héloïse* at several points in the novel before the narrator informs us that 'il n'avait pas même lu de romans' (he had not even read novels) (p. 355).

The incoherence and inscrutability of Julien's character become an explicit problem at the end of the novel. Julien's defence lawyer believes his crime to have been motivated by jealousy, while Mathilde prefers the hypothesis of 'une noble vengeance' (a noble vengeance) (p. 606). Julien himself tells Mathilde that his crime was an act of vengeance, and appears privately to agree with this assessment, telling himself: 'J'ai été offensé d'une manière atroce, j'ai tué, je mérite la mort' (I was offended in a brutal way, I killed, I deserve death) (p. 457). However, he cannot decide whether his vengeance was inspired by his ambition or by his love for Mathilde: 'j'ai voulu la tuer par ambition ou par amour pour Mathilde' (I wanted to kill her for ambition or for love of Mathilde) (p. 485). His motivation is, ultimately, 'inexplicable', in the eyes of the women of Besançon and in the eyes of the Abbé de Frilair (pp. 504, 464), and arguably in his own eyes too.

The protagonist's various inconsistencies and contradictions are part of what makes him so fascinating for both readers and other characters. In the final chapters of the novel, Julien is described as an object of popular fascination; crowds throng to the Besançon courtroom to see and hear the man who tried to kill his former lover. It is his 'étrange aventure' (strange adventure) (p. 469) that appeals to the crowds; they are attracted to the strangeness of his act, its resistance to understanding. Readers, like the Besançon hordes, are fascinated by the inexplicability of Julien's action, an inexplicability that is exacerbated by the fact that he insists on its premeditated character. Readers are also often intrigued by his unexplained switch of affections from his fiancée to his former lover.[31] But this is not the place to consider the different critical interpretations of the hero that have been offered over time. Instead, I would like to ask how the novel's two infatuated heroines read Julien's mind, in the hope that this may help us to understand how the text unconsciously programmes its own reading.

Madame de Rênal as a Mind-Reader

Madame de Rênal is a very poor reader of her own motivations – she fails, for example, to understand the implications of her newfound interest in low-cut dresses, is astonished to discover that she loves Julien, and misinterprets her 'malheur' (misfortune), during Julien's time in Paris, as remorse for her affair with him rather than as lovesickness (p. 455). However, she is a shrewd reader of others, capable of manipulating her husband when she considers it necessary, of divining Valenod's complex political machinations and of explaining these machinations to Julien.

Madame de Rênal is also a highly intuitive reader of Julien. The first time she sees him, she feels 'pitié' (pity) for him (p. 36), closely followed by 'bonheur' (happiness) (p. 37) when she realises that this gentle-seeming person is the new tutor whose sternness she had feared. Even in the course of this first encounter, she divines something of Julien's feelings, though incorrectly identifies the cause of these feelings: 'Mme de Rênal en était déjà à saisir les moindres nuances de ce qui se passait dans l'âme du précepteur; elle prit ce mouvement de tristesse pour de la timidité' (Madame de Rênal was already capable of grasping the slightest movements within the soul of the tutor; she took this sad turn for shyness) (p. 38). In the days that follow, she notices the efforts that he makes to keep his clothes clean, and accurately detects a poverty that shocks her at first but which then provokes her pity: 'Peu à peu, elle eut pitié de tout ce qui manquait à Julien, au lieu d'en être choquée [. . .] Souvent, en songeant à la pauvreté du jeune précepteur, Mme de Rênal était attendrie jusqu'aux larmes' (Gradually, she felt pity for Julien's hardship, instead of being shocked by it. [. . .] Often, thinking about the young tutor's poverty, Madame de Rênal was moved to tears) (pp. 46, 48). She has only to see the look in his eyes when he tells her about a 'pauvre chien écrasé' (poor trampled dog) in order to deduce his generosity and to feel drawn into sympathetic relation with him:

> Elle trouva des jouissances douces, et toutes brillantes du charme de la nouveauté, dans la sympathie de cette âme noble et fière. [. . .] La générosité, la noblesse d'âme, l'humanité lui semblèrent peu à peu n'exister que chez ce jeune abbé. Elle eut pour lui seul toute la sympathie et même l'admiration que ces vertus excitent chez les âmes bien nées. (p. 47)

> (She found sweet pleasures, shining with the charm of novelty, in the sympathy of this noble and proud soul. [. . .] Generosity, nobility of the soul, humanity gradually seemed to her to exist only in this young abbé. She felt for him alone all the sympathy and even admiration that those virtues excite in well-born souls.)

Repeatedly, Madame de Rênal interprets, in an approximate way, the affect conveyed by Julien's demeanour or facial expressions, and responds emotionally to what she perceives:

> Elle [. . .] était inquiète, car son instinct de femme lui faisait comprendre que cet embarras n'était nullement tendre. (p. 51)

> (She [. . .] was worried, because her womanly instinct gave her to understand that this discomfiture had nothing tender about it.)

> Elle avait surpris la crainte sur cette physionomie [. . .] Ce surcroît de douleur [chez elle] arriva à toute l'intensité de malheur qu'il est donné à l'âme humaine de pouvoir supporter. (p. 74)

(She had surprised fear on that face. [...] Her additional anguish reached an intensity of misery that is at the limit of what a human soul can tolerate.)

Elle le regardait aller, atterrée de la hauteur sombre qu'elle lisait dans ce regard si aimable la veille. (p. 76)

(She watched him go, stricken by the somber aloofness that she read in his eyes, which had been so affable the previous day.)

These instances of mind-reading are all affective in character: Madame de Rênal discerns the hero's feelings and responds feelingly to what she discerns.

The heroine also occasionally reads Julien in a more dispassionate way; impressed, for example, by his accurate interpretation of Monsieur de Rênal's response to an anonymous letter, she decides that his 'tact parfait' (perfect discernment) will get him far in society (p. 132). However, Madame de Rênal's style of reading is not especially concerned with Julien's thoughts and motivations, tending to concentrate on his feelings rather than on their potential causes. This means that Madame de Rênal fails to understand that Julien will react angrily to her offer of money after she notices his poverty, and then makes the mistake of telling her husband about his refusal; she half intuits Julien's irony when he claims to be pleased with the monetary gift subsequently bestowed on him by her husband – 'Mme de Rênal le regarda comme incertaine' (Madame de Rênal looked at him uncertainly) (p. 49) – just as she correctly divines 'un air de supériorité intellectuelle' (an air of intellectual superiority) in his eyes whenever he meets visitors to the household, but she does not appear to analyse her own perceptions in any depth. Madame de Rênal's affective style of mind-reading also allows her to think of Julien as candid and charming while Madame Derville, more alert to his possible motivations, judges him to be 'un sournois' (a sly one) (p. 87). Madame de Rênal occasionally experiences '[d]es inquiétudes' (anxieties) (p. 94) about the possible discontinuation of his feelings for her, and at one point tells him that she cannot 'read' him: 'Il est des moments où je crois n'avoir jamais lu jusqu'au fond de ton âme. Tes regards m'effrayent' (There are moments when I think that I have never read as far as the depths of your soul. The look in your eyes frightens me) (p. 123). However, she never asks herself whether Julien's love for her is authentic, even when the evidence of its deficiencies is most apparent, for example when he fails to seek her out among the faces in the crowd during the king's visit to Verrières.

In those cases where Madame de Rênal does attempt to interpret Julien's intentions, she is prone to misreading them. She imagines, for example, that he is in love with her maid, Élisa. When he kisses her hand in the garden at Vergy, she erroneously imagines that his intentions are sincere: 'Julien couvrait la main qu'on lui avait laissée de baisers passionnés ou du moins qui semblaient tels à Mme de Rênal' (Julien covered the hand that had been left to him with passionate kisses, or at least kisses that seemed such to Madame de Rênal) (p. 72). The heroine wilfully blinds herself to the fact that Julien's social situation is very different from her own. When he tries to tell her about his feelings of social dispossession and his admiration for Napoleon, his focus on money displeases her and runs counter to her idealised image of him. In general, indeed, Madame de Rênal is blind to those aspects of Julien's personality that she condemns in the letter that her eventual confessor pushes her to write, in response to the Marquis de La Mole's request for a reference:

> Pauvre et avide, c'est à l'aide de l'hypocrisie la plus consommée, et par la séduction d'une femme faible et malheureuse, que cet homme a cherché à se faire un état et à devenir quelque chose. C'est une partie de mon pénible devoir d'ajouter que je suis obligée de croire que M. J. . . . n'a aucun principe de religion. En conscience, je suis contrainte de penser qu'un de ses moyens pour réussir dans une maison, est de chercher à séduire la femme qui a le principal crédit. Couvert par une apparence de désintéressement et par des phrases de roman, son grand et unique objet est de parvenir à disposer du maître de la maison et de sa fortune. (p. 452)

> (Being poor and greedy, it was by means of the most consummate hypocrisy, and through the seduction of a weak and unfortunate woman, that this man sought to establish himself and become something. It is part of my painful duty to add that I am obliged to believe that Monsieur J. . . . has no religious principles. In good conscience, I am compelled to think that one of the means by which he succeeds in a house is by trying to seduce the woman of highest standing therein. Under cover of an appearance of disinterestedness and quotations from novels, his one great objective is to gain power over the master of the house and over his fortune.)

There is very little in this analysis that can be easily refuted on the basis of the textual facts: the letter offers an unsympathetic but accurate account of Julien's behaviour. However, even after the shooting, Madame de Rênal appears to turn a blind eye to Julien's possible motivations either in seducing her earlier in the novel or in returning to her at its end. When Julien tells her that he has never loved anyone but her, she chooses to believe him, despite the fact that believing him on this point amounts to an acceptance of the idea that his engagement to Mathilde was a cynical act of social climbing, as her letter had incriminatingly proposed. Again, Madame de Rênal reads Julien selectively, seeing in him only what she wishes to see. In sum, she is an intuitive and subjective reader of Julien; she does not appear to question his sincerity, or the authenticity of his feelings for her, despite the statements made in the pivotal letter to the Marquis de La Mole. It has occasionally been pointed out how strange it is that this letter is never produced as a piece of evidence during Julien's trial. What seems equally strange is that, despite its content, she never appears to question Julien's sincerity, either past or present, in the final chapters of the novel.

Nevertheless, there is some evidence to suggest that Madame de Rênal develops as a reader of other characters' minds in the course of the novel. When we meet her first, the heroine refrains from judging her husband, but after Julien's arrival she begins to regard her husband with a more critical eye: 'Mme de Rênal fut humiliée de cette manière de voir; elle ne l'eût pas remarquée avant l'arrivée de Julien' (Madame de Rênal was humiliated by this way of seeing things; she would not have noticed it before Julien's arrival) (p. 46). The narrator tells us that she has become 'un peu adroite depuis qu'elle aimait' (a little shrewd since falling in love) (p. 56), and this astuteness is well illustrated in the scene involving the dropped scissors, and in the anonymous letter episode, where she outwits her husband and saves both herself and Julien from grave danger. The narrator even suggests that Madame de Rênal arrives, eventually, at certain insights with regard to Julien:

> Mme de Rênal eut un instant l'illusion que Julien pourrait accepter les offres de M. Valenod et rester à Verrières. Mais ce n'était plus cette femme simple et timide de l'année précédente; sa fatale passion, ses remords l'avaient éclairée. [. . .] Loin de moi, Julien va retomber dans ses projets d'ambition si naturels quand on n'a rien. [. . .] Il m'oubliera. Aimable comme il est, il sera aimé, il aimera. (p. 158)

> (Madame de Rênal had for a moment the illusion that Julien could accept Monsieur Valenod's offers and remain in Verrières. But this was no longer the simple, timid woman of the previous year; her fatal passion, her remorse had enlightened her. [. . .] Distant from me, Julien will fall back upon his ambitious plans, so natural when one has nothing. [. . .] He will forget me. Lovable as he is, he will be loved, and he will love.)

Interestingly, in this moment of lucidity, Madame de Rênal also berates herself for her own lack of insight into other characters' minds; she imagines that greater understanding of her maid's priorities might have prevented the need for Julien's departure:

> Il ne tenait qu'à moi de gagner Élisa à force d'argent, rien ne m'était plus facile. Je n'ai pas pris la peine de réfléchir un moment, les folles imaginations de l'amour m'absorbaient tout mon temps. (p. 159)

> (All I had to do was win Élisa over with money; nothing would have been easier for me. I did not bother to reflect for a moment; love's extravagant fantasies absorbed all my time.)

Despite this textual evidence that her mind-reading skills have improved, on account of her relationship with Julien, overall Madame de Rênal appears to continue to choose to deceive herself. As Julien puts it, she seems 'à la fois éclairée et aveuglée par [son] amour' (simultaneously enlightened and blinded by her love) (p. 138). For example, after the crucial conversation with her husband during which she places herself in significant danger and demonstrates her shrewdness, she signals news of the positive outcome to Julien, who is walking in the woods with her children; she wonders how he can have failed to find any means to signal his relief back to her, but stops short of drawing the conclusion that he is less concerned than she is by the threat of Monsieur de Rênal discovering the truth of their affair. Similarly, she never asks Julien, in the prison cell, why he tried to kill her, appearing not to be interested in his intentions. In short, Madame de Rênal does not manifest much curiosity about Julien; she responds emotionally to his emotional states, and does not interrogate them.

While the improvement in Madame de Rênal's mind-reading skills, on account of her relationship with Julien, is debatable, this heroine who had previously thought of passion only in terms of 'duperie certaine et bonheur cherché par des fous' (certain dupery and a happiness sought by madmen) (p. 56) certainly does undergo a sentimental education. Madame de Rênal is, from the beginning of the novel, a generous and compassionate character who, we are told, would sacrifice her own life willingly to save that of her husband. It is probably unsurprising then that at the end of the novel Madame de Rênal, 'cette âme naïve et si timide' (this naive and so timid soul), is on the point of throwing herself at the feet of King Charles X to secure Julien's pardon, an idea suggested to her by an 'amie intrigante' (a plotting friend) (p. 504). The heroine may not become more self-abnegating or compassionate in the course of the novel, but she has become more passionate than she was before Julien's arrival, when she was presented as virtually oblivious to the world beyond her children. She may even become more capable of affective sharing, as a result of her relationship with Julien. Certainly, in prison, Madame de Rênal enters a semi-fusional relationship with Julien, where the boundaries of her own identity begin to become unclear:

Dès que je te vois, tous les devoirs disparaissent, je ne suis plus qu'amour pour toi, ou plutôt le mot amour est trop faible. [. . .] En vérité, je ne sais pas ce que tu m'inspires. Tu me dirais de donner un coup de couteau au geôlier, que le crime serait commis avant que je j'y eusse songé. (p. 491)

(When I see you, all duties disappear, and I am nothing but love for you, or rather the word 'love' is too weak. [. . .] In truth, I do not know what you inspire in me. If you were to tell me to stab the prison guard, the crime would be committed before I had even thought about it.)

Par un étrange effet de cette passion, quand elle est extrême et sans feinte aucune, Mme de Rênal partageait presque son insouciance et sa douce gaieté. (p. 504)

(By a strange effect of this passion, when it is extreme and entirely without pretence, Madame de Rênal almost shared his carelessness and his sweet gaiety.)

The first passage, in particular, suggests the lack of critical reflection that characterises the heroine's passion. These quotations describe the intensity of Madame de Rênal's love, but they also suggest a form of empathy that resembles emotional contagion and self-loss, wherein the boundaries of the self become blurred.[32] She appears to merge her consciousness with Julien's so fully that it seems fitting that she should die just three days after his execution.

What has Madame de Rênal gained from her relationship with Julien? Any improvement in her mind-reading skills appears moot, but she does appear, for better or worse, to have deepened her capacity for passion and for affective fusion.

Mathilde as a Mind-Reader

Our first insight into Mathilde's view of Julien comes in the fourth chapter of the second volume, when we read her astute internal response upon overhearing his objection to having to dine with Madame de La Mole: 'elle prit quelque considération pour Julien. Celui-là n'est pas né à genoux, pensa-t-elle' (she began to hold Julien in some regard. That one was not born on his knees, she thought) (p. 256). After Julien's period of intimacy with the Marquis, and his two-month stay in London, Mathilde notices a change in him: he has lost his provincial bearing, though it persists in his conversation, and she sees 'qu'il était homme à soutenir son dire' (that he was a man to act upon his words) (p. 282). Having decided that Julien 'n'était pas exactement comme un autre' (was not exactly like any other) (p. 283), she invites him to a ball. It is at this ball, where she formulates her *bon mot* about the death sentence ('Je ne vois que la condamnation à mort qui distingue un homme' (I see only the death sentence that distinguishes a man) (p. 289)), that Mathilde's perspicacity and even 'génie' (genius) (p. 289) are most dramatically revealed to the reader. Speaking to Julien at that ball, she compares his attitude to that of Jean-Jacques Rousseau, and is 'étonnée' (astonished)

(p. 288) upon subsequently being treated coolly by her interlocutor, for whom this comparison, however incisive, is less than flattering. She decides that Julien's apparent disdain for her is 'singulier' (singular) (p. 292), and subsequently notices that 'il a l'air d'un prince déguisé; son regard a redoublé d'orgueil' (he has something of a disguised prince; the pride in his eyes has doubled) (p. 294). She scrutinises him carefully, 'étudiant ses traits pour y chercher ces hautes qualités qui peuvent valoir à un homme l'honneur d'être condamné à mort' (studying his features to seek out those fine qualities that can win a man the honour of being condemned to death) (p. 294). Hearing him declare admiration for one of the leaders of the French Revolution, she wonders if he may be a Danton, realises that 'ce Sorel a quelque chose de l'air que mon père prend quand il fait si bien Napoléon au bal' (this Sorel has something of my father's manner when he imitates Napoleon at the ball) (p. 294), and fascinatedly eavesdrops on and interjects into his conversation with Altamira. Unlike Madame de Rênal, Mathilde is soon privy to Julien's thoughts about Napoleon: the two begin to enjoy 'une singulière amitié' (a singular friendship) (p. 310), discussing politics and history. She is, moreover, alert to his 'ambition étonnante' (astounding ambition) (p. 321) which is 'sans bornes' (limitless) (p. 358): 'elle fut étonnée de son orgueil; elle admira l'adresse de ce petit bourgeois. Il saura se faire évêque comme l'abbé Maury, se dit-elle' (she was astonished by his pride; she admired the shrewdness of this petty bourgeois. He will know how to make himself a bishop like the Abbé Maury, she thought) (p. 315). Mathilde correctly deduces his rebellious qualities and political leanings, noting that 'il méprise les autres' (he disdains others) (p. 318), and admiring his 'énergie' (energy) (p. 318), his 'audace' (boldness) (p. 321), and his Danton-like spirit. To sum up, Mathilde's mind-reading abilities leave even the quasi-omniscient Henri de Marsay in the shade.

Furthermore, Mathilde is keenly alert to the protagonist's feelings towards her, being 'profondément choquée' (deeply shocked) (p. 298), for example, by the contemptuous look that Julien shoots at her at the ball at the Hôtel de Retz. She notices the disappointed look in his eyes, the next day, when he sees her in the library, and draws the correct conclusions: 'Mathilde vit avec évidence qu'elle l'avait troublé, et qu'il eût mieux aimé songer à ce qui l'occupait avant son arrivée, que lui parler. [. . .] [E]lle venait de sentir vivement qu'elle n'était rien pour ce jeune homme' (Mathilde saw clearly that she had perturbed him, and that he would have preferred to think about whatever was on his mind before her arrival, than to talk to her. [. . .] She had just had the strong sense that she was nothing for this young man) (p. 301). She soon decides that she loves him, but is a good enough mind-reader to see that he does not love her. In a later episode, she correctly divines, to Julien's great surprise, that he wishes to speak to her:

> Il lui semblait qu'une chose apporterait à sa douleur un soulagement infini: ce serait de parler à Mathilde. Mais cependant qu'oserait-il lui dire?
> C'est à quoi un matin à sept heures il rêvait profondément lorsque tout à coup il la vit entrer dans la bibliothèque.
> — Je sais, monsieur, que vous désirez me parler.
> — Grand Dieu! Qui vous l'a dit?
> — Je le sais, que vous importe? (p. 369)

> (It seemed to him that one thing would give infinite relief to his suffering: this would be to speak to Mathilde. But what would he dare say to her?
> This is what he was thinking intensely about one morning at seven o'clock, when suddenly he saw her enter the library.
> 'I know, Sir, that you wish to talk to me.'
> 'Good God! Who told you?'
> 'I know it, what does it matter to you?')

In sum, then, Mathilde may idealise Julien's character, as we shall see, but she is rarely mistaken with regard to his feelings or intentions, or indeed with regard to the feelings or intentions of other characters. When she does initially misread someone, or draw a false conclusion, she quickly corrects herself, as when she revises her previously high estimation of Count Altamira.

Mathilde's ability to decipher the minds of others means that she is very good at manipulating them. The narrator tells us that much of Mathilde's social capital, or 'empire sur tout ce qui l'entourait' (power over those around her), comes from her ability to hurt the feelings of people who displease her, or who might prove to be amusing victims (p. 313): 'Elle avait infiniment d'esprit, et cet esprit triomphait dans l'art de torturer les amours-propres et de leur infliger des blessures cruelles' (She had infinite wit, and this wit triumphed in the art of torturing the self-regard of others and inflicting cruel injuries upon them) (p. 369). The narrator suggests that the young heroine enjoys tormenting Julien by telling him, in lingering detail, of her former feelings for other men: 'Elle continua à torturer Julien, en lui détaillant ses sentiments d'autrefois [. . .]; ils semblaient tous deux [y] revenir avec une sorte de volupté cruelle' (She continued to torture Julien, by detailing her feelings of before [. . .]; they both seemed to come back to these with a sort of cruel pleasure) (pp. 354–5). Her father, the Marquis de La Mole, in his own right a shrewd and powerful reader of other people, recognises his daughter's ability to predict and manipulate his own thought processes: 'Mathilde est clairvoyante' (Mathilde is clairvoyant), he remarks (p. 446).

Despite Mathilde's great skills as a mind-reader, however, there are elements of truth to the speculations about her character made by Korasoff, a friend who offers Julien advice about how to manage a character of her type:

> Mme de Dubois est profondément occupée d'elle-même, comme toutes les femmes qui ont reçu du ciel ou trop de noblesse ou trop d'argent. Elle se regarde au lieu de vous regarder, donc elle ne vous connaît pas. Pendant les deux ou trois accès d'amour qu'elle s'est donnés en votre faveur, à grand effort d'imagination, elle voyait en vous le héros qu'elle avait rêvé, et non pas ce que vous êtes réellement . . . (p. 398)

> (Madame de Dubois is deeply concerned with herself, like all women who have been endowed with too much nobility or too much money. She looks towards herself instead of looking at you, so she does not know you. During the two or three amorous bouts that she has allowed herself in your favour, thanks to a great effort of the imagination, she saw in you the hero that she had dreamed up, and not what you really are . . .)

Certainly, Korasoff is justified in speculating that Mathilde (a.k.a. Madame de Dubois) blinds herself to Julien's reality, choosing to see in him a hero of her own making. In her fantasies, he is alternately an anti-monarchist revolutionary and an aristocratic counter-revolutionary. The evidence of the text shows that Mathilde overestimates Julien's heroism, or at least misreads his style of heroism: she believes, erroneously as it turns out, that he would fight to save himself from the guillotine, and that, unlike her male aristocratic peers, he would never adopt 'la résignation sublime' (sublime resignation), nor ever be worried about looking ridiculous (p. 320). The first bedroom scene between Mathilde and Julien shows her struggling to keep her illusions intact; she initially decides that Julien's bravery makes him 'digne de tout mon amour' (worthy of all my love) (p. 344); but when he subsequently informs her that he has had copies made of her letters to protect himself from potentially plotting rivals, she is astonished by all of his precautions, telling him somewhat half-heartedly that he has 'un cœur d'homme' (a man's heart) (p. 345). In the days after this first night, she worries about Julien's 'vanité' (vanity) (p. 349), but upon nearly being killed by him decides again that 'il est digne d'être mon maître' (he is worthy of being my master) (p. 353). Arguably, then, Mathilde's perception of Julien is faulty, on account of the wilful idealisations which motivate her passion for him. However, this is something of a moot point, given that many esteemed critics of the text also argue for a flattering reading of the protagonist.

What does seem clear is that Mathilde is not an entirely dispassionate mind-reader of Julien, despite the narrator's description of her heart as 'naturellement froid, ennuyé, sensible à l'esprit' (naturally cold, bored and cerebral) (p. 326). Her interpretations of Julien are sometimes inflected with a level of affect that makes them unreliable: 'mon imagination folle m'a trompée' (my mad imagination tricked me) (p. 369). The intensity of her affect can also prevent her from applying her skills as a reader to Julien: 'Elle était loin d'avoir le sang-froid nécessaire pour chercher à deviner dans ses yeux ce qu'il sentait pour elle en cet instant' (She was far from having the self-possession necessary to try to detect in his eyes what he felt for her in that moment) (p. 422). Another element that throws doubt upon the reliability of her interpretations of the hero's character is her regular questioning of her own conclusions about that character, on account of changes in her feelings, as well as her doubts about the legitimacy of her feelings. The text represents these fluctuations as the result of a battle between Mathilde's heart, which would enslave her to Julien, and her reason, which resists his domination of her: 'Je renonce à l'exercice de ma raison, sois mon maître' (I renounce the use of my reason; be my master) (p. 365). While Madame de Rênal, as Julien reflects, lets her heart dominate her head, Mathilde's head generally rules her heart.[33] The head–heart opposition is, of course, highly conventional, but Stendhal complicates the usual dynamic by having Mathilde's head not just resist her heart, but also lead her into bed with Julien, even when her heart is not fully engaged. The complex intrication of reflection and feeling, in Mathilde, contributes to the instability of her conclusions about Julien, whom she judges to be 'un homme de mérite' (a man of merit) (p. 359) or 'un être commun' (a common being) (p. 405) as a function of her current feelings about him. Even when most enamoured of the hero, she is reflective enough to acknowledge the possibility that he may only have 'les apparences d'un homme supérieur' (the appearance of a superior man) (p. 333), and to admit to a certain 'doute' (doubt) (p. 333) about his character. And when she changes her mind about his merit, her feelings about him are liable to change, and even turn to contempt, as for example when she realises that, despite loving her, he has listened meekly to her accounts of her former feelings for other men.

Mathilde does have certain shortcomings, therefore, as a mind-reader, but what compensates for the unreliability of her readings is her recognition of the limits of her own understanding of Julien. In fact, his resistance to easy interpretation, what she calls 'la profondeur, l'*inconnu* du caractère de Julien' (the depth, the *obscurity* of Julien's character) (p. 334), appeals to her greatly. While her 'incertitude' (uncertainty) about Julien's feelings for her (pp. 321, 322) causes her anxiety, it is also partly responsible for her continued interest in him. It is arguably for this reason, and not because of her vanity, as Korasoff had supposed, that Julien's strategy of duplicity has the desired effect on her. It is true that this strategy makes Mathilde jealous of her supposed rival, but her feelings for him appear to be rekindled at least as much by by his wilful deceitfulness as by any wounded vanity:

> Ce qui l'étonnait surtout, c'était sa fausseté parfaite; il ne disait pas un mot à la maréchale qui ne fût un mensonge, ou du moins un déguisement abominable de sa façon de penser, que Mathilde connaissait si parfaitement sur presque tous les sujets. Ce machiavélisme la frappait. Quelle profondeur! se disait-elle (p. 418)

> (What especially surprised her was his perfect duplicity; every word he said to the Maréchale was a lie, or at least a montrous travesty of his way of thinking, which Mathilde knew so perfectly on almost all subjects. This Machiavellianism struck her. 'What great depth!' she thought.)

Korasoff is wrong, then, about Mathilde's lack of any real interest in or understanding of Julien's character. However, he is superficially correct, in the sense that he predicts that Julien's feigned interest in Madame de Fervacques will win Mathilde back to him. Julien concludes from his successful application of Korasoff's strategy that the only way to ensure that her love for him endures is to make her afraid of losing him: 'l'ennemi ne m'obéira qu'autant que je lui ferai peur, alors il n'osera me mépriser' (the enemy will obey me only insofar as I make her frightened of me, then she will not dare disdain me) (p. 429). Effectively, he wins her over by making his love unreadable to her: 'Julien ne s'abandonnait à l'excès de son bonheur que dans les instants où Mathilde ne pouvait en lire l'expression dans ses yeux' (Julien abandoned himself to the excesses of his happiness only in those moments when Mathilde could not read its expression in his eyes) (p. 433). When he does eventually reveal his feelings, she is surprised: 'Julien avait suivi son rôle avec tant d'application qu'il était parvenu à lui faire penser qu'elle était celle des deux qui avait le plus d'amour' (Julien had played his role with such application that he had succeeded in making her think that she, of the two of them, was the one who loved more) (p. 435). Even when Mathilde subsequently feels most sure of Julien's love for her, she continues to be enchanted by the idea that he is unreadable to her:

> *Je ne connais pas Julien*; ce mot la jeta dans une rêverie, qui bientôt finit par les suppositions les plus enchanteresses; mais elle les croyait la vérité. L'esprit de mon Julien n'a pas revêtu le petit *uniforme* mesquin des salons, et mon père ne croit pas à sa supériorité, précisément à cause de ce qui la prouve . . . (p. 447)

(*I do not know Julien*; this idea threw her into a daydream, which soon led her to the most enchanting suppositions; but she believed them to be the truth. Julien's mind has not taken on the niggardly little *uniform* of the salons, and my father does not believe in his superiority, precisely because of what proves it . . .)

Mathilde acknowledges the limits of her knowledge of Julien and makes of these limits a point of departure for her interpretations of his character as heroic.

Mathilde continues to believe in Julien's great qualities after his shooting of Madame de Rênal: 'tu es toujours l'homme supérieur, celui que j'ai distingué!' (you are still the superior man, he whom I singled out!) (p. 466); again, whether or not this judgement constitutes a misreading is debatable, but it is certainly a reading that has its roots in feeling as well as reason. She continues to feel 'une curiosité vive' (a keen curiosity) about the fiancé she now considers to be even more heroic than Boniface de La Mole (p. 466). Her enactment of the Marguerite and Boniface story after Julien's execution suggests, indeed, that she continues, until the end of the novel, to play out the heroic, affect-driven fantasy in which she assumes the role of beloved soulmate. Despite this play-acting, Mathilde is simultaneously very clear-eyed about Julien's motivations: she never deludes herself about his changed feelings for her, realising that her position has been usurped by Madame de Rênal, even while Julien, a consummate actor, attempts to hide this fact from her:

> Ces dispositions qui s'accroissaient rapidement furent en partie devinée par la jalousie de Mathilde. [. . .] Mathilde, déjà fort jalouse des visites de Mme de Rênal, et qui venait d'apprendre son départ, comprit la cause de l'humeur de Julien et fondit en larmes. [. . .] [L]a jalousie de Mathilde s'exalta jusqu'à l'égarement. [. . .] [I]l ne pouvait venir à bout de persuader Mathilde de l'innocence des visites de sa rivale [. . .] Une jalousie furieuse et impossible à venger [. . .] av[ait] jeté Mlle de La Mole dans un silence morne. (pp. 472, 495, 502–3)

> (These tendencies, which increased rapidly, were in part detected by Mathilde's jealousy. [. . .] Mathilde, already very jealous of Madame de Rênal's visits, and having learned of her departure, understood the cause of Julien's bad humour and began to weep. [. . .] Mathilde's jealousy intensified to the point of distraction. [. . .] He could not manage to persuade Mathilde of the innocence of her rival's visits [. . .] A furious jealousy, impossible to avenge [. . .], had thrown Mademoiselle de La Mole into a gloomy silence.)

In the final chapters of the novel, the young heroine is simultaneously disenchanted, calling herself 'une veuve qui méprise les grandes passions' (a widow disdainful of grand passions) (p. 503) and disbelieving what Julien tells her about Madame de Rênal's visits, and wilfully self-

deluding, in that she continues to mould him in the image of her fantasised heroic lover. Previously, she had alternated successively between
impassioned idealisation and dispassionate critique; now she appears to
occupy the two positions simultaneously.

The narrator suggests in one of the final chapters that Mathilde is too
socially privileged to understand easily the kind of passion that motivated Julien's shooting of Madame de Rênal. This, the narrator tells us,
is why she is thrown into disarray by the all-too-rational interpretation
of Julien's crime that is formulated by Monsieur de Frilair:

> Ce raisonnement, si juste en apparence, acheva de jeter Mathilde hors d'elle-
> même. Cette âme altière, mais saturée de toute cette prudence sèche qui passe
> dans le grand monde pour peindre fidèlement le cœur humain, n'était pas faite
> pour comprendre vite le bonheur de se moquer de toute prudence, qui peut
> être si vif pour une âme ardente. Dans les hautes classes de la société de Paris,
> où Mathilde avait vécu, la passion ne peut que bien rarement se dépouiller
> de prudence, et c'est du cinquième étage qu'on se jette par la fenêtre. (p. 469)

> (This ostensibly sound reasoning succeeded in pushing Mathilde over the
> edge. This noble soul, so steeped in all the sterile prudence that passes in high
> society for a faithful representation of the human heart, was not designed to
> understand quickly the happiness of casting aside all prudence, which can be
> so intense for a passionate soul. In the upper classes of Parisian society, where
> Mathilde had lived, passion can only very rarely shake off all prudence, and
> it is from the fifth floor that one jumps from the window.)

In other words, Mathilde listens to Frilair's rational explanation, in this
instance, because her upbringing has not allowed her much exposure
to souls as passionate as Julien's; she has never inhabited a fifth-floor
lodging, where such souls are more likely to be found. However, just a
few pages later, Mathilde is compared to just such a fifth-floor dweller:
'Mathilde, ce jour-là, était tendre sans affectation, comme une pauvre
fille habitant un cinquième étage' (Mathilde, that day, was tender
without affectation, like a poor girl living on the fifth floor) (pp. 486–7).
Furthermore, in the final chapters, Mathilde's love for Julien is described
as 'la passion la plus extraordinaire et la plus folle' (the most extraordinary and mad passion) (p. 470), and as having 'désormais ni bornes, ni
mesure' (henceforth neither boundary nor restraint) (p. 472). Certainly,
there may be sarcasm in such statements on the part of the narrator; nevertheless, the latter also notes that 'elle était parvenue à aimer
réellement' (she had achieved real love) (p. 444) and that her 'douleur'
(suffering) is both 'vraie' (true) (p. 487) and 'réelle' (real) (p. 495).

At the end of the novel, then, Mathilde arguably becomes a reader in
the mould of the Abbé Chélan, another character sceptical enough to
recognise Julien's duplicity while also remaining emotionally attached

to him. Chélan is both fond of Julien and an excellent reader of his character, as seen at an early point in the novel, when he tearfully advises Julien against the priesthood, and again in the episode when he disapprovingly guesses at the hero's intention to visit Madame de Rênal during a visit to Verrières, and later in the prison cell when, again tearfully, he addresses the hero as: 'mon enfant . . . Monstre! devrais-je dire' (my child . . . Monster! I should say) (p. 461). Mathilde's combination of lucidity and emotion also likens her to Madame Derville, who is both sympathetic and 'raisonnable' (reasonable) (p. 58) in her treatment of Madame de Rênal: she is a highly perceptive observer, noticing her friend's feelings for Julien even before the heroine does, but she remains loyal to the latter until the end, remaining her companion after Julien's departure, and later attending his trial, where she surprises him by becoming emotional. Her friendship with Madame de Rênal is described by the narrator as 'hardie et incisive' (bold and incisive) (p. 94). It is no accident that Chélan, despite his poverty, has a lodging full of books, or that Madame Derville is an admirer of Mozart who teaches Julien lines from Corneille: this is Stendhal's shorthand way of indicating that both Chélan and Madame Derville are signed-up members of the Happy Few. If Mathilde's skills as a mind-reader have improved in the course of her relationship with Julien, it is insofar as she too has become a member of the Happy Few, capable of straddling two opposed attitudes.

The Two Opposing Attitudes

While emotion does sometimes enlighten Stendhal's heroes and heroines, there is a constant opposition in his writing between clear-headed judgement and emotion. This opposition is marked even within *Le Rouge et le Noir* itself. Julien, for example, notes of Korasoff that his judgement can be relied upon because 'l'enthousiasme, la poésie sont une impossibilité dans ce caractère' (enthusiasm and poetry are an impossibility for this character) (p. 400). We read at one point that Julien's judgement at one particular moment 'n'était troublé par aucune passion' (was troubled by no passion) (p. 76). It is not a coincidence either that it is in a moment when her passion is in abeyance that Madame de Rênal is capable of recognising the fact that she has fallen in love with Julien: 'Son âme, épuisée par tout ce qu'elle venait d'éprouver, n'avait plus de sensibilité au service des passions' (Her soul, exhausted by all that it had just felt, had no more sensibility left in the service of her passions) (p. 56). If Madame de Rênal reads her husband very well, in the scene where she confronts him with a fake anonymous letter, it is no doubt because she feels little 'sympathie' (sympathy) for him in his suffering (p. 137). Because of the antithesis between judgement and emotion in Stendhal's work, it is difficult for a character to be a good mind-reader, in Stendhal's novels, when she is under the influence of emotion: 'Julien était trop malheureux et surtout trop agité pour deviner une manœuvre de passion aussi compliquée [. . .]: il en fut la victime' (Julien was too miserable and especially too agitated to guess at such a complicated passionate manoeuvre [. . .]: he was its victim) (p. 362).

While any binary reading of Mathilde as led by her head and Madame de Rênal as led by her heart is excessively simplistic, Madame de Rênal and Mathilde do broadly embody two different reading stances, one naive and affect-driven, the other critical and detached. These divergent attitudes might be aligned with affective sharing and mind-reading, or seduction and suspicion, as discussed earlier in this book, and compared with Jean-Louis Dufays's 'two essential styles of reading, two opposing ways of orienting meaning', which he calls '*participation* and *distancing*'.[34] In an article of 1832, indeed, Stendhal suggests that his novel was designed to appeal to two antithetical readers, and describes the difficulty of writing a novel capable of satisfying 'ces deux *exigences opposées*' (these two opposed requirements):

> Dans les romans de *femmes de chambre*, peu importe que les événements soient absurdes, calculés à point nommé pour faire briller le héros, en un mot ce qu'on appelle par dérision *romanesques*. Les petites bourgeoises de province ne demandent qu'à l'auteur que des scènes extraordinaires qui les mettent toutes en larmes, *peu importent les moyens* qui les amènent. Les dames de Paris au contraire, qui consomment les romans in-8°, sont sévères en diable pour les événements *extra-ordinaires*. Dès qu'un événement a l'air d'être amené à point nommé pour faire briller le héros, elles jettent le livre et l'auteur est ridicule à leurs yeux. (p. 559)

> (In novels for *chambermaids*, it matters little that events are absurd, conveniently calculated to make the hero shine, or, in a word, what is mockingly called *novelistic*. The provincial petty bourgeoisie asks only extraordinary scenes of its author, scenes that will make them weep, *whatever methods* are used to bring them there. Parisian ladies, by contrast, as consumers of 8° novels, are devilishly severe regarding *extraordinary* events. As soon as an event appears to have been conveniently calculated to make a hero shine, they cast the book away and the author is ridiculous in their eyes.)

Stendhal categorises those who desire affective immersion in a story as chambermaids or women of the provincial petty bourgeoisie, and those who need accurate depictions of the world as the better-educated ladies who inhabit Parisian salons. While Madame de Rênal is not a novel-reader, and is hardly either a chambermaid or a *petite bourgeoise*, the parallel with the two female leads of *Le Rouge et le Noir* seems clear. Does the reader therefore need to choose between these two reading attitudes? If so, how might the novel's presentation of these heroines help us to make this choice?

Stendhal's novel explicitly presents Madame de Renal's style of love as preferable to that of her Parisian counterpart. The narrator tells us that Mathilde's love, being 'amour de tête' (love of the head), has only occasional flashes of enthusiasm. One such moment takes place at the opera, when she thinks of Julien 'avec les transports de la passion la plus vive' (with raptures of the most intense passion), and where a sung lyric 'pénétra son coeur' (penetrated her heart) (p. 360) so forcefully that she spends part of the night, subsequently, singing and playing the same passage on her piano. Madame de Rênal's love, by contrast, is constantly at this level of intensity, according to the narrator:

> Grâce à son amour pour la musique, elle fut ce soir-là comme Mme de Rênal était toujours en pensant à Julien. L'amour de tête a plus d'esprit sans doute que l'amour vrai, mais il n'a que des instants d'enthousiasme; il se connaît trop, il se juge sans cesse; loin d'égarer la pensée, il n'est bâti qu'à force de pensées. (p. 361)

> (Thanks to her love of music, she was that night like Mme de Rênal always was when thinking of Julien. Love of the head has more wit, no doubt, than true love, but it only has moments of enthusiasm; it is too self-aware, it judges itself endlessly; far from leading thought astray, it can only be constructed by sheer force of thought.)

If Madame de Rênal's style of love is rated more highly than Mathilde's by the narrator, does this mean that the former is closer than the latter to Stendhal's ideal lover and reader? Not necessarily. Stendhal did not always rate 'amour-passion' (passionate love) all that highly, and indeed claimed to be particularly pleased with the originality of his representation of 'amour de tête' (love of the head) in *Le Rouge et le Noir*.[35] In addition, Stendhalian love is always to some extent constructed 'à force de pensées' (by dint of thought), like Mathilde's love as described in the opera passage; it is precisely these 'pensées' (thoughts) that create 'enthousiasme' (enthusiasm) through the process of 'cristallisation' (crystalisation), defined by the author of *De l'Amour* as '[un] ensemble d'illusions charmantes' (a collection of charming illusions) and, crucially, as '[une] opération de l'esprit' (an operation of the mind).[36] What distinguishes Mathilde's cerebral love from Madame de Rênal's 'amour vrai' (true love) is the former's tendency to reflect on itself: 'il se juge sans cesse' (it judges itself endlessly). Constant self-judgement is problematic from a Stendhalian point of view, being associated with vanity.

However, thought and reflection are nevertheless represented as crucial components of a successful life in the works of this author.

Stendhal had great fondness for gullible, naive readers, those to whom he refers in *Racine et Shakspeare* as '[des] aimables paresseux' (likable idlers): 'These tender souls, exalted and eloquent, the only ones in the world that I love.'[37] However, he was also a strong proponent of the need to 'pense[r] au lieu de croire' (think instead of believe), as he noted in the margins of *Le Rouge et le Noir* (p. 227) and as stated in many of his writings. It is precisely because he worried about his younger sister's passionate nature that he advised her to hone her judgement, and specifically her understanding of other people's motivations. This understanding could be acquired from observation: in his many letters to her, he regularly exhorts his sister to study those she meets in her everyday life, and write descriptions of them. Stendhal also frequently expressed the idea that extensive reading, provided the books were of good quality, could impart a deepened understanding of other people's motivations.[38] According to Stendhal, books could offer 'deep and reasoned knowledge of man and his passions', and this knowledge could provide an 'immense advantage' in 'the conduct of life'.[39]

It was historical and philosophical works that tended to offer the best understanding of human beings and their motivations, according to Stendhal.[40] However, fictional works too offered a means to acquire an understanding of other people. The peculiar advantage of novels and plays, for Stendhal, was that, as well as developing a person's social intelligence, they could act upon 'l'âme' (the soul):[41] they could, in other words, offer not just 'new perspectives [. . .] for knowledge of the human heart' but also 'the reverie that is the true pleasure of the novel'.[42] It is because of the dual action of fictional works that Stendhal recommends them so warmly to Pauline. Referring to plays by Voltaire and Racine, for example, he tells her that such works 'will shape both the mind and the heart'[43] and that 'it is in reading works of the mind that one learns to think and feel in one's turn'.[44]

Precisely because of the appeal of art to the emotions, however, fictional works could also lead unreflective readers astray, according to Stendhal. They could have dangerous effects on readers likely to be taken in by their seductive illusions. Women, being 'more sensitive' than men,[45] and young girls, being 'toutes à *sensation*' (given over to *sensation*),[46] were in greater danger than men of being 'spoilt by the futilities of society and novels'.[47] Nevertheless, Stendhal considered novel-reading to be important for women on account of the fact that narrative fiction could inspire reflection. Women, he argued, needed to be 'much more distrustful' than men because love exposed them more than men to the dangers of public opinion.[48] He suggests, in various places, that works of the imagination, by seducing readers, can also train them to resist seduction:

> Amiable mother and superior spirit, books are like Achille's lance, which alone could heal the injuries it inflicted; teach your daughter the art of avoiding error, if you want her one day to resist the seductions of love, or those of hypocrisy at the age of forty.[49]

> Only imagination can offer resistance to itself [. . .] It is therefore the imagination that must be retained in a young girl whom one wishes to protect from love.[50]

Paradoxically, then, exposure to the seductions of novels and plays can train a person to be less prone to seduction.

If this ostensibly virtuous message seems un-Stendhalian, consider *Ernestine*, the story appended to *De l'Amour*, where the young heroine falls for a rakish but besotted suitor, but ultimately resists his efforts to seduce her, marries another man and becomes an influential and independent-minded woman in her later life. This was the kind of future that Stendhal wanted for his younger sister, as he repeatedly asserts in his letters to her: he advises her to marry not for love but in order to acquire independence. In those letters, he repeatedly beseeches her to send him her reflections on her reading material and social milieu:

> You have the makings of a charming woman, but you must get used to reflection. This is the great secret.[51]

> I would like you to get used to reflecting, as only good sense endures. The more I see of women, the more I feel that they are wrong not to study.[52]

Stendhal worried that, in the absence of an appropriate habit of reflection, his imaginative sister might be led astray by the illusions of novels, and consequently allow herself to be seduced by an unsuitable man:

> I fear that you have formed several of your opinions from *these damned books*. Beautiful souls alone suffer from such illusions; but these are almost all miserable, and I worry that you might be adding to their number.[53]

Illusions are a great source of happiness, in Stendhal's writing; but when unaccompanied by reflection, they can be damaging. While this damage affects women in particular, he claims, Stendhal tells his sister that he himself was led astray by fictional representations of men, and was subsequently disappointed by the reality. Nevertheless, seduction by illusions can have positive consequences, once a person has been cured of her madness:

This madness is the natural and inevitable effect of book education. Once they have been cured, those who were afflicted are sought out, because they are the cream of society.[54]

If one is of an emotional and imaginative temperament, the habit of reflection is particularly crucial, according to this author.

What distinguishes superior souls is their own sensibility, their interior enemy [. . .] To avoid this obstacle, it is necessary to reason with oneself and as, in reasoning with oneself, it is very easy to lose one's way, it is necessary to make oneself very capable in the art of reasoning, that is, to take up *a sustained habit* of sound reasoning, in such a way that emotion cannot pull you from the accustomed path.[55]

For Stendhal, it is difficult though not impossible to be both susceptible and resistant to seduction, both emotional and sceptical. Novel-reading could help a person to achieve this difficult balance.

As Roger Pearson points out, 'the Stendhalian novel is designed to be both passionate *and* reflective, both emotional *and* intellectual'.[56] In *Le Rouge et le Noir*, the shifts of narrative perspective among primary and secondary characters, as well as the frequent narratorial intrusions, the lengthiest of which appears in one of the most emotionally intense chapters of the novel, all require a separation from narrative immersion, a rupture of the illusion, to borrow a phrase often associated with Romantic irony.[57] The interplay of illusion and detachment is also a theme in Stendhal's thinking about the arts. In writing about the pleasure of attending the theatre, the author emphasises the centrality of moments of pure naivety, from which reflection and analysis are absent. During these moments, the spectator is entirely caught up in the emotions being represented on the stage:

To have illusions, to be *under an illusion*, is to be deceived, according to the Dictionary of the Academy. An *illusion*, for Monsieur Guizot, is the effect of a thing or an idea that deceives us by a misleading appearance. An *illusion* is therefore the action of a man who believes a thing that does not exist, as in dreams, for example. Theatrical illusion is the action of a man who truly believes in the existence of the things that happen on the stage. [. . .] It seems to me that these moments of *perfect illusion* are more frequent than is generally believed, and certainly more than is accepted as true in literary discussions. But these moments are infinitely short, for example the half or quarter of a second. [. . .] They last longer in young women, and this is why the latter shed so many tears before a tragedy. [. . .] These delicious and so rare moments of *perfect illusion* can only be encountered in the heat of an animated scene. [. . .] All of the pleasure that one finds in tragic spectacle depends upon the frequency of these little moments of illusion, *and upon the state of emotion in which, in their intervals, they leave the spectator's soul.*[58]

Moments of self-deception are essential to the enjoyment of theatre, for Stendhal, but they are not sustainable; the majority of the time spent at the theatre is populated by the intervals between these moments. During these intervals, the spectator is fully cognisant that the illusion is an illusion and yet continues to feel the emotions produced by the brief instants during which she believes in the illusion. It seems reasonable to conclude that, for Stendhal, enjoyment of the theatre involves a kind of dialectic between immersion and detachment, seduction and suspicion, the illusion of affective fusion and critical distance. He writes in *De l'Amour*, again in the context of the theatre, of 'cette illusion qui renaît et se détruit à chaque seconde' (this illusion that is reborn and destroyed every second).[59] Fiction could therefore appeal to an individual's capacity to fall for illusions, while also training that individual to cultivate suspicion.

In *Le Rouge et le Noir*, Madame de Rênal, who we are told cannot recognise the nature of her attraction to Julien on account of the fact that she has read no novels, puts up very little resistance to Julien's attempts to seduce her, is blind to his hypocrisy, and ultimately sacrifices everything for the hero, including her life. She is repeatedly presented as a victim of her love for Julien: in the early stages of their relationship, her old friend, Madame Derville, sees the effort she is making with her appearance and concludes: 'Elle aime, l'infortunée!' (She loves, the unfortunate woman!) (p. 82). Madame de Rênal imagines herself being pilloried as an adulteress and thinks her son's illness is a divine punishment for what she consistently thinks of as her 'crime'; she languishes in Julien's absence, and writes him letters stained with tears. She would appear to be intended as an example of 'ces malheureuses femmes de province' (these unfortunate women of the provinces), described in Stendhal's draft article on *Le Rouge et le Noir*, 'que l'amour a un peu compromises aux yeux de leurs voisines' (whom love has compromised a little in the eyes of their neighbours), and for whom life has consequently become 'insupportable' (intolerable) (p. 556).

Mathilde, who has read many novels as well as historical works, also lets herself be seduced by Julien, but she differs from Madame de Rênal, as we have seen, in that she is considerably more reflective. Both heroines are madly in love with Julien, both sacrifice their reputations for Julien and both acquiesce in his last wishes by riding away in a carriage together before his execution; however, Mathilde alone returns to claim the hero's severed head and hijack his funeral plans. As the young heroine tells herself when she worries about what might become of her independence, should she surrender to Julien's seductions, 'Eh bien! je me dirai comme Médée: *Au milieu de tant de périls, il me reste* MOI'

(Well then! I will say to myself like Medea: *Amidst so many perils, I remain MYSELF*) (p. 334). It is perhaps no coincidence that it is a work of fiction that Mathilde calls upon to remind herself of her inner strength. At the end of the novel, the young heroine may resemble, as the narrator says, a besotted young girl who lives on the fifth floor, but she has, as she predicted, maintained her 'moi', along with her ability to reason and reflect. She has not experienced Madame de Rênal's loss of boundaries, and she does not die three days after Julien's execution. Mathilde ultimately learns her limitations as a reader of other people – the limits of her understanding of Julien are revealed to her. Despite this apparent failure, she survives his seduction of her. She manages to combine both critical distance from and affective attachment to the hero. Are Stendhal's Happy Few, his ideal addressees, naively empathetic readers or critical mind-readers, then? I would argue that, like Mathilde, they are both.

Julien Sorel poses difficulties for reading, and these difficulties argu-ably account for a good deal of the reason why Stendhal's novel contin-ues to fascinate readers, just as it goes a long way towards explaining why at least one of the heroines, Mathilde, falls for him. What crucially differentiates Madame de Rênal and Mathilde, as readers of Julien, is that the Parisian heroine proves herself a far more sceptical, critical mind-reader of her love object than her rival.

If we take seriously the idea that fictional strangers can serve as figures of fiction, then our analysis of fictional responses to the fictional stranger in *Le Rouge et le Noir* only weakly suggests that encounters with fiction can hone mind-reading skills: Madame de Rênal becomes a little more adroit, according to the narrator, thanks to her love for Julien. However, our analysis does suggest that encounters with fiction enable readers to experience intense feelings, while also potentially training them to resist narrative seduction. *Le Rouge et le Noir* offers two different models for responding to the seductions of fiction (or to the seductions of fictional strangers). The first is broadly naive, in the style of Madame de Rênal, who puts up little critical resistance to Julien, but who responds feelingly and empathetically towards him. The second style of reading, embodied by Mathilde, combines naivety and reflection, heart and head. Both styles of reading can prompt self-transformation, just as both Madame de Rênal and Mathilde are changed by their encounter with Julien. However, it is surely no accident that one heroine ends up so closely emotionally bound to the hero that his death is also effectively hers, while the other ends the novel literally pregnant with new possibilities. Self–other boundaries have become porous for both heroines, thanks to their experience of love, but in the case of Madame de Rênal this porousness has led to transformative self-expansion followed by self-loss, while in the case of Mathilde it has led to transformative self-expansion followed by something more hopeful. My argument in this chapter has been that a difficult combination of seduction and suspicion, affective sharing and mind-reading, is tacitly advocated by *Le Rouge et le Noir*, where Balzac's *La Fille aux yeux d'or* had focused rather upon the limitations of each attitude. In the next chapter, it will be proposed that these limitations are emphasised by George Sand's *Indiana*, too, but here the warning against the seductions of narrative is more explicitly sounded than it is in either Stendhal's or Balzac's texts, while suspicious mind-reading is presented both as a social survival skill, as in Stendhal's *Le Rouge et le Noir*, and as having practical and ethical limitations, as in Balzac's *La Fille aux yeux d'or*.

Notes

1. Stendhal, *Histoire de la peinture*, p. 84.
2. 'A novel is like a bow, the body of the violin, which makes the sounds, is the reader's soul.' Stendhal, *Œuvres intimes*, vol. 2, p. 699 (*Vie de Henry Brulard*).
3. Stendhal, *Histoire de la peinture*, pp. 397–8.
4. Ibid. p. 397.
5. Ibid. p. 251.
6. Stendhal, *Journaux et papiers*, pp. 250, 418. See also Stendhal, *Molière, Shakspeare*, p. 278. Stendhal was interested in the *Lettres sur la sympathie* of Adam Smith's French translator, Sophie de Grouchy. See the letter to Pauline of 9 March 1806, in which he defines sympathy as '*souffrance avec*' (suffering with). Stendhal, *Correspondance*, vol. 1, p. 306. He also associates it in his writing with 'pitié' (pity). See R 5896 Rés., volume 24, feuillet 10, verso and R. 5896 Rés., volume 24, feuillet 11, recto (Manuscrits de Stendhal). On the link between sympathy and compassion, see also Stendhal, *De l'Amour*, p. 319.
7. Stendhal, *De l'Amour*, p. 91; Stendhal, *Chroniques italiennes*, p. 341 ('La Comédie est impossible en 1836'). See also 'Des deux sympathies' in Stendhal, *Molière, Shakspeare*, pp. 306–7.
8. Stendhal, *Racine et Shakspeare*, p. 111.
9. Stendhal, *Œuvres romanesques complètes*, vol. 3, p. 279 (*La Chartreuse de Parme*).
10. Ibid. vol. 2, p. 721 (second preface to *Lucien Leuwen*).
11. Stendhal, *Racine et Shakspeare*, p. 316.
12. Stendhal, *Histoire de la peinture*, p. 478. See also Stendhal, *Promenades dans Rome*, vol. 2, p. 116.
13. Kristeva, *Histoires d'amour*, p. 325.
14. Stendhal, *Œuvres intimes*, vol. 2, p. 466 (*Souvenirs d'égotisme*).
15. Jefferson, *Reading Realism in Stendhal*, p. 130.

16. On sympathy as a law of nature, see *De l'Amour*, pp. 138, 230.
17. Stendhal, *Le Rouge et le Noir*, p. 356. This edition will be cited, alongside my translations, henceforth in this chapter. Stendhal, *Promenades dans Rome*, vol. 1, p. 300.
18. Stendhal, *De l'Amour*, p. 412.
19. Ibid. p. 286.
20. Ibid. pp. 138, 133.
21. 'The landscapes were like a *bow* playing on my soul.' Stendhal, *Œuvres intimes*, vol. 2, p. 542 (*Vie de Henry Brulard*); 'A lover sees the woman he loves on the horizon of all landscapes.' Stendhal, *De l'Amour*, p. 258.
22. Stendhal, *De l'Amour*, p. 86.
23. See for example *Le Rouge et le Noir*, pp. 88, 89, 90, 91, 92.
24. See for example Gormley, '"Mon roman est fini"'.
25. See Scott, *Stendhal's Less-Loved Heroines*, pp. 59–61.
26. Also arguing against Julien's shrewdness is the case that Francesco Manzini makes for his fanatical credulousness. 'Reading Julien Sorel'.
27. 'Ce fut en vain qu'il [Pirard] interrogea Julien pour tâcher de deviner s'il croyait sérieusement à la doctrine de M. de Maistre.' (It was in vain that Monsieur Pirard quizzed Julien to find out if he seriously believed in Monsieur de Maistre's doctrine.) Stendhal, *Le Rouge et le Noir*, p. 175.
28. See Stendhal, *Le Rouge et le Noir*, pp. 66–7, 78, 142, 262.
29. 'Cette figure de jeune fille, si pâle et si douce, cachait la résolution inébranlable de s'exposer à mille morts plutôt que de ne pas faire fortune.' (This young girl's face, so pale and sweet, hid the unshakeable determination to risk a thousand deaths rather than fail to make his fortune.) Stendhal, *Le Rouge et le Noir*, p. 32.
30. Ansel and Kheyar Stibler, *Stendhal*, p. 139.
31. I have discussed the difficulty of explaining both the shooting and the switch of love object in *Stendhal's Less-Loved Heroines* and in '*Le Rouge et le Noir*'.
32. 'Self-loss can be described as a possible effect of simulating, adapting, or otherwise engaging with the perceived perspective, state, or identity of another and thereby losing, ignoring, or forgetting one's own perspective, interests, or state.' Breithaupt, 'A Three-Person Model of Empathy', p. 85.
33. Julien reflects that 'Mme de Rênal trouvait des raisons pour faire ce que son coeur lui dictait: cette jeune fille du grand monde ne laisse son coeur s'émouvoir que lorsqu'elle s'est prouvé par bonnes raisons qu'il doit être ému' (Mme de Rênal found reasons to do as her heart dictated; this young high-society girl lets her heart be moved only when it has been proven to her with good reasons that it should be moved) (p. 425).
34. Dufays, *Stéréotype et lecture*, p. 122. Dufays observes that 'each of the two operations can be privileged' (p. 180).
35. 'Ordinarily passionate love is found in those people who are a little simple in the Germanic style.' *De l'Amour*, p. 132. See also the author's references in his draft article on *Le Rouge et le Noir* to the originality of his portrait of Mathilde's style of love (*Le Rouge et le Noir*, pp. 559, 569).
36. Stendhal, *De l'Amour*, pp. 165, 64.
37. Stendhal, *Racine et Shakspeare*, p. 106.
38. However, Stendhal occasionally argued that reading could diminish the

critical faculties. See for example Stendhal, *Correspondance*, vol. 1, p. 105: 'Knowledge of society is so difficult! For this reason, one cannot learn anything of it from books; on the contrary, the more one reads, the more one goes wrong. There is however a book that is useful because it is a model of conversation: La Bruyère.' As this translated quotation indicates, the choice of book was important; the narrator of *Féder* notes that Valentine's mind has been weakened by her reading of books that promulgate Restoration mores. Stendhal, *Œuvres romanesques complètes*, vol. 3, p. 795.

39. Stendhal, *Correspondance*, vol. 1, p. 177.
40. Ibid. pp. 12, 16, 27.
41. See for example ibid. p. 136. While Stendhal notes that 'a book cannot change a person's soul' (*Histoire de la peinture en italie*, p. 71), he also writes about the influence of Ariosto and the theatre over his own character. Stendhal, *Œuvres intimes*, vol. 2, p. 619 (*Vie de Henry Brulard*); *Œuvres intimes*, vol. 1, p. 736 (*Journal*).
42. Stendhal, *De l'Amour*, pp. 86–7.
43. Stendhal, *Correspondance*, vol. 1, p. 29.
44. Ibid. p. 2.
45. Stendhal, *De l'Amour*, p. 109. See also Stendhal, *Correspondance*, vol. 1, pp. 137, 148.
46. Stendhal, *Correspondance*, vol. 1, p. 184.
47. Ibid. p. 231. He repeatedly suggests that reading novels disposes a person to love (though this theme is often treated ironically by Stendhal, the kind of love that is inspired by novels often being presented as an imitation of an imitation). See for example Stendhal, *De l'Amour*, p. 322.
48. Stendhal, *De l'Amour*, p. 77.
49. Stendhal, *Racine et Shakspeare*, p. 78.
50. Stendhal, *De l'Amour*, p. 168.
51. Stendhal, *Correspondance*, vol. 1, p. 38.
52. Ibid. p. 61. See also ibid. pp. 48, 54–5, 66.
53. Ibid. p. 371.
54. Ibid. p. 162.
55. Ibid. pp. 341–2.
56. Pearson, *Stendhal's Violin*, p. 18. For Stendhal, 'the only authentic mirror will be one that is also a bow'. Jefferson, *Reading Realism*, p. 37.
57. On Stendhal's version of Romantic irony, see Jefferson, 'Stendhal (1783–1842): Romantic Irony'.
58. Stendhal, *Racine et Shakspeare*, pp. 13–16.
59. *De l'Amour*, p. 303. As Patrizia Lombardo puts it, for Stendhal 'the experience of the work is not a continuum or a metamorphosis of the subject into the object, but a complex combination of diverse reactions that sometimes, though rarely, attain the emotive maximum'. 'Empathie et simulation', p. 30.

Chapter 6

Sand and the Necessity of Suspicion

Of all of George Sand's novels, only one – her first as a solo author – can be considered predominantly realist in its style, even if it is true that aspects of this first novel also undermine its realism.[1] From its first chapter, *Indiana* presents a world that is, ostensibly at least, legible in its every detail, not least because it is mediated by a narrator who adopts the recognisably all-knowing and seductive tone of the Balzacian omniscient narrator.[2] Both narrator and characters regularly decipher facial expressions and the messages conveyed by glances or bodily movement, and in fact the performance of, and obstacles to, mind-reading are central to the novel's plot. The novel also makes a theme of narrative seduction, in its depiction of the charming but duplicitous Raymon de Ramière. This chapter will argue that *Indiana* both suggests that narrative seduction is to be resisted and highlights the limits of mind-reading.

There are two very obvious figures of the stranger in *Indiana*: both the eponymous heroine and Noun, her childhood companion and maid, are designated as 'créoles' (creoles) from Île Bourbon (now Réunion). Indiana is of European origin, her father having moved from Spain to the French colony, while there are numerous suggestions that Noun is of African origin. In Sand's representation, both heroines are perceived by other characters as foreign to different degrees.[3] These figures will not be the main focus of study in this chapter, however, because there are two other stranger figures who are more closely associated in the novel with pretence, and who might therefore serve as more appropriate figures of fiction in the text.

The ability to seduce others is particularly closely linked, in this novel, to the ability to arouse the sympathy of others. One male protagonist has no difficulties in attracting either erotic partners or friends, while the other is defined by his lack of erotic charm as well as by his inability to inspire any feelings of sympathy in those around him. This chapter will begin by arguing that the character of Raymon, in *Indiana*, is one of two fiction-connoted figures of the stranger in the novel, and that he embodies the dangerous seductions of fiction. Indiana and Noun both fall for him; only the former survives the encounter, due at least in part to a capacity for resistance that appears to be innate. The novel's warnings against the seductive illusions of fiction are more or less explicit. The chapter will go on to examine the depiction of Ralph, as a second fiction-associated stranger figure who inhabits *Indiana*. This second stranger is characterised by a complete absence of seductive appeal, at least until the closing chapters of the novel. The presentation of Ralph exercises the mind-reading skills of the reader and eventually rewards anyone expert enough to read between the novel's lines. In other words, the reader who is capable of suspicion with regard to the text's presentation of Ralph will be rewarded for his or her diligence. This formal strategy reinforces the novel's more explicit warnings against fiction's seductions. However, Ralph's narrative depiction also suggests the limits of mind-reading – not only because the character who knows him best in the world turns out to know him not at all, but also because his own character undergoes a radical change which makes him problematically readable. Ralph is not only a rounder, more three-dimensional character at the novel's end than he was at its beginning, but he is also a less coherent entity.[4] Finally, the chapter will ask how *Indiana* depicts the interaction of mind-reading skills and affective sharing, and how they each relate to the themes of generosity and selfishness in the novel.

Raymon as Fiction-Associated Stranger: Narrative Seduction

Raymon de Ramière makes his first appearance in the second chapter of the novel, when he is shot by Monsieur Delmare as he attempts to climb over a wall into the latter's residence, Lagny. He is, at this point in the story, a stranger in the sense that he is an impostor, and in the sense that his identity and motivations are at least initially mysterious: his refined appearance, and the fact that his pockets are filled with money, suggest that his intention is not, in fact, to steal coal, as had been suspected at first by Delmare and others. Raymon is represented as being out of place at various other points in the story too: in the home of Madame de Carvajal, which he twice visits unexpectedly (the second time clandestinely); at Ralph's hunt, where the host's welcome is strained; in Lagny, where Delmare welcomes him because he does not wish to have '[des] obligations envers un étranger' (obligations towards a stranger)

(p. 122), without realising that he is inviting a rival into his home; and in Indiana's bedroom, more particularly, where at one point he recognises that he is not 'à [sa] place' (in his place) (p. 102), and in which he is twice discovered by Indiana in circumstances that are shocking to her.

Raymon is associated with fiction, or what the 1832 preface refers to as '*l'illusion*' (p. 39), in various ways.

Firstly, he is presented throughout the novel as a skilled producer of fictions. When Monsieur Delmare demands an explanation of his presence in the grounds of Lagny, he spins a story about industrial espionage, which the narrator later refers to as 'la fiction qu'il avait heureusement improvisée' (the fiction that he had fortunately improvised) (p. 72), and which Delmare describes as 'une intrigue admirablement tissue' (an admirably woven plot) (p. 69). When Raymon recovers from his injury, he returns to Lagny to tell his lover, Noun, falsely, that 'il la préférait aux reines du monde, et mille autres exagérations qui seront toujours de mode auprès des jeunes filles pauvres et crédules' (he preferred her to the queens of the world, and a thousand other exaggerations that will always be fashionable among poor, credulous young girls) (p. 74). The narrator alludes to Noun's later suicide as the climax of Raymon's complex seduction plot, 'le tragique dénouement de sa double intrigue' (the tragic climax of his double plot) (p. 131). Indiana, meanwhile, refers to his clandestine visit to her bedroom as an indelicate 'projet romanesque' (novelistic project) (p. 147).

Secondly, Raymon is compared at various points to a fictional character. The narrator refers to him as '[le] héros de cet exploit galant' (the hero of this gallant exploit) (p. 70) and, in an allusion (similar to those already encountered in the Balzac narrative) to the play (or opera) *Le Barbier de Séville*, as 'l'Almaviva de cette aventure' (the Almaviva of this adventure) (p. 71), while Laure de Nangy, referencing Samuel Richardson's *Clarissa*, calls him 'un Lovelace' (p. 79). Raymon is also compared to both a dramatic author and an actor immersed in his role:

> A force de réfléchir à son projet de séduction, il s'était passionné comme un auteur pour son sujet, comme un avocat pour sa cause, et l'on pourrait comparer l'émotion qu'il éprouva en voyant Indiana, à celle d'un acteur bien pénétré de son rôle, qui se trouve en présence du principal personnage du drame et ne distingue plus les impressions factices de la scène d'avec la réalité. (p. 143)

> (By virtue of reflecting on his seduction plan, he had become passionate like an author for his subject, or like a solicitor for his case, and one might compare the emotion he felt upon seeing Indiana to that of an actor steeped in his role, who finds himself in the presence of the main character of a drama

and who no longer distinguishes the artificial impressions of the scene from reality.)

Raymon appears, indeed, to view his own life as a form of narrative with distinctly fictional elements. He seems to be interested in Noun only for as long as their 'intrigue amoureuse' (amorous intrigue) retains its fairy-tale elements: 'Noun, en déshabillé blanc, parée de ses longs cheveux noirs, était une dame, une reine, une fée; [. . .] il la prenait volontiers pour une châtelaine du moyen âge' (Noun, in white underclothes, adorned with her long black hair, was a lady, a queen, a fairy; [. . .] he could have mistaken her for a medieval chatelaine) (p. 74). Raymon feels looked after by a magical Providence, and upon being introduced to Laure, whose expression reminds him of a character from Shakespeare's *The Merry Wives of Windsor*, 'il remercia la destinée ingénieuse qui con-ciliait tous ses intérêts en lui offrant, à l'aide d'incidents romanesques, une femme de son rang à la tête d'une belle fortune plébéienne' (he thanked the ingenious destiny that reconciled all his interests by offering him, through novelistic turns of event, a woman of his social standing in control of a large plebeian fortune) (p. 288).

Thirdly, there are numerous evocations in the text of Raymon's active imagination, including the interior monologue in which he compares the effect on Indiana of virtual contact with Noun's sexual body to the lethal effect of Deianira's tunic on Heracles, his apparent fear of encountering the ghosts of Noun and her unborn baby as he wanders through the moonlit, misty grounds of Lagny, his sense on leaving the park later that Ralph appears and disappears by magic, and his belief, prompted by 'sa riante et fertile imagination' (his playful and fertile imagination) (p. 266), in the possibility of making Indiana his mistress while he is married to someone else.

Another aspect of Raymon's association with fiction is his duplic-ity. In the 1832 preface to the novel, Sand writes that 'Raymon [. . .] c'est la fausse raison, la fausse morale' (Raymon [. . .] is false reason, false morality) (p. 41). In his conversations with Monsieur Delmare, he pretends to be someone he is not in order to win the latter's trust: 'Il se fit même un caractère différent du sien propre, afin d'attirer sa confiance' (He even made himself a character different from his own, in order to win his trust) (p. 139). When he meets Indiana after a lengthy period during which she has refused to see him, he feigns sorrow at the sight of her physical frailty, speaking to her with 'une assurance secrète parfaitement cachée sous un air de tristesse profonde' (a secret confi-dence perfectly hidden beneath an air of profound sadness) (p. 144). Elsewhere, too, Raymon proves himself gifted at simulating emotion, both in person ('Il affecta quelques instants une profonde tristesse, une rêverie sombre' (He feigned for a few moments a profound sadness, a gloomy reverie) (p. 194)) and in writing: 'Il feignait de regarder le retour d'Indiana comme un bonheur inespéré' (He pretended to view the return of Indiana as an impossible happiness) (p. 267). Directly after we learn that Raymon no longer loves Indiana, he writes a letter telling her that he would give his life for an hour in her arms. So talented, indeed, is Raymon at expressing emotion that, as already seen in one of the quotations above, he tends to persuade himself that he actually feels it: 'ce n'était pas la passion qui le rendait eloquent, c'était l'éloquence qui le rendait passionné' (it was not passion that made him eloquent, it was eloquence that made him passionate' (p. 83). Raymon is, furthermore, very capable of ingenious improvisations when the situation requires it, for example when he tells a surprised Noun that it is to see her that he has visited Indiana's home in Paris, or when he manages to avoid recriminations after the latter discovers his role in Noun's suicide. In an episode described by the narrator as a 'scène d'amour' (love scene), Raymon embodies 'la fiction théâtrale' (theatrical fiction), while Indiana incarnates 'la réalité' (reality) (p. 206); later, when she comes to his home, he braces himself for 'encore un effort d'imagination, encore une scène d'amour' (another imaginative effort, another love scene) (p. 217), but finishes triumphantly: 'Il joua la passion à s'y tromper lui-même' (He performed passion so well that he deceived himself) (p. 220).

As well as being closely associated with fiction and duplicity, Raymon is consistently associated with seduction, and is even compared by Ralph to a hypnotic snake: 'il savait éblouir les yeux et tromper la raison; c'est que son regard de vipère fascinait' (he knew how to dazzle the eyes and trick reason; his viper eyes could fascinate) (pp. 326–7). In his first conversation with Delmare, he tells the latter that his plan on entering Lagny was to 'séduire les ouvriers' (seduce the workers) (p. 68) and thereby steal his industrial secrets. He is universally liked in the high-society circles he frequents; the narrator refers repeatedly to his almost magical power to inspire affection in others. He succeeds easily in winning Delmare over to his side in political arguments, even where little common ground is in evidence. Raymon is also presented as an unusually gifted seducer of women: 'Il se sentait du goût pour une femme, et devenait éloquent pour la séduire et amoureux d'elle en la séduisant' (If he felt an inclination for a woman, he would use his eloquence to seduce her and would then fall in love with her while seducing her) (p. 83). He launches a 'projet de séduction' (seduction plan) (p. 143) with regard to Indiana, showering her with 'les séductions d'une éloquence brûlante' (the seductions of ardent eloquence) (p. 220).

This is not to say that every woman is taken in by Raymon's charms: some are 'assez fines pour se méfier de ces chaleureuses improvisations' (astute enough to distrust his heated improvisations) (p. 83).

Raymon's linguistic persuasiveness is his most powerful instrument of seduction; as the narrator puts it, 'le plus puissant [des hommes] est celui qui sait le mieux écrire et parler' (the most powerful of men is he who writes and speaks best) (p. 130). In speaking and writing to Indiana, he knowingly adopts a courtly, platonic register, repeatedly referring to her as an angel and comparing her to a divinity. He asserts, to somewhat comical effect, that were he Indiana's husband he would force the air to caress her lightly and golden dreams to throw flowers to her. The style adopted by Raymon is overblown and novelistic, eminently well designed to appeal to a reader of sentimental fiction: 'ce ne sont pas des circonstances vulgaires qui nous ont réunis, vois-tu; ce n'est ni le hasard ni le caprice, c'est la fatalité, c'est la mort' (it is not vulgar circumstances that have brought us together, you see; it is neither chance nor luck, it is fate, it is death) (p. 96), Raymon tells a credulous Indiana. However, this style is not always or necessarily adopted for manipulative purposes; Raymon's internal monologue is also, at least occasionally, presented in a very similar idiom, as when he imagines that his activities in Indiana's bed, in her absence, will have frightened away the angel that keeps watch by her pillow. The seductiveness of Raymon's language is not confined to his sexually interested relationships; it extends to his everyday interactions. The narrator tells the reader that he will have been 'entrainé, en lisant les journaux du temps, par le charme irrésistible de son style, et les grâces de sa logique courtoise et mondaine' (carried away, in reading newspapers of the time, by the irresistible charm of his style, and the grace of his courtly and urbane logic) (p. 128). Raymon is a gifted writer, valued by the government for his 'rare faculté [. . .] de réfuter par le talent la vérité positive' (rare ability [. . .] to refute, with his talent, factual truth) (p. 130). Raymon's mastery of language, 'une reine prostituée qui descend et s'élève à tous les rôles, qui se déguise, se pare, se dissimule et s'efface' (a prostituted queen who lowers and raises herself to all roles, who disguises herself, adorns herself, hides herself from sight and disappears) (p. 130), is bound up with his seductiveness, his duplicity and his close association with fiction.

Indiana tells the story of two women who fall for Raymon's charms. Indiana's maid and childhood companion, Noun, abandons herself entirely to her passion for this dashing young noble: 'la pauvre Noun [. . .] s'y jetait avec toute la violence de son organisation ardente' (poor Noun [. . .] threw herself into it with all the violence of her passionate constitution) (p. 71). She conducts a clandestine affair with him over a period of some months, but on informing him of the fact that she is pregnant with his child receives no offers of help until after she has seduced him one last time. She refuses his subsequent proposal to relocate her and provide financial assistance, deciding that if marriage is not an option she will declare her situation to Indiana, and trust in her benevolence. Unfortunately, before she has the chance to explain her circumstances to her mistress, she learns of the relationship between Indiana and Raymon, and drowns herself in the grounds of Lagny. Indiana herself is the other heroine who falls in love with Raymon. The willingness of both heroines to be seduced by him is tacitly attributed to their naivety and ignorance.[5] However, if Noun's naivety and ignorance are linked to her lack of education, Indiana's are associated with her type of education, and more specifically with her reading habits.

There are strong suggestions in the novel that Indiana's openness to being seduced by Raymon is related to a naively extravagant, book-fed imagination. Raymon thinks of her as 'sa romanesque maîtresse' (his fanciful mistress), driven by what he considers to be 'l'exagération des sentiments qu'elle avait puisée dans les livres' (the exaggerated feelings that she had found in books) (p. 205). The text itself indicates that it is Raymon's own seductively novelistic rhetoric that has encouraged her delusions; as Margaret Waller notes, he 'unscrupulously parrots the eloquent passion typical of the genre [of romance novel]' even while denouncing that genre.[6] On receiving a letter from her, Raymon attributes Indiana's declared willingness to leave her husband, and thereby flout public opinion, to her 'tête romanesque' (fanciful mind): 'Exaltation de femme! dit Raymon en froissant le billet. Les projets romanesques, les entreprises périlleuses flattent leur faible imagination, comme les aliments amers réveillent l'appétit des malades' (Female fanaticism! said Raymon as he crumpled the note. Romantic plans and dangerous undertakings appeal to their weak imaginations, as bitter foods whet the appetite of the sick) (pp. 224, 203). When she shows up in his bedroom, having believed the seductive fictions about love which he himself had spun her, he asks her (indirectly recalling Stendhal's words about the reading habits of chambermaids): 'Où avez-vous rêvé l'amour? dans quel roman à usage des femmes de chambre avez-vous étudié la société, je vous prie?' (Where did you find your dreams of love? In what chambermaids' novel have you learned about society, I ask you?) (p. 217). Writing to Raymon subsequently from Île Bourbon, having been disappointed by his unwillingness to face a public scandal, Indiana tells him that he was right to say that she learned about life from 'les romans à usage des femmes de chambre, [. . .] ces riantes et puériles fictions où l'on intéresse le cœur au succès de folles entreprises et d'impossibles félicités' (chambermaids' novels, [. . .] those playful and childish fictions that interest the heart in the success of mad undertakings and impossible joys) (p. 247). However, she turns the insult around by asking how it is that she, 'faible femme' (a weak woman), was able to place herself 'dans une situation d'invraisemblance et de roman' (in an implausible and fanciful situation), while he was not (p. 247). While the narrator never quite catches Indiana in the act of reading, her favoured way of passing the time seeming instead to be tapestry, there are numerous allusions in the text to her taste for sentimental fiction. In her bedroom, Raymon spies '[d]es livres d'amour et de voyages, épars sur les planches d'acajou' (books about love and travel, scattered over the mahogany shelves) (p. 101) as well as prints showing scenes from Bernardin de Saint-Pierre's *Paul et Virginie*. Her aunt explains to those disappointed not to see Indiana at a ball that 'elle a voulu rester seule, un livre à la main dans le salon, comme une belle sentimentale' (she wanted to remain alone, a book in her hand in the salon, like a beautiful romantic) (p. 92). Delmare claims to be bored by her 'phrases de roman' (novelistic utterances) (p. 232), and tells her that her low estimation of Ralph is on account of her reading preferences: 'vous ne le trouvez pas assez sentimental, le pauvre diable! vous le traitez d'égoïste parce qu'il n'aime pas les romans et ne pleure pas à la mort d'un chien' (you do not find him sentimental enough, the poor devil! you think him selfish because he does not like novels and does not weep over the death of a dog) (p. 142). Having accompanied the bankrupted Delmare back to Île Bourbon, she dreams of escape, and according to the narrator conceives 'mille projets d'établissement romanesque dans les terres désertes de l'Inde ou de l'Afrique' (countless plans for a romantic existence in the deserts of India or Africa), is captivated by the 'récits' (stories) told by visitors from Madagascar, and abandons herself to '[d]es préoccupations romanesques' (romantic preoccupations) (p. 273) and the construction of 'un avenir selon sa fantaisie' (a future moulded by her fantasy) (p. 274).

Indiana's willingness to be seduced is linked not just to the effervescent activity of her overactive imagination but also to a certain lack of activity on the part of her critical faculties, a lack that is explicitly related by the text to the exertions of her novelistic imagination: 'Elle le vit comme elle le désirait, comme elle l'avait rêvé, et Raymon eût pu la tromper, s'il n'eût pas été sincère' (She saw him as she desired him, as she had dreamed him, and Raymon could have tricked her had he not been sincere) (p. 90). Put simply, Indiana believes the fictions she is fed by Raymon. She unquestioningly swallows, for example, his story about entering the grounds of Lagny to steal industrial secrets: 'elle avait ingénument ajouté foi aux explications de M. de Ramière' (she had ingenuously given credence to Monsieur de Ramière's explanations)

(p. 71). When he speaks to her amorously for the first time, 'l'ignorante Indiana s'abandonnait, sans comprendre que tout cela n'avait pas été inventé pour elle' (the ignorant Indiana surrendered, without understanding that none of this had been invented for her) (p. 83). As this quotation indicates, Indiana demonstrates a lack of reflection in her engagements with Raymon. The narrator tells us that 'elle ne pensa pas [. . .] que cet homme pouvait être menteur ou frivole' (she did not think [. . .] that this man could be dishonest or frivolous) (p. 90) and that 'elle ne songeait nullement au danger de se perdre' (she did not think at all about the danger to herself) (p. 91). The narrator describes Indiana as 'la crédule femme' (the credulous woman) (p. 178), and indeed extends this accusation of 'idiote crédulité' (idiotic credulity) (p. 251) to all women, who are only too ready to believe flattery when it is offered to them. Even the male character who knows her best expresses surprise at the extent of her gullibility: 'Ce qui m'a toujours étonné, dit-il, c'est que vous n'ayez pas deviné le véritable motif qui amenait ici M. de Ramière par-dessus les murs' (What has always astonished me, he said, is that you never guessed Monsieur de Ramière's true motivation for climbing over the walls) (p. 183).

At least some of Indiana's credulity or 'aveuglement' (blindness) (pp. 173, 251) is, however, wilful: she deliberately suspends her disbelief, just as a reader of fiction, and particularly sentimental fiction, is often said to do. 'Elle était facile à tromper; elle ne demandait qu'à l'être, tant sa vie réelle était amère et désolée!' (She was easy to deceive; she asked only for that, so bitter and sad was her actual life) (p. 207). Indiana believes Raymon's fairy tales not because of an unavoidable cognitive failing but because she needs to: 'Raymon fut éloquent; Indiana avait tant besoin de croire, que la moitié de son éloquence fut de trop' (Raymon was eloquent; Indiana needed so much to believe him that half of his eloquence was unnecessary) (p. 150); 'elle ne pouvait plus se passer de croire en lui, d'espérer l'avenir qu'il lui avait promis' (she could no longer give up her belief in him, nor her hope in the future that he had promised her) (p. 213). Even after he refuses to take her in and has consigned her to years of exile, Indiana cannot confront 'la sèche vérité' (the hard truth) about Raymon, because to do so could cost her her life (p. 251); instead, she clings to 'une certaine faculté d'illusions' (a certain skilfulness with illusions) (p. 254). The various references in the text to Indiana's self-abandonment in Raymon's company – to cite just a few examples, 'l'ignorante Indiana s'abandonnait' (the ignorant Indiana surrendered herself) (p. 83), 'madame Delmare, qui, s'abandonnant aux transports de son amant, l'écoutait avec délices' (Madame Delmare who, surrendering herself to the ecstasies of her lover, listened to him with delight)

(p. 96), and she trusts him 'avec tant d'abandon et d'aveuglement' (with such abandon and blindness) (p. 173) – reinforce the impression that her gullibility is an at least partially conscious decision to set aside her scepticism in the interest of her happiness:

> Honte à cette femme imbécile! Elle s'abandonna avec délices à ces trompeuses démonstrations; elle se sentit heureuse, elle rayonna d'espérance et de joie; elle pardonna tout, elle faillit tout accorder. (pp. 220–1)

> (Shame on this imbecilic woman! She surrendered herself with delight to these deceitful demonstrations; she felt happy, she shone with hope and joy; she forgave everything, she almost offered everything.)

The narrator explicitly tells us, indeed, that Indiana has, with regard to Raymon, 'fermé son âme à toute méfiance' (closed her soul to all distrust) (p. 189).

The fact that Indiana so often, nevertheless, finds the means to resist Raymon itself suggests that she retains at least some mental distance from him, despite her choice of affective openness. In one episode, after directly challenging the veracity of one of Raymon's stories, Indiana's laying aside of her critical defences is expressed as a physical gesture of submission; but her moral resistance, also expressed through a physical movement, stages a revolt:

> Quand il la vit à ses genoux, mourante, épuisée, attendant la mort d'un mot, il la saisit dans ses bras avec une rage convulsive et l'attira sur sa poitrine. Elle céda comme une faible enfant; elle lui abandonna ses lèvres sans résistance. Elle était presque morte.
> Mais tout à coup, s'éveillant comme d'un rêve, elle s'arracha à ses brûlantes caresses, s'enfuit au bout de la chambre, à l'endroit où le portrait de sir Ralph remplissait le panneau [. . .]
> [. . .] Raymon s'arrêta, frappé de cette résistance morale qui survivait à la résistance physique. (pp. 194–5)

> (When he saw her at his knees, dying, exhausted, ready to die at a word from him, he seized her in his arms with a convulsive rage and drew her against his chest. She surrendered like a weak child; she abandoned her lips to him without resistance. She was nearly dead.
> But suddenly, waking up as if from a dream, she tore herself away from his passionate caresses, ran to the end of the room, to the place where the portrait of Sir Ralph occupied the wall panel. [. . .]
> [. . .] Raymon stopped, struck by this moral resistance that was outliving physical resistance.)

This passage suggests that Indiana is capable of snapping out of her trance when she needs to; just after the above passage, when she once again begins to succumb to Raymon's eloquence, 'tout à coup elle se souvint' (suddenly she remembered herself) (p. 195). Later, when Indiana has run away from Delmare and finds herself on the point of being physically overpowered in Raymon's bedroom, 'un bon ange étendit ses ailes sur cette âme chancelante et troublée; elle se réveilla et repoussa les attaques du vice égoïste et froid' (a good angel spread his wings over this wavering and troubled soul; she came to her senses and repelled the attacks of selfish, cold vice) (p. 221). Like any minimally skilled reader of fiction, the heroine knows how to maintain a degree of critical distance, however slight. She resembles the reader who, as suggested in our second chapter, both willingly suspends her disbelief and keeps it active in the background.

Like Indiana, in a sense, Raymon voluntarily switches off his reflective faculties. The narrator tells us that Raymon is, unusually, 'un homme capable de folie en amour' (a man capable of madness in love) (p. 84), but his rare openness to seduction is deliberate rather than involuntary:

C'était un homme à principes quand il raisonnait avec lui-même; mais de fougueuses passions l'entraînaient souvent hors de ses systèmes. Alors il n'était plus capable de réfléchir, ou bien il évitait de se traduire au tribunal de sa conscience: il commettait des fautes comme à l'insu de lui-même, et l'homme de la veille s'efforçait de tromper celui du lendemain. (p. 72)

(He was a principled man when he reasoned with himself; but fiery passions often drew him outside of his systems. At these times he was no longer capable of reflection, or rather he avoided appearing before the court of his conscience: he committed faults as if unaware of his actions, and the man of yesterday strove to deceive the man of tomorrow.)

Dans le kiosque rempli de fleurs exotiques où elle venait l'enivrer des séductions de la jeunesse et de la passion, il oubliait volontiers tout ce qu'il devait se rappeler plus tard. (p. 74)

(In the summer-house filled with exotic flowers where she intoxicated him with the seductions of youth and passion, he readily forgot all that he would remember later.)

Quand Raymon commençait à se sentir amoureux, il avait coutume de s'étourdir, non pour étouffer cette passion naissante, mais, au contraire, pour chasser la raison qui lui prescrivait d'en peser les conséquences. Ardent au plaisir, il poursuivait son but avec âpreté. (p. 84)

(When Raymon began to feel the stirrings of love, he was in the habit of diverting himself, not in order to to stifle this nascent passion, but on the contrary to chase away reason, which would require him to weigh the consequences of that passion. Pleasure-loving, he pursued his goal inflexibly.)

What is it that enables both Raymon and Indiana to resist total domination by their feelings, despite their attempts to quell their critical faculties? In Raymon's case, he is aware that his feelings for Indiana could jeopardise his future independence: 'il faudra[it] que ma destinée succombe, et que je sacrifie mon avenir à son présent' (my destiny would have to succumb, and my future sacrifice itself to her present) (p. 163). Later, the narrator tells us that 'depuis longtemps, il avait prévu qu'un instant viendrait le mettre aux prises avec cet amour de femme, qu'il faudrait défendre sa liberté contre les exigences d'une passion romanesque' (for a long time, he had predicted that a moment would come when he would need to deal with this woman's love, and to defend his freedom against the demands of a romantic passion) (p. 234). It would appear that Raymon has too keen an appreciation of his own freedom to abandon himself entirely to his passions.

This is the case for Indiana too: she, like Raymon, instinctively rebels against any kind of domination, in defence of her freedom. The entire novel stages a tension between freedom and domination, in whatever form the latter takes. The first paragraph of the first chapter depicts Indiana and Ralph absorbed in watching the fire ('[ils] semblaient s'abandonner en toute *soumission* au vague ennui qui pesait sur eux' (they seemed to surrender themselves, in complete submission to the vague boredom that weighed upon them)), while Delmare 'donnait des marques de rébellion ouverte' (showed signs of open rebellion), indicating 'l'intention marquée de lutter contre l'ennemi commun' (the clear intention to struggle against the common enemy), that is, boredom (p. 49). It is Indiana's resistance, however, rather than Delmare's, that is at the centre of the novel. The Preface of 1832 describes Indiana as an embodiment of 'la volonté aux prises avec la nécessité' (the will struggling against necessity), of 'l'amour heurtant son front aveugle à tous les obstacles de la civilisation' (love flinging her head blindly against all the obstacles of civilisation) (p. 40). Indiana demonstrates a capacity for resistance when she experiences any threat to her freedom. The narrator tells us that the heroine is in possession of 'une volonté de fer, une force de résistance incalculable contre tout ce qui tendait à l'opprimer' (an iron will, an incalculable force of resistance to all that tended to oppress her) (p. 88), and that 'résister mentalement à toute espèce de contrainte morale était devenu chez elle une seconde nature, un principe de conduite, une loi de conscience' (mental resistance to every kind of moral constraint had become second nature for her, a principle of conduct, a law of conscience) (p. 89). Her subjugation to her husband is only apparent, because she does not bend her will to his. The narrator compares the heroine's position, in her marriage to a man capable of '[la] domination violente' (violent domination) (p. 244) and whose mastery over her is sanctioned by French law, to that of a king chained up in a dungeon. When her husband attempts to find out where she has spent the morning, Indiana refuses to say, telling him that 'sur ma volonté, monsieur, vous ne pouvez rien' (over my will, sir, you have no power) (p. 232) and that her escape from the house was 'pour vous prouver que ne pas régner sur la volonté d'une femme, c'est exercer un empire dérisoire' (to prove to you that not to govern the will of a woman is to exert a derisory power) (p. 233). She tells him that his physical strength will never secure her 'volonté' (will) (p. 233). The narrator attributes Indiana's resistance to oppression to 'ce besoin de bonheur' (this need for happiness), 'cette haine de l'injustice' (this hatred of injustice), and cette 'soif de liberté' (thirst for freedom) that rebel against 'les lois sociales' (social laws) (p. 272). The novel consequently frames Indiana's resistance to domination in terms of 'cette grande et terrible lutte de la nature contre la civilisation' (this great and terrible struggle of nature against civilisation) (p. 272).

Indiana is less good, admittedly, at resisting domination when it takes the form of persuasion rather than oppression. The narrator tells us that 'Madame Delmare, qui savait si bien résister à la violence de son mari, cédait toujours à sa douceur' (Madame Delmare, so able to resist her husband's violence, always gave in to his gentleness) (p. 70), and that if her husband had been 'impérieux' (imperious) rather than affectionate on the night of her flight from Île Bourbon, she would have found it easier to defy him: 'la résistance eût semblé douce et légitime' (resistance would have seemed sweet and legitimate) (p. 278). Indiana is portrayed as completely defenceless, 'sans défense possible, [. . .] dénuée de protection, exposée de tous côtés' (without any possible defence, [. . .] devoid of protection, exposed on all sides) when Raymon makes his first amorous 'attaque' (attack) on her, in the Parisian residence of her aunt (pp. 87–8). The heroine does subsequently put in place a 'plan de résistance' (resistance plan) (p. 93) against her seducer, by not attending a ball at which she is likely to meet him, but she is very happy to see it fail. When she subsequently discovers Raymon in her bedroom and imagines that he has intended to surprise her there, she decides that henceforth she will be 'en garde contre cette passion orageuse et funeste qui fermentait dans son sein' (on guard against this stormy and fatal passion which smouldered in her heart), and distrustful of 'cette éloquence menteuse que les hommes savent dépenser avec nous' (this dishonest eloquence that men know how to use with us) (pp. 118–19); nevertheless, she realises how difficult it will be to resist Raymon's particular brand of domination: 'il n'[a] qu'à étendre la main pour dire: "Elle est à moi! Je troublerai sa raison, je désolerai sa vie; et, si elle me résiste, je répandrai le deuil autour d'elle, je l'entourerai de remords

[. . .]"' (he has only to put out his hand to say: 'She is mine! I will trouble her reason, ravage her life; and, if she resists me, I will spread suffering around her, envelope her in remorse [. . .]') (pp. 125–6). The heroine realises that Raymon will attempt to lure her into a 'piège' (trap) (p. 141), and initially 'lutta contre cette puissance magique qu'il exerçait autour de lui' (struggled against that magical power that he exercised over those around him) (p. 150). However, she soon allows herself once more to succumb to his charms: 'Indiana se laissait entraîner au besoin d'aimer et de respecter tout ce qu'aimait et respectait Raymon' (Indiana let herself give in to the need to love and to respect all that Raymon loved and respected) (p. 175).

Raymon recognises, nevertheless, from the moment he sees her astride a horse, that Indiana will not make his conquest of her easy: 'Ce n'était pas le cœur résigné de la pauvre Noun, qui aimait mieux se noyer que de lutter contre son malheur' (This was not the resigned heart of poor Noun, who preferred to drown herself than to fight against her misfortune) (p. 162). Indiana's psychological resistance to Raymon appears to arise from innate, childlike wisdom. When he tries to give her lessons in contemporary politics, she questions his logic:

> Malgré l'empire qu'il exerçait sur son âme neuve et ingénue, ses sophismes rencontrèrent quelquefois de la résistance.
> Indiana opposait aux intérêts de la civilisation érigés en principes, les idées droites et les lois simples du bon sens et de l'humanité; ses objections avaient un caractère de franchise sauvage qui embarrassait quelquefois Raymon, et qui le charmait toujours par son originalité enfantine. (p. 174)

> (Despite the power that he exercised over her pure and gullible soul, his sophisms sometimes met with resistance.
> Indiana opposed the self-interested principles of civilisation with the straightforward ideas and simple laws of good sense and humanity; her objections had a quality of primitive candour that sometimes embarrassed Raymon, and that always charmed him with its childlike originality.)

Even through the haze of her intense infatuation with Raymon, Indiana is aware that from his point of view she may be merely 'le caprice de trois jours' (a three-day whim) (p. 150), and that his eyes appear to express 'l'amour-propre triomphant' (triumphant vanity) rather than anything more noble (p. 175). When Ralph informs Indiana of Raymon's affair with Noun, the narrator tells us that 'ce n'était pas la première fois qu'un soupçon vague jetait ses clartés sinistres sur le frêle édifice de son bonheur' (it was not the first time that a vague suspicion cast its sinister beams over the fragile edifice of her happiness) (p. 188). Indiana's scepticism about Raymon's good intentions may have lain dormant, but it is not absent. It is because she wants proof of the sincerity of Raymon's love that she insists on a platonic relationship: 'j'aime mieux mourir que de descendre à n'être plus que votre maîtresse' (I would prefer to die than to descend to being no more than your mistress) (p. 200).

Indiana's resistance to Raymon's attempts to seduce her is also a resistance to his will to dominate her, however persuasion-based that domination would be. The narrator draws an explicit analogy between her brutish husband, who effectively enslaves her, and her cruel, slave-owning father: 'En épousant Delmare, elle ne fit que changer de maître' (In marrying Delmare, she changed only her master) (p. 88). While Raymon appears to 'cette femme esclave' (this woman slave) (p. 90) as a saviour, he is tacitly aligned, throughout the text, with these tyrannical masters. His first kiss marks her hand, the narrator tells us, 'comme un fer rouge' (like a red-hot iron) (p. 90), a phrase that calls to mind, beyond its suggestion of erotic intensity, the brutal branding of slaves. He flatters himself that, in his relationship with Indiana, 'il était le maître' (he was the master) (p. 93) and in the same conversation tells her that were he to 'possess' her ('vous posséder' (p. 93)) as his wife, she would have 'béni [sa] chaîne' (blessed her chain) (p. 94). He goes on to say that, were he to be her husband, he would guard her 'en maître jaloux' (as a jealous master) (p. 95), and even declares that he owns her – 'tu m'appartiens' (you belong to me) (p. 95) – and that she is his 'bien' (good) (p. 96).[7] Later in the text, Indiana calls him 'maître de son sort' (master of her destiny) (p. 219), and aligns him with all men, who she claims believe themselves to be 'les maîtres du monde' (the masters of the world) when they are simply '[d]es tyrans' (tyrants) (p. 249). Raymon's desire to own Indiana as if she were a piece of property, and his jealousy of Ralph's portrait because of its presence in her bedroom – 'il la possède à toute heure' (he possesses her at all times) (p. 109) – recalls Delmare's jealous surveillance of his wife, 'un trésor fragile et précieux' (a fragile and precious treasure) (p. 50), in the opening chapters of the novel. It also recalls Henri de Marsay's desire to possess Paquita, but this time the protagonist's emphasis is less on finding out the heroine's secrets than on physically and psychologically establishing his 'empire' (authority) over her (p. 203). This desire to assert mastery over Indiana long outlives his love for her: driven by resentment now, he vows to make her his, and he very nearly succeeds. When Indiana throws herself at Raymon's feet in the final scene at Lagny, she appears to accept his domination unreservedly: 'Dispose de moi, de mon sang, de ma vie; je suis à toi corps et âme. J'ai fait trois mille lieues pour t'appartenir, pour te dire cela; prends-moi, je suis ton bien, tu es mon maître' (p. 297) (Dispose of me, of my blood, of my life; I am yours body and soul. I have travelled three thousand leagues to belong to you, to tell you that; take me, I am your good, you are my master). Thankfully for Indiana, there is another master in town: Raymon's wife. His plans to take advantage of the heroine, finally on her knees, are foiled by Laure's entry on the scene.

The most obvious lesson imparted by *Indiana*, in relation to the workings of fiction, is that stories, like seducers, must always be suspected of falsehood and of a will to domination. Shira Malkin notes that *Indiana* 'reads like a cautionary tale about the rhetoric of love that gullible, inexperienced female readers find in tragic novels or in real-life encounters with manipulative men'.[8] I would argue that while *Indiana* certainly does explicitly warn its readers to distrust the rhetoric of love, wherever it is found, it also warns of the dangers of seductive stories more generally. In other words, Raymon's duping of Indiana thematically foregrounds the need for critical vigilance with regard to seductive storytellers of all kinds, even those who, like the realist narrator himself, present themselves as trustworthy.

The reader is repeatedly invited by the narrator of *Indiana* to feel sympathy with Raymon, whose shortcomings are, initially at least, made light of. Despite the plentiful evidence of the character's duplicity, for example, the narrator tells us that Raymon is 'aussi fran[c] qu'il soit possible de l'être dans le monde' (as frank as it is possible to be in the world) (p. 165), that 'il ne savait pas tromper' (he knew not how to deceive), and that 'son coeur était sincère' (his heart was sincere) (p. 99). In addition, events are often focalised by Raymon, such as the moment when he prevents Ralph from committing suicide:

> Dans cet instant d'effroi, les yeux de Raymon rencontrèrent le visage pâle et morne de M. Brown. Il ne criait pas, il n'écumait point, il ne se tordait pas les mains; seulement, il prit son couteau de chasse, et, avec un sang-froid vraiment britannique, il s'apprêtait à se couper la gorge, lorsque Raymon lui arracha son arme et l'entraîna vers le lieu d'où partaient les cris. (p. 163)

> (In that horrible moment, Raymon's eyes fell on the pale and doleful face of Monsieur Brown. He was not crying out, he was not foaming at the mouth, he was not wringing his hands; he simply took out his hunting knife and, with a truly British *sang-froid*, he was preparing to cut his throat, when Raymon seized his weapon and dragged him towards the place from which the shouts were emanating.)

Indeed, the narrator's internal focalisation on Raymon is so frequent that (as in the case of *La Fille aux yeux d'or*) it is often difficult to differentiate the narratorial perspective from the character's, as in the above passage, or in the one where Indiana's cheeks, eyes and figure are viewed through infatuated eyes that could belong either to Raymon or to the narrator. The paragraph begins with 'Raymon vit madame

Delmare en amazone' (Raymon saw Madame Delmare in her riding-habit) but ends with a generalisation that the narrator assumes as his own: 'Le principal charme des créoles, selon moi, c'est que l'excessive délicatesse de leurs traits et de leurs proportions leur laisse longtemps la gentillesse de l'enfance' (The principal charm of Creoles, in my view, is that the extreme delicacy of their features and proportions gives them for a long time the gentle appearance of children) (p. 153). Similarly, when the narrator exclaims at the contrast between Indiana's innocence and the sexual wiliness of most women, and admires her 'sourire des anges' (angel's smile), it is not clear whether he is voicing Raymon's thoughts or his own (p. 173). Readers' sympathy for or empathy with Raymon is also encouraged through the regular direct (though arguably ironic) encouragements to take the character's side, for example with regard to his decision not to marry Noun: 'Non, vous conviendrez avec lui que ce n'était pas possible' (No, you will agree with him that it was not possible) (p. 76). The narrator overtly encourages us, moreover, to take Raymon's side over Ralph's, in their political debates: 'Ne valait-il pas mieux croire Raymon, qui avait une âme si chaleureuse, si large et si expansive?' (Was it not better to believe Raymon, who had so warm, broad and expansive a soul?) (p. 175). Such incitements occur even where the narrator is explicitly highlighting Raymon's shortcomings, for example the selfish reasons for his silence about Ralph's suicide attempt: 'Il y eut dans cette discretion désobligeante quelque chose d'égoïste et de haineux que vous pardonnerez peut-être au sentiment de jalousie amoureuse qui l'inspira' (There was in this ungenerous discretion something selfish and hateful that you will perhaps forgive in view of the amorous jealousy that was its cause) (p. 164). The reader may find Raymon difficult to read, then, partly because she is encouraged to feel with, or empathise with, him; she is invited to be seduced by him, much as Noun and Indiana are seduced by him.

What helps the reader to gain some critical distance from Raymon is the evidence in the text of a gap between his self-image and his reality. For example, he is convinced that he is principled and honourable, but consistently behaves in ways that suggest otherwise, most notably by neglecting his pregnant former mistress, by allowing himself to be seduced by her in Indiana's bedroom, by playing the role of friend to Delmare while he attempts to seduce the latter's wife and by professing his love to Indiana for selfish reasons and to devastating effect. Nevertheless, he does feel a degree of guilt about his behaviour; he is 'accablé de honte' (overwhelmed with shame) (p. 105), for example, after sleeping with Noun in Indiana's bed. He is so horrified by his own role in Noun's suicide that he loads his pistols 'dans l'intention bien réelle de se brûler la cervelle; mais un sentiment louable l'arrêta. Que deviendrait sa mère . . . sa mère âgée, débile!' (with the very real intention of blowing his brains out; but a praiseworthy feeling stopped him. What would become of his mother . . . his elderly, feeble mother!) (p. 127). Raymon argues himself out of suicide for altruistic reasons: he tells himself that he must live to look after his mother. Though the narrator does not explicitly invite alternative interpretations of Raymon's decision, the suspicious reader will have been alerted to irony by subtle clues in the text, such as the hyperbolic pluralisation of 'pistolets', the back-handed undertones of 'intention bien réelle' (very real intention) and the speed with which the entire project is despatched. The gap between Raymon's self-image and his reality is further underlined when the protagonist writes to Indiana, tacitly inviting her to return to him from Île Bourbon. He tells himself that his intentions are innocent and that his letter will have no real consequences: 'enfin il réussit à s'abuser lui-même et à ne se pas croire coupable' (he finally succeeded in deceiving himself and in not believing himself guilty) (p. 289). Sand anticipates Sartre's theorisation of bad faith in her presentation of Raymon's careful avoidance of self-knowledge:

> Le vice ne se mire pas dans sa propre laideur, car il se ferait peur à lui-même, et le Yago de Shakspeare, personnage si vrai dans ses actions, est faux dans ses paroles, forcé qu'il est par nos conventions dramatiques de venir dévoiler lui-même les replis secrets de son cœur tortueux et profond. L'homme met rarement ainsi de sang-froid sa conscience sous ses pieds. (p. 289)

> (Vice does not gaze at its own ugliness, as it would frighten itself, and Shakespeare's Iago, a character so true in his actions, is false in his speech, obliged as he is by stage conventions to reveal, himself, the secret recesses of his deep and tortuous heart. Man rarely treads upon his conscience with such calm indifference.)

Iago's knowledge of his own evil (what Baudelaire would call his 'conscience dans le mal' (consciousness in evil)) may make his motivations understandable to viewers and readers of *Othello*, but it makes him less credible as a character, according to Sand's narrator. By this logic, Raymon is credible as a character precisely because his motivations are so elusive, even and perhaps especially to himself. In his resistance to understanding, which endures regardless (and because) of the access we have to his thought processes, he resembles a human being more than a fully readable fictional character.

Arguably, Raymon's contradictions and lack of self-knowledge do more than elicit our suspicion of his motivations, and do more than make his character plausible: they also make his character at least sporadically sympathetic. His incoherence is not, after all, intentionally evil. The narrator tells us repeatedly that Raymon does authentically love Indiana. However, Raymon's love is also fickle. Intending to seduce Indiana, for example, he obtains an invitation to visit her bedroom under cover of dark; but on seeing her naive trust in his good intentions, he changes his mind, telling himself that he will spend the night chastely in her bedroom. However, he again changes his mind as he makes his way, the same night, through the grounds of Lagny, feeling haunted by memories of Noun and insulted by Ralph. He goes on opportunistically and manipulatively to tell Indiana that the trick she played on him, upon his arrival, is the reason why he has given up on his chaste intentions. This most transparently disingenuous of characters proves impossible to pin down: did he ever truly intend to behave honourably during his clandestine visit to Indiana, or was this an expedient lie he told himself in order to keep his self-image intact? Raymon's most intimate thoughts and feelings are regularly laid bare by the narrator, but the character remains both resistant to understanding and oddly sympathetic.

To sum up, Indiana falls under Raymon's sway but manages to maintain a minimal resistance to him. Readers resemble Indiana to the extent that we are seduced by the rhetoric of a narrator who encourages us both to feel complicity with the young protagonist and to maintain a critical distance from him. The narrator's accounts of the workings of Raymon's mind help to elicit readers' affective empathy, to the extent that the apparently authoritative narrator presents his motivations in a sympathetic light and shows that his intentions are opaque even to himself. However, the protagonist's thought processes and general character, as relayed by the narrator, also heighten readers' suspicion of him. This suspicion does not necessarily extinguish readers' sympathy for, or empathy with, Raymon, just as readers can be alternately, and to varying degrees, seduced by the persuasive, apparently omniscient narratorial voice and alert to its potential biases, falsehoods and ruses, including its disingenuous portrayal of Ralph.

Mind-Reading and Opacity: Ralph as Fiction-Associated Stranger

Raymon de Ramière is a paradoxical stranger figure in *Indiana*, in that he is introduced as an impostor and regularly intrudes into places where he does not belong, but is nevertheless represented as an individual who is at home everywhere, 'l'homme d'intelligence qui appartient à tous et pour qui la société est une patrie' (the man of intellect who belongs to everyone and for whom society is a kind of homeland) (p. 207). Ralph Brown is an equally paradoxical figure of the outsider, in that he is presented as an insider in the Delmare household (so close an intimate is he that he has the right to kiss Indiana on the lips, and can come and go as he pleases in her home), but is simultaneously marked as a stranger. Certainly, at the beginning of the novel Ralph appears to be very much an insider in the Delmare household; he is almost literally a piece of the furniture, his portrait hanging on Indiana's bedroom wall, and the narrator's opening description of him comparing his face to the one that features on a fireplace engraving. For at least the first third of the novel, Ralph is only superficially an outsider, then, and is so purely on account of his nationality and what Nigel Harkness calls his 'linguistic inaptitude': despite having been brought up on Île Bourbon, a French colony, Ralph Brown, as his name suggests, speaks English as his first language, and is not at home in French.[9]

The extent of Ralph's isolation is, however, revealed as the novel progresses. He is an outsider not just because of his foreignness, and not just because his presence at Lagny is inconvenient for Raymon and Indiana, while Delmare is absent on business. Ralph's long-standing sense of estrangement is conveyed in four lengthy passages prior to the conclusion. In the first such passage, Indiana tells Raymon how Ralph was spurned by his own parents, and subsequently by the wife he was forced to marry. In the second, he is revealed by the narrator to be an 'être isolé qui avait eu un père et une mère comme tout le monde, un frère, une femme, un fils, une amie' (isolated being who had had a father and a mother like everyone, a brother, a wife, a son, a friend), but who 'n'avait jamais rien recueilli, rien gardé de toutes ces affections' (had never reaped or retained any benefit from these affections); he is '[un] étranger dans la vie, qui passait mélancolique et nonchalant, n'ayant pas même ce sentiment exalté de son infortune qui fait trouver du charme dans la douleur' (a stranger in life, passing by with melancholy and nonchalance, lacking even the exalted sense of his misfortune which allows one to find charm in suffering) (p. 176). In the third character sketch, the narrator explains that Ralph was a victim of his family's 'injustices' to such an extent that he spent much of his youth hiding his 'secrètes angoisses' (secret agonies) from the eyes of others (p. 256). In the fourth account of his life, Ralph himself explains that in his childhood he had been pushed away by his mother, virtually exiled from his family home and deprived, beyond his friendship with Indiana, of any 'voix amie' (friendly voice) (p. 315): 'J'ai grandi seul, j'ai vécu seul' (I grew up alone, I lived alone) (p. 316). The effect of the repeated retelling of Ralph's story is that the latter's outsider status is gradually but insistently impressed upon the reader.

Ralph is a stranger, then, in that he is, or rather becomes, a figure of the exiled outsider; but he is also a stranger in that he is other than he seems. Ralph tells Indiana, towards the end of the novel, that he needs to reveal to her the secret of his life, and announces that she has never known anything of the life story she thought she knew so well: this secret is his love for her, but also the story of his isolation. It is only late in the novel, therefore, that we learn of the condition that has afflicted him since birth: he has always been incapable of communicating his feelings through his facial expressions, so that there is a perpetual mismatch between his inner emotions and his blank face. Ralph's affliction, which makes him other than he seems, also gives him outsider status. The strange impassivity of his face means that other people, including his own mother, have always rejected him as different or strange. In other words, his innate otherness is perceived as a difference from other people, and this leads to his social isolation, reinforcing his status as a stranger. After his brother's death, for example, he attempts to comfort his father but is so unhelpful an emotional presence that the latter accuses him of 'insensibilité' (insensitivity), leaving 'le pauvre Ralph plus malheureux et plus méconnu que jamais' (poor Ralph more miserable and misunderstood than ever) (p. 158). Raymon, who finds him difficult to decipher, refers to him as 'étrange' (strange) (p. 202).

Even when Ralph does successfully convey his emotions, he comes across as strange to other characters. When he learns that Raymon has nearly caused Indiana's death, he expresses his anger in terms that make him seem a stranger to Madame de Ramière: 'Il était si différent de ce qu'elle l'avait toujours vu, qu'elle pensa presque à la possibilité d'une subite aliénation mentale. [. . .] [L]'étrangeté de cette disposition [. . .] en rendait l'aspect terrible' (He was so different from what she had always seen of him that she almost considered the possibility of a sudden outburst of insanity. [. . .] The strangeness of this disposition [. . .] made him terrible to behold) (p. 238). It gradually becomes clear that Ralph is not the unemotional character he appears to be; when Indiana agrees to let him come to Île Bourbon with her and Delmare, he nearly faints, a fact that the narrator explains as follows: 'dans ce corps robuste, dans ce tempérament calme et réservé, fermentaient des émotions puissantes' (within this robust body, within this calm and reserved temperament, powerful emotions were simmering) (p. 243). It is only in the chapter just before the conclusion that the reader is explicitly told that he has, all along, been passionately in love with Indiana.

It is by overcoming his strange inability to communicate, which had set him apart from others and rendered him a stranger in the world, that Ralph reveals the extent of his disability. In other words, it is upon revealing the difference between his inner and outer reality that Ralph becomes expressive, thereby seeming to heal the rift between appearance and reality. The character remains a stranger, however, in two senses. Firstly, he is now marked out as superior to other men. He is described as 'cet homme si vulgaire en apparence, homme d'exception pourtant' (this man so outwardly common, but so exceptional) (p. 313). The character is a figure of some fascination in the conclusion to the novel, again suggesting his difference from other men. Secondly, in the conclusion Ralph is depicted as living in a remote place, with Indiana, on Île Bourbon. Instead of being ostracised by others, he chooses, now, to remove himself from the company of other men.

Ralph's long account of his life, towards the end of the novel, shows him to have been, all along, other than he seemed, and also shows him, in the present moment, to be other than he himself realised, in that he is now capable of expressing himself eloquently. This pivotal monologue places Ralph in the position of seductive storyteller. The story Ralph tells is certainly not a fiction, but it arguably has fictional elements, insofar as something magical appears to happen to both him and Indiana as he speaks. Previous to Ralph's monologue, Raymon had been the character most closely and overtly associated with fiction and storytelling; he tells lies designed to deceive others, and even presents himself, in the language he uses with Indiana, as a hero-saviour of the sort that might be found cutting a dash in sentimental fiction. Ralph, by contrast, seems the very antithesis of a hero or creator of fiction when we first meet him; he appears to embody frank and unadorned actuality, a reality principle unembellished by artful language. He certainly has none of the seductive charm or curiosity-provoking mysteriousness that characterises the other fictional strangers included in this study. Ralph embodies the prosaic antithesis of art and the imagination. The narrator tells us that the least artistic of men would prefer Delmare's countenance to Ralph's 'traits régulièrement fades' (regular but lacklustre features) (p. 51). Indiana observes that the latter's late brother was endowed with all the wit and expressiveness that he lacks. The narrator notes that Ralph has no quality capable of attracting 'une tête romanesque' (a romantic mind), though he might appeal to 'une tête positive' (a factual mind), somebody who looks with their eyes only (p. 108). We are told that his destiny is 'vraiment maudite, mais sans poésie, sans aventure' (truly cursed, but without poetry or aventure) (p. 176). Another aspect of Ralph's anti-fictional persona is his apparent inability to be untruthful. He is unjustly suspected of 'fausseté' (duplicity) by Raymon until

Indiana points out that 'Ralph n'a jamais menti' (Ralph has never lied) (p. 197). The narrator too asserts that 'le pauvre Ralph ne savait pas mentir' (poor Ralph did not know how to lie) (p. 231). In the course of verbal sparring with Raymon, he becomes painfully conscious of his linguistic ineptitude; he does not know how to 'envelopper [s]es idées dans des mots qui en altèrent le sens' (wrap his ideas in words that change their meaning) (p. 243), or how to '[s]e jouer de [s]a parole' (make a mockery of his word), which means that he is perceived by others as 'ce crétin sans intelligence et sans voix' (that idiot with neither brain nor voice) (p. 324).

Despite his apparent allegiance to mundane truth, however, there are suggestions that all is not as it seems. Ralph has, after all, named his beloved dog after one of Shakespeare's most poetic creations: Ophelia. Further suggesting the existence in Ralph of a hidden life of the imagination is the fact that the narrator characterises his political beliefs as utopian, referring to 'son rêve de république' (his dream of a republic) (p. 167). In addition, despite the narrator's insistence on Ralph's 'franchise' (frankness) (p. 167) and guilelessness, the character gradually reveals a capacity for duplicity, as when he tells Raymon and Delmare that Indiana is indisposed, or knowingly hides Raymon's shocked reaction when the latter learns that he is standing beside the place where Noun drowned. He even manages to simulate friendship with Raymon, despite his deep suspicion and dislike of his rival. A rift between Ralph's appearance and his reality is further suggested by Madame de Ramière's realisation that she has been deceived by his calm demeanour, and by the narrator's observation, after the protagonist's return to the Île Bourbon with Indiana and Delmare, that 'il continuait à se donner toutes les apparences de la froideur et de l'égoïsme' (he continued to give himself all of the appearances of coldness and selfishness) (p. 255); it is suggested here that at least some degree of pretence is involved. As all of this suggests, Ralph becomes a more incoherent and therefore enigmatic character as the story progresses, certainly for the observant reader who is alert to the various hints, in the text, that he is a more complex character than he initially appears. It seems appropriate, then, that the novel should describe him occasionally in terms suggestive of mystery. As Raymon makes his way in the moonlight through the grounds of Lagny, for example, Ralph takes on, for him, 'l'aspect d'un fantôme' (the appearance of a ghost) (p. 186), and the narrator compares him to a forbidding shade posted at the entrance to the Elysian Fields.

Towards the end of the novel, once the decision to commit joint suicide has been taken by Indiana and Ralph, the narrator refers to the 'changement [. . .] extraordinaire [qui] s'opéra dans l'âme et dans l'extérieur de Ralph' (extraordinary [...] change that took place in Ralph's soul and bearing) (p. 309; see also p. 312). In the course of a long monologue, Ralph effectively metamorphoses into the novel's hero. He becomes the saviour fantasised, earlier in the story, by Indiana: she now sees him as 'un ami qu'elle avait vu jadis dans ses rêves et qui se réalisait enfin pour elle sur les bords de la tombe' (a friend whom she had seen once in her dreams and who was finally materialising before her on the brink of the grave) (p. 313). The idea that 'the mutating Ralph'[10] undergoes a transformation at the end of *Indiana* is strongly suggestive of fiction and even fairy tale. The narrator's comparison of the protagonist to 'un bon génie' (a good genie) (p. 312) is further suggestive of a magical metamorphosis.[11]

However, there is also a strong suggestion towards the end of Sand's novel that Ralph's transformation is illusory only, and that he is, in fact, finally revealing his true self, which is a self that he had kept voluntarily hidden. The moment that Ralph prepares for his own suicide is presented by the narrator as 'le moment d'être lui, de mettre à nu tout son être moral, de se dépouiller, devant le Juge, du déguisement que les hommes lui avaient imposé' (the moment to be himself, to lay his entire inner self bare, to strip himself, before the Judge, of the disguise that men had imposed upon him) (p. 313). Ralph claims now that he made a decision, when he moved to France to be close to Indiana, to wear a 'déguisement' (disguise) and to erect 'un triple mur de glace' (a triple wall of ice) between himself and Indiana, in order to restrain his passion for her (p. 324). He refers repeatedly to his dissimulation, using terms such as 'feinte' (pretence), 'travestissement' (disguise) and 'rôle' (p. 324). He insists upon his own agency: he has fashioned himself, he says, 'pour être méconnu' (to be misunderstood) (p. 324). This character who could not lie is thus revealed to be a master of disguise. The disguise has finally been abandoned, however, and the blindfold finally falls from Indiana's eyes: 'Rendue à la vérité, à la nature, elle vit le coeur de Ralph tel qu'il était' (Awoken to truth, to nature, she saw Ralph's heart as it was) (p. 329).

As well as revealing his past aptitude for fiction or dissimulation, Ralph finally discovers, in his monologue, an eloquence that, we are told, surpasses Raymon's own and that leads the narrator to compare his 'étranges discours' (strange words) to 'les mystérieuses visions de l'anachorète' (the anchorite's mysterious visions), or 'les rêves du poète' (the poet's dreams) (p. 313). This newly fluent speech enables Ralph to tell Indiana 'une longue histoire' (a long story), the story of his life (p. 314). The narrator states that the force of Ralph's story comes from its truthfulness, from 'la puissance que possède la voix d'un homme profondément vrai dans sa passion' (the power possessed by the voice of a man who is profoundly true in his passion) (p. 329). This potency is also associated with a force of seduction that Sand's own fictional narrator explicitly envies.

In the course of telling his life story, Ralph gives further evidence of his affinity with fiction: he refers four times to the workings of his 'imagination', claiming to have been in love, as an adolescent, not with the heroine as a little girl, but with an imagined future Indiana (p. 317; see also pp. 316, 325). Ralph also reminds Indiana that he once read her the story of *Paul et Virginie*, a story that had made him shiver in 'sympathie' (sympathy); they had recounted it to one another on one occasion when, in their younger lives, they were lost in the woods after nightfall (p. 320). Ralph identifies strongly with Paul, and indeed there are strong parallels between his story and that of Bernardin de Saint-Pierre's hero. Ralph goes on, in his monologue, to evoke 'les félicités' (the joys) (p. 328) that await him in the afterlife, when he and Indiana will finally be together as man and wife; he has even asked her to wear a white dress to prepare for their joint suicide. He claims that, in death, they will finally be rid of 'les fictions menteuses de cette vie' (the deceitful fictions of this life) (p. 329); that his dream of a posthumous honeymoon might be one such fiction does not appear to occur to him. In the conclusion, we learn that the pair had stopped before they threw themselves into the waterfall, and that Ralph chooses retrospectively, against any more plausible medical explanation, to believe that an angel saved them. Further cementing Ralph's reinvention as expressive and imaginative, the (now personal, no longer omniscient-seeming) traveller-narrator refers to the presence on his face of 'une expression de rêverie' (a dreamy expression) (p. 336). Ralph is presented by the narrator, in this conclusion, as a focal point for a range of conflicting fictions spun by the islanders; he is 'le héros de tant de contes étranges' (the hero of so many strange tales) (p. 336). According to one source, Ralph is an uneducated and utterly uninteresting man whose only admirable quality is his silence; according to another, he is highly educated but supercilious; another claims that he is mediocre, selfish and unsociable; a particularly unreliable source affirms that Ralph is a scoundrel who poisoned his friend to marry his wife, and a substantially more reliable one simply recounts the story of Delmare's death, Ralph and Indiana's departure and their later return to Île Bourbon. The pair have 'un odieux soupçon' (an odious suspicion) hanging over them; rumour has it that they are on the island to escape condemnation by public opinion, according to which they killed Delmare to permit 'leur criminel attachement' (their criminal attachment) (p. 335). But other, better informed voices throw doubt upon this version with their claim that Indiana had never seemed particularly fond of her cousin, Ralph. It is little wonder that the latter is a source of fascination for the first-person narrator-traveller.

In the course of *Indiana*, Ralph goes from being a slightly odd insider in the Delmare household to a heroic outsider, from a passionless secondary character to a passionate protagonist, and from a figure strongly associated with prosaic reality to a figure invested with all the charms and seductions of fiction. As he gradually is revealed, and finally reveals himself, as other than he seems, he takes on more of a fictional aura. To the extent that Ralph conceals his true nature, at least until the novel's final pages, he is an embodiment of realist fiction, which characteristically denies its fictive status; and to the extent that his nature magically transforms at the end of the story, he arguably embodies a more fantastical mode of fiction, the kind towards which Sand's novel veers in its final pages. In either case, by the end of the novel, the opening references to Ralph as 'le personnage vermeil et blond de cette histoire' (the blond and rose-cheeked protagonist of this story) (p. 51), and to both him and Indiana as 'fixes et pétrifiés comme les héros d'un conte de fées' (fixed and petrified like the heroes of a fairy tale) (p. 53) seem considerably less ironic than they initially appeared.

Whereas Raymon's character appears to embody the seductions of fiction, Ralph more obviously and consistently demonstrates the way in which fiction engages the reader's mind-reading skills.[12] The reader is always privy to Raymon's intimate thoughts and feelings, not least because the narrative is so often focalised by him. We know, for example, that he is appalled by Noun's illiteracy, and that Indiana's show of strength and courage, on her horse, worries him greatly; we know that after she presents Noun's tresses to him he no longer loves her and simply wants to complete his seduction of her; we know that the letter he sends her when she is in Île Bourbon is intended to provoke her return to him; and we know that when she finally returns and presents herself at his feet, he considers making her his adulterous mistress. We know all of these things and more. If Raymon provokes our curiosity, as readers, it is only on account of the occasional incoherence of his thoughts and actions. Ralph, by contrast, is opaque not only to other characters, but also to readers. This is not the kind of overt illegibility, characteristic of Paquita and Julien, that seduces readers and other characters by stimulating interest, but rather the covert kind, where there appears to be nothing to decipher: Ralph appears to be entirely legible, and therefore absolutely devoid of interest. His portrait may be protected by a veil while Indiana is absent from Lagny, but his character is presented without any hint of concealment. The narrator states that his face is utterly 'insignifiante' (insignificant) (p. 69) and that the only thing more 'insignifiant' (insignificant) than the portrait of him that hangs in Indiana's bedroom is the 'original' (p. 108). Raymon's description of Ralph is particularly revealing of the latter's lack of appeal:

> Sa figure [. . .] annonce un homme complètement nul; cependant il y a du bon sens et de l'instruction dans ses discours quand il daigne parler; mais il s'en acquitte si péniblement, si froidement, que personne ne profite de ses connaissances, tant son débit vous glace et vous fatigue. Et puis il y a dans ses pensées quelque chose de commun et de lourd que ne rachète point la pureté méthodique de l'expression. (p. 156)

> (His face [. . .] announces a completely uninteresting man; however, his words show good sense and education when he deigns to talk; but he speaks so painfully, so coldly, that nobody can benefit from his knowledge, so paralysing and tiring is his delivery. And then there is a commonplace, tedious quality to his ideas which the measured purity of his expression cannot redeem.)

Ralph's face is repeatedly described as impassive, inscrutable, inexpressive, the suggestion being, for much of the novel, that there is nothing much of interest going on behind the façade. Not only does this face not inspire curiosity, it fails to elicit any kind of sympathy: Ralph will claim later that he never provoked 'un regard de pitié' (a compassionate look) from anyone (p. 322). This is a character who knows himself to be devoid of interest for other people: 'il faisait peu de cas de sa personne, qu'il savait être insipide et commune. Il comprenait l'indifférence dont il était l'objet' (he cared little for his own character, which he knew to be insipid and common. He understood the indifference to which he was subjected) (p. 177).

Indiana, who has known Ralph all her life, in assuming that she knows his mind entirely, reveals her own shortcomings as a mind-reader. However, she does at least acknowledge some uncertainty; she tells Raymon that she has certain 'doutes' (doubts) about the dullness the latter so quickly attributes to the Englishman: 'Vous tranchez hardiment des doutes que je n'oserais pas résoudre, moi qui connais Ralph depuis que je suis née' (You boldly pronounce upon questions that I would not dare to answer, I who have known Ralph since I was born) (pp. 156–7). She authoritatively explains his character by referring to the Englishman's past suffering, which has meant that 'une invincible timidité paralysa toutes ses facultés' (an invincible shyness paralysed all his faculties) (p. 157) and that he now avoids feeling love for anyone: 'Ralph n'aime plus rien afin de ne plus souffrir' (Ralph no longer loves anything so as not to suffer) (p. 160). Indiana understands Ralph's feelings for her to be a merely instinctual product of 'l'habitude' (habit) and of a selfish need to be loved by someone. She feels certain that she knows how he thinks, and believes that one word suffices to sum up his character: 'il faut dire le mot: Ralph est égoïste' (the word must be spoken: Ralph is selfish) (p. 161). Ralph's alleged selfishness explains his character entirely, for Indiana. It is what accounts, in her eyes, for what she perceives as his indifference towards her own inner life, and his avoidance of any discussion with her of her relationship with Raymon:

> Ralph n'a pas besoin de mon coeur; pourvu que mes mains sachent apprêter son pouding et faire résonner pour lui les cordes de la harpe, que lui importent mon amour pour un autre, mes angoisses secrètes, mais impatiences mortelles sous le joug qui m'écrase? Je suis sa servante, il ne m'en demande pas davantage. (p. 213)

> (Ralph does not need my heart; as long as my hands are capable of preparing his pudding and of making the harp strings vibrate for him, what does he care about my love for another, my secret agonies, my deathly impatience under the yoke that crushes me? I am his servant, he asks for nothing more of me.)

However, as the novel progresses, the narrator increasingly hints that there is something not quite right about the way in which Ralph is perceived by Indiana. Even the credulous Noun questions Indiana's description of Ralph as 'égoïste' (selfish) after witnessing the care he takes of Raymon, when the latter is injured (p. 109).

For the astute mind-reader who engages with *Indiana*, small but significant narrative details suggest that Ralph's bland exterior may conceal hidden depths. The narrator notes that his 'contenance' (countenance), 'au travers de son apparente imperturbabilité' (beyond its apparent impassivity), shows a quality of attention 'qu'on aurait pu appeler de l'intérêt ou de la sollicitude, si sa physionomie eût été capable de refléter un sentiment déterminé' (that could have been called interest or concern, if his face were capable of reflecting a definable feeling) (p. 151); the word 'apparente' suggests that all may not be as it seems, as does the reference to the inability of Ralph's face to convey feeling. In a formula that again suggests a mismatch between appearances and reality, the narrator tells us that Ralph subsequently displays 'un sang-froid tout à fait bizarre' (a completely bizarre sang-froid) when purchasing a horse from Raymon (p. 152). His suicidal gesture in response to the (fake) news that Indiana has been fatally thrown from this horse is described, and Raymon's observation of the gesture is registered, but the conclusions that might be drawn from Ralph's action are not spelled out by the narrator. Despite the latter's insistence on his own ability to deduce a man's entire character from his 'opinion politique' (political opinion), and vice versa (p. 166), Ralph's republican beliefs present, according to the disingenuous narrator, a contradiction between his generous ideas and his selfish spirit, between 'son esprit et son cœur' (his mind and his heart) (p. 175). The narrator suggests, subsequently, that his selfishness is merely apparent, and that Ralph is in fact 'capable de ressentir tout ce qu'il n'inspirait pas' (capable of feeling all that he did not inspire) (p. 177). The reader again suspects that appearances are deceptive when the narrator later tells us that Raymon's mother, Madame de Ramière, who is 'la seule personne, peut-être, qui jugeât bien Ralph' (the only person, perhaps, who judged Ralph accurately), produces an 'altération profonde' (deep alteration) in Ralph's facial features (p. 236). She is shocked, we learn, to observe the transformation of his character. The narrator tells us a few pages later that powerful emotions lurk within Ralph, and slightly later again refers to the character's 'secrètes ango-isses si longtemps couvées, si cruellement méconnues' (secret agonies, so long fostered and so cruelly misunderstood) (p. 256). Further informa-tion about Ralph's upbringing is introduced with the equally suggestive words 'pour que vous compreniez le caractère de Ralph' (so that you understand Ralph's character) (p. 256). We read, in the course of this narrative portrait, that Ralph perpetually watches over and protects Indiana 'sans jamais laisser deviner que telle fût son intention' (without ever letting it be suspected that his intention was such) (p. 258). For the watchful and suspicious reader, therefore, Ralph's character has always been far less bland and insignificant than we are told it is.

Nevertheless, until the final chapters of *Indiana*, the suspicious, mind-reading reader has no proxy in the text other than Raymon, who strongly suspects that Ralph is secretly in love with Indiana. Raymon asks Indiana 'qui pourrait pénétrer sous son masque de pierre?' (who could penetrate his stone mask?) (p. 156), in a formulation that suggests that there is more to Ralph than meets the eye, and also asks Indiana to explain her cousin's character to him. It is only at the novel's conclusion, however, after the revelation to both Indiana and the reader of his secret love, that Ralph is explicitly presented as an object genuinely worthy of the interest of other characters. He is now perceived by the newly individualised and homodiegetic traveller-narrator, as by the inhabitants of the Île Bourbon, as a man with a secret, for why else would he choose to live in remote isolation? The narrator claims to have been made curious by Ralph's appearance when he first saw him, and the answers offered in response to his requests for information about him were 'si étranges, si contradictoires' (so strange, so contradictory) (p. 334) that he becomes even more intrigued. A severe glance thrown in his direc-tion by Ralph bothers him so much that he begins to dream about the Englishman. The hieroglyph-loving narrator feels a very strong 'désir de connaître sir Ralph' (desire to know Sir Ralph) (p. 336). On stumbling across his dwelling during a storm, and having been welcomed into the home of Ralph and Indiana, the narrator asks his host for 'son histoire' (his story) (p. 338). Ralph is now presented explicitly, in the text, as a worthy object of curiosity. Ralph does tell his story to the traveller-narrator in the conclusion, but it is in the previous chapter that he dramatically reveals 'le secret de [s]a vie' (the secret of his life) (p. 314) to both Indiana and the reader. By disclosing that Ralph has always loved the heroine passionately, *Indiana* does what novels often do at their climax: it gives up a secret whose revelation the novel's plot has postponed.[13] The reader who has been at least minimally alert to the clues in the text is now rewarded for her wariness. She has proven herself a competent mind-reader. Indeed, even the least suspicious reader is placed, in the conclusion, in the flattering position of knowing more about Ralph than the narrator does. Nevertheless, the conclusion of the novel leaves some questions unanswered for the most suspicious of mind-readers.

Ralph's self-revelation is a moment of 'embodied transparency'[14] to the extent that his words and gestures finally express his feelings without obstacle or blockage. Ralph suddenly makes complete sense: his appearance corresponds to his reality. This process has already begun during the voyage to the Île Bourbon, and is attributed to the character's decision to commit suicide: 'Ses paroles prirent l'empreinte de ses sentiments, et, pour la première fois, Indiana connut son véritable caractère' (His words took on the imprint of his feelings, and for the first time Indiana saw his true character) (p. 309). On the night of the planned suicide, the narrator states that Ralph's thought communicates itself to his lips for the first time: 'cette âme n'avait plus ni entraves, ni mystères; [. . .] le voile qui cachait tant de vertus, de grandeur et de puissance, tomba tout à fait, et l'esprit de cet homme s'éleva du premier bond au niveau de son cœur' (this soul had no more fetters or mysteries; [. . .] the veil that obscured so many virtues, so much greatness and power, fell completely, and the mind of this man rose with one leap to the level of his heart) (p. 312). This is a liberatory moment of unveiling and unmasking, a moment when Ralph's hairshirt ('cilice') can finally be removed. It is the culminating moment of what Barthes would refer to as a narrative striptease. Previously, Ralph was presented as an insignificant character, but now he signifies: the 'contre-sens' (error) (p. 315) that had been nature's legacy to him has resolved itself into a permanent harmony between his appearance and his feelings, so that in the conclusion the traveller-narrator describes him variously as 'souriant avec bonhomie' (smiling cheerfully) (p. 339), as showing on his face 'une expression non équivoque de hauteur et de mécontentement' (an unequivocal expression of superiority and displeasure) (p. 338) and ultimately as very far indeed from insignificant.

However, for the suspicious reader, Ralph's moment of self-revelation is in some ways just as ambiguous as those of Paquita and Julien. Firstly, the idea of radical transformation is problematic from the perspective of realist verisimilitude.[15] Certainly, a couple of the metaphors used by the narrator present Ralph's transformation in terms of naturally occuring physical processes, a device that operates to naturalise the protagonist's change of state: his personality bursts into life like a hot but dormant flame, and the altitude has an effect upon him analogous to that of electricity. However, a couple of the other metaphors used to describe Ralph's change liken it to a mystical or quasi-mystical occurrence, comparisons that suggests that the change in Ralph is resistant to rational understanding: his inspired speech is compared to an anchorite's mysterious vision and a poet's dream. Secondly, the protagonist's self-revelation is presented in contradictory terms, both as a transformation of his character and as the unveiling of his true character. The hypothesis of unveiling helps to make the change seem plausible, but is incompatible with the notion of fundamental transformation. The idea that Ralph's true character has, all along, been suppressed and dissimulated, and can now be revealed, is relatively acceptable within the logic of realist narrative, where characters regularly reveal themselves to be other than they seem. However, the hypothesis of a radical transformation, as distinct from an unveiling, is necessary to account for Ralph's previous emotional and verbal obtuseness, which was, after all, so convincing that it appeared to fool even the omniscient narrator. There is nothing particularly coherent, in other words, about the protagonist's newfound coherence.

Ralph's previous obtuseness is itself highly ambiguous; it is presented by the character himself as arising from an ambiguous combination of the disabling consequences of other people's misreading of his inner truth and a form of natural disability that prevented him, from birth, from expressing his truth:

J'étais né pour aimer; aucun de vous n'a voulu le croire, et cette méprise a décidé de mon caractère. [. . .] [La nature] avait mis sur mon visage un masque de pierre et sur ma langue un poids insurmontable; elle m'avait refusé [. . .] le pouvoir d'exprimer mes sentiments par le regard ou par la parole. Cela me fit égoïste. On jugea de l'être moral par l'enveloppe extérieure, et, comme un fruit stérile, il fallut me dessécher sous la rude écorce que je ne pouvais dépouiller. [. . .] Ma mère m'éloigna de son sein avec dégoût, parce que mon visage d'enfant ne savait pas lui rendre son sourire. (p. 315)

(I was born to love; none of you wanted to believe it, and this misunderstanding determined my character. [. . .] Nature had put on my face a mask of stone and on my tongue an insurmountable weight; it had refused me [. . .] the power to express my feelings through my eyes or through my speech. That made me selfish. The inner being was judged by the external envelope and, like a sterile fruit, I necessarily became dry under the rough husk that I could not remove. [. . .] My mother cast me from her breast with disgust, because my childish face could not return her smile.)

While a twenty-first-century reader might be tempted to use the above passage to place Ralph somewhere on the autism spectrum, his extraordinary mind-reading skills complicate this reading.[16] Further problematising any clear diagnosis of the reasons for Ralph's lack of expressiveness is the fact that, during his monologue, he claims that he deliberately assumed his disguise in order to prevent any possibility of a dangerous complicity establishing itself between him and Indiana, once he moved to Paris to be close to her. Ralph's previous lack of verbal or physical expressiveness is variously presented by him, therefore, as a natural physical disability, as imposed by other people and as a consciously chosen attitude. This explains why the protagonist's sudden eloquence is presented by Sand's text in terms capable of accounting for both a profound organic transformation and an act of self-emancipation and self-revelation. However, these explanations are not compatible with one another.

A further element that lends a certain obscurity to Ralph's moment of self-revelation is the suggestion that Ralph's feelings towards Indiana may be morally ambiguous. He denies that there ever was any impurity in his feelings for Indiana as a child, but moral ambiguity nevertheless characterises his feelings for the adult heroine: he effectively claims, in the course of his monologue, that he would not have hesitated to enslave and isolate Indiana, if she were to have presented herself to him as she had done to Raymon. Is this what he has successfully done, at the end of the novel?

It seems clear that the novel is intended to finish happily, with the triumph of freedom over domination. Indiana discovers Ralph's true nature, and the two live happily ever after in a remote part of Île Bourbon, immunised against society's tyranny, and using any money they can spare to buy slaves from their masters. However, as numerous commentators have pointed out, Indiana seems strangely dominated by Ralph in the conclusion of the novel. The eponymous heroine effectively fades into the background, while the traveller-narrator's attention is focused on Ralph, a character who had previously played a crucial but background role. This formerly uninteresting character undergoes a strange transformation of his personality, a transformation that he himself does not understand, and in the process becomes interesting and even seductive. It is the telling of his life story that changes Ralph, transforming him into a character worthy of being the hero of a novel. Eloquence, for Ralph as for Raymon, bestows power on the speaker: it seduces other characters, whether in the weak sense of inviting their sympathy (Raymon's political arguments win Delmare's acquiescence), or in the stronger, more literal sense (Raymon's rhetoric encourages Indiana to fall in love with him, while Noun's naive 'éloquence' inspires 'un moment d'amour' (a moment of love) in Raymon (p. 103)). The process is especially clear in Ralph's telling of his story: his storytelling wins him Indiana's love, and also appears designed to win the sympathy of the reader: the narrator claims that if the reader does not love Ralph after hearing him recount his life story, this is because he himself has failed to reproduce the 'puissance' (power) of the character's voice along with 'toutes les séductions molles et enivrantes d'une nuit des tropiques' (all of the gentle and intoxicating seductions of a night in the tropics) (p. 329), as the character recounts his life to the heroine. In acquiring eloquence, Ralph has arguably succeeded in seducing and dominating Indiana and in winning the reader's sympathy.

However, the explicit message of the novel until this point has been that it is important to maintain a sceptical and independent attitude with regard to the seductions of fiction, embodied for most of the duration of the text by Raymon. On one level, by uniting Indiana with Ralph, the novel tells us that prosaic, unseductive reality, as embodied by Ralph, may ultimately be preferable to, and is certainly more reliable than, the superficial excitements offered by novels. To the extent, however, that Ralph himself becomes a seductive, eloquent character, the novel complicates its own message. It suggests that we may need to be suspicious of this apparently happy ending. Unsurprisingly, then, just as Sand's three prefaces appear to contradict one another in their presentation of the message of *Indiana*, conflicting interpretations of the novel's ending have been offered. On the one hand, the conclusion indicates that happiness and freedom are to be found in turning one's back on what Ralph calls deceitful fictions, and in seeking contentment rather than passion. On the other hand, the end of the novel can be understood to suggest that complete happiness and freedom are impossible, and that fiction and lies are inescapable: false gossip finds its way to the cabin, via the narrator; it transpires that Ralph has been hiding these stories from Indiana all along. The traveller-narrator notes of Indiana, moreover, that when she smiles 'il y a encore de la mélancolie dans son regard, mais une mélancolie qui semble être la méditation du bonheur ou l'attendrissement de la reconnaissance' (there is still melancholy in her eyes, but a melancholy that seems to come from reflection upon happiness or the tenderness of gratitude) (p. 337). This seems far enough from a description of romantic bliss to raise questions about Indiana's happiness.

What lends particular ambiguity to the novel's conclusion, and what may only be visible to the reader who resists the seductions of the text and maintains a certain suspicious attitude, is that Ralph, like Delmare and like Raymon, appears to harbour a fantasy of domination with regard to Indiana. Support for this reading is present at different points in the text. For example, Ralph's insistence on accompanying Raymon out of Lagny, while Delmare is away, makes Indiana resentful of what she perceives not only as a slight on her character, but also of 'l'intention de s'arroger un pouvoir despotique sur sa conduite' (the intention to assume a despotic power over her behaviour) (p. 179). In the months after Ralph rescues her from the Paris hotel and before they find themselves in Île Bourbon, Indiana follows him around as if she is in his thrall; he appears to exercise almost complete control over her. In Ralph's long monologue, he tells the heroine that, as an adolescent ten years older than her, he considered her his personal possession and prize:

> Je fis de vous ma soeur, ma fille, ma compagne, mon élève, ma société [. . .] [V]ous étiez la jeune plante que je cultivais, le bouton que j'étais impatient de voir fleurir. [. . .] Je n'avais dans la vie qu'un bien, un espoir, une pensée, celle que vous m'apparteniez pour toujours. (pp. 316, 317, 322)

> (I made of you my sister, my daughter, my companion, my pupil, my society [. . .] You were the young plant that I cultivated, the bud that I was impatient to see flower. [. . .] I had in my life only one good, one hope, one idea, namely that you belonged to me forever.)

He admits to having felt '[une] joie cruelle' (a cruel joy) (p. 323) on first meeting Delmare, on account of his realisation that Indiana would never love her husband. Ralph even refers to his own murderous jealousy of Raymon, and his suffering at the idea that her love 'appartint à un autre' (belonged to another) (p. 325). The following passage, in which Ralph details how he would have responded had Indiana left Delmare for him, makes his proprietorial desire particularly evident:

> A sa place, je n'aurais pas été vertueux; j'aurais fui avec vous dans le sein des montagnes sauvages, je vous aurais arrachée à la société pour vous *posséder à moi seul*, et je n'aurais eu qu'une crainte, c'eût été de ne vous voir pas assez maudite, assez abandonnée, afin de vous tenir lieu de tout. J'eusse été jaloux de votre considération, mais dans un autre sens que lui; c'eût été pour la détruire, afin de la remplacer par mon amour. J'eusse souffert de voir un autre

homme vous donner une parcelle de bien-être, un instant de satisfaction, c'eût été *un vol* que l'on m'eût fait; car votre bonheur eût été ma tâche, *ma propriété*, mon existence, mon honneur! [. . .] C'est moi maintenant qui suis ton frère, ton époux, ton amant pour l'éternité. Depuis le jour où tu m'as juré de quitter la vie avec moi, j'ai nourri cette douce pensée que *tu m'appartenais*, que *tu m'étais rendue* pour ne jamais me quitter; j'ai recommencé à t'appeler tout bas ma fiancée. (pp. 327–8; my emphasis)

(In his place, I would not have been virtuous; I would have fled with you into the heart of the wild mountains, I would have torn you from society *to possess you for myself*, and I would have had only one fear, that of not seeing you accursed enough, abandoned enough, to allow me to be everything to you. I would have been jealous of your consideration, but in a different way from him; it would have been to destroy it, to replace it by my love. I would have suffered to see another man give you a morsel of well-being, a moment of satisfaction, it would have been *a theft* visited upon me; since your happiness would have been my task, *my property*, my existence, my honour! [. . .] It is I now who am your brother, your husband, your lover for eternity. Since the day you vowed to end your life with me, I have nurtured this sweet thought that *you belonged to me*, that *you had been given back to me* so as never to leave me; I started again to call you, quietly, my fiancée.)

The violence of Ralph's language in this passage is striking: he would have torn Indiana from society, would have wanted to see her utterly cursed and abandoned, would have destroyed her social reputation . . . and all so that he could have her entirely to himself. He goes on to declare that in death she will finally belong to him: 'c'est là que tu seras *mienne*, ô *mon* Indiana! [. . .] [S]i j'ai mérité d'être sauvé, j'ai mérité de *te posséder*' (it is there that you will be *mine*, oh *my* Indiana! [. . .] If I have earned my salvation, I have earned my *possession of you*) (p. 329; my emphasis). It is true that, as Peter Dayan observes, the conclusion of the novel ostensibly suggests the possibility, or at least the dream, of a world in which ownership, and particularly ownership of other people, plays no role.[17] However, it is also true that the conclusion can be read as the outcome of Ralph's fantasy of mastery over Indiana. Indeed, Aimée Boutin goes so far as to say that 'Ralph's story is predicated on female submission and silence.'[18]

Indiana thus encourages its most suspicious readers to penetrate Ralph's opaque and uninteresting mask in order to decipher his motivations and feelings, and the novel ultimately reveals these motivations and feelings to its readers. However, the novel also suggests, albeit indirectly, like *Le Rouge et le Noir* and *La Fille aux yeux d'or*, that full transparency is impossible. The readability of character is a central theme of this novel. The narrator explicitly claims, for example, to be able to deduce a man's character from knowledge of his political opinions. But the notion that other people are endlessly ambiguous is also repeatedly underscored in the course of the novel. The difference between appearances and reality is regularly emphasised: the burglar who arrives over the wall is not, in fact, a burglar; the Marquise de Carvajal, Indiana's aunt, is not as kind and virtuous as she seems; Indiana's frail physique belies her psychological strength; the friendship between Ralph and Raymon is a sham; and Ralph is far more perceptive and passionate than he seems. However, some of the ambiguity surrounding personality is more deep-rooted, and ultimately impossible to resolve. Indiana is presented by the narrator as both weak-willed and strong-willed; Delmare is a gullible brute, but can also be tender and insightful; Raymon is sincere, but also duplicitous; Ralph's alleged selfishness is indistinguishable from generosity.[19] Interestingly, too, the text not only resists any certain conclusions being drawn about Noun's racial origins,[20] it also avoids quoting her spoken and written words verbatim, opting instead for paraphrase, so that she too becomes problematically legible.

The superficially omniscient narrator himself admits, on occasion, to the limits of his own mind-reading abilities. He never fully confirms that Noun's drowning was a suicide, though admits that this episode is 'à peu près prouvé pour le lecteur et pour moi' (more or less proven for the reader and me) (p. 124). Of Delmare's feelings towards Indiana, he notes that 'il l'aimait ou il la plaignait, je ne sais lequel' (he loved her or he pitied her, I do not know which) (p. 209). Regarding the question of whether or not Ralph witnesses an intimate moment between Indiana and Raymon at the hunt, the narrator simply comments: 'Une fanfare voisine les avertit de s'observer; c'était sir Ralph qui les voyait ou ne les voyait pas' (A blast of the horn, nearby, warned them to watch out; it was Sir Ralph, who saw them or did not see them) (p. 161). The narrator speculates about the reason for Indiana's continuing attachment to a character who has proven himself unworthy: 'Peut-être ne perdit-elle jamais un reste de confiance en l'amour de Raymon' (Perhaps she never lost part of her faith in Raymon's love) (p. 251). When the heroine receives Raymon's letter three months after he sent it from Paris to Île Bourbon, the narrator highlights not only the limits of his own mind-reading capabilities but also the limits of Indiana's self-knowledge: 'Elle sentit, ou elle crut sentir qu'elle l'aimait plus que par le passé. Pour moi, je me plais à croire qu'elle ne l'aima jamais de toutes les forces de son âme' (She felt, or believed she felt, that she loved him more than in the past. For my part, I like to believe that she never loved him with all the force of her soul) (p. 274).

The narrator's own voice is problematically legible. It is not clear, for example, whether the above examples demonstrate the partial nature of his knowledge, or whether they suggest that he is disingenuously with-holding information. In either case it becomes clear, as the story goes on, that the narrator is unreliable.[21] In an externally focalised passage in the first chapter, it is impossible even in retrospect to say whether the narrator is imparting truths about the current state of the relationship between Indiana and Ralph, speculating idly on the basis of appear-ances, or deliberately misrepresenting that relationship:

> Peut-être la jeune et timide femme de M. Delmare n'avait-elle jamais encore examiné un homme avec les yeux; peut-être y avait-il, entre cette femme frêle et souffreteuse et cet homme dormeur et bien mangeant, absence de toute sympathie. (p. 51)

> (Perhaps the shy young wife of Monsieur Delmare had never before examined a man with her eyes; perhaps there was, between this frail, sickly woman and this sleepy, well-fed man, a complete absence of sympathy.)

Here, as so often elsewhere, the narrator either misinterprets or encour-ages us to misinterpret Ralph; later, for example, the latter will be described, in a possible instance of free indirect speech, as 'un Anglais passionné seulement pour la chasse du renard!' (an Englishman passion-ate only about fox hunts!) (p. 90). The ambiguity of the narratorial voice in *Indiana* is an aspect of the challenge it poses to the mind-reading, suspicious reader.

Various textual devices foster the reader's wariness of the narrator. A couple of delayed revelations early in the novel, for example, discreetly encourage the reader to pay particular attention to what the narrator shows us, as well as to what the latter tells us: the confirmation that the intruder, Raymon, is having an affair with Noun and the disclosure of the fact that Noun is pregnant both occur only after a number of textual clues, in each case, have been offered to the reader, who may consequently learn to listen for what the narrator does not tell us as much as for what he does tell us. The latter notes of Ralph, for example, that he is radi-cally lacking in the quality we might describe as empathy ('cet homme comprenait si peu le chagrin d'autrui [. . .] [I]l se hasardait rarement à s'apercevoir des afflictions de ses amis' (this man understood so little of the suffering of others. [. . .] He rarely ventured to notice his friends' afflictions) (pp. 58–9)), but the text shows us that Ralph regularly treats others with great sensitivity, for example by helping to support Raymon when the latter is overcome close to the place where Noun drowned. As early as the first chapter, it is possible to find a discreet indication, in the form of Ralph's lighting of a mood-influencing candle, that he acts as Indiana's protector. The reader is explicitly advised, again in the very first chapter, to find a hidden meaning in apparently insignificant details: 'Si quelqu'un alors eût observé de près madame Delmare, il eût pu deviner, dans cette circonstance minime et vulgaire de sa vie privée, le secret douloureux de sa vie entière' (If someone were to have observed Madame Delmare closely then, he might have detected, in this trivial and ordinary detail of her private life, the painful secret of her whole life) (p. 53). In other words, the reader's suspicion, and her mind-reading skills, are regularly solicited by this text.

The narrator's access to Ralph's thoughts and feelings appears to be particularly restricted for much of the novel.[22] It is Ralph himself who retrospectively confirms, in conversation with Madame de Ramière, that he had in fact witnessed the first kiss, at the hunt, between Indiana and Raymon, a question about which the narrator had speculated. Ralph also refers in this conversation to amorous messages previously intercepted by him in the woods, about which the narrator has mentioned nothing. Ralph reveals, furthermore, that he had actually seen his rival cross the bridge to visit Indiana, when the narrator's internal focalisation on Raymon had suggested that he had successfully eluded the former's vigilance.

These postponed revelations about Ralph, like the dramatic one that forms the novel's denouement, suggest that while his character poses problems for reading, he ultimately gives up his secrets. However, as we have seen, the end of the novel problematises the idea that full legibility, of Ralph or any other character, is achievable. The resistance of (even fictional) human beings to understanding is particularly strongly foregrounded in the novel's conclusion where, as Naomi Schor notes, 'everything about the couple bears the mark of indeterminacy', including 'Indiana's existence', 'her guilt or innocence', 'Ralph's intellect as well as his guilt or innocence'.[23] The apparently omniscient narrator has now been replaced by a traveller-narrator who offers a merely partial portrait of the private lives of Ralph and Indiana. For example, as various commentators have noted, there is no clear indication as to whether the relationship between Ralph and Indiana, in the conclusion to the novel, is a sexual one or not.[24] It is true that, in his monologue, Ralph reproaches Indiana for having treated him previously as a eunuch, but the absence of any reference to children or to a shared bedroom in the conclusion leaves the reader wondering if their relationship continues to be platonic.[25] Ralph draws a veil over their relationship, in his words to the traveller-narrator – 'Je ne vous parle pas de mon bonheur' (I shall not speak to you about my happiness) – on the pretext that there are some joys, like some sorrows, that cannot be expressed by 'une voix de la terre' (an earthly voice) (p. 341).

The limit of the traveller-narrator's understanding is in fact a theme of the final part of the novel. Towards the beginning of the conclusion, the traveller-narrator writes about how, at the moment that a fateful storm descended on the Île Bourbon, he was meditating on the 'impressions hiéroglyphiques' (hieroglyphic imprints), like '[des] lettres cabalistiques' (cabbalistic letters), inscribed by nature on the volcanic stone: 'Je restai longtemps dominé par la puerile pretention de chercher un sens à ces chiffres inconnus' (I remained a long time dominated by the childish aspiration to find the meaning of these unknown figures) (p. 333). This episode prepares, not least by its use of some of the same or similar words,[26] the narrator's subsequent description of his first encounter with Ralph Brown about a year previous, including the contradictory accounts received in response to his requests for information. He learns that 'un odieux soupçon' (an odious suspicion) (p. 335) continues to hang over Ralph and Indiana, because of the incriminating circumstances of Indiana's previous flight from the island, and the failure of the legal system to put the two on trial. The narrator claims that he initially interpreted, apparently unproblematically, the expression on Ralph's face: 'j'aurais juré [. . .] que son cœur et ses mains étaient purs comme son front' (I would have sworn [. . .] that his heart and his hands were as pure as his brow) (p. 336). However, when the man he studies with 'une avide et indiscrète curiosité' (an avid and indiscreet curiosity) suddenly returns his gaze, the narrator goes on to wonder if Ralph might in fact be capable of dark crimes: 'La transparence cristalline de ses yeux me glaçait de crainte. Il devait y avoir chez cet homme une telle supériorité de vertu ou de scélératesse, que je me sentais tout médiocre et tout petit devant lui' (The crystalline transparency of his eyes filled me with fear. There seemed to be, in this man, such superior virtue or villainy that I felt completely mediocre and small before him) (p. 336). The narrator's sense of being reduced to nothing by Ralph's transparent but somehow inscrutable gaze recalls his previous sense of awe before the ambiguously signifying but ultimately indecipherable rockface.

When the narrator finally asks Ralph to tell his story, the latter admits that he does not know what prevented him from jumping to his death, with Indiana in his arms, on the night of their planned suicide. As already indicated by our analysis of Raymon's bad faith, a character who does not understand his own motivations is unlikely ever to be fully readable by others. In short, the novel encourages readers to engage in mind-reading exercises that never do lead to full disclosure.

Mind-Reading, Affective Sharing and Their Consequences in *Indiana*

The ability or failure accurately to decipher the words and expressions of other people is a key theme of *Indiana*. As Lauren Pinzka puts it of the text, 'The reader is constantly confronted with references to things either hidden or buried [. . .]; the impossible desire of penetrating another's thoughts and secrets.'[27] As in *Le Rouge et le Noir*, the more skilled a mind-reader each character is, the more power she appears to wield over other characters.

Delmare is a successful, self-made industrialist on the one hand, but he is also unhappily married, and dies as an exiled bankrupt. He is occasionally good at deducing the truth about other people's intentions: he is correct, for example, to suspect Raymon of amorous intentions when he discovers him entering the grounds of Lagny, and correctly discerns the nature of the relationship between Raymon and Noun when he spies on them from behind a curtain. Indiana, moreover, describes him as 'si clairvoyant' (so clairvoyant) (p. 90) and believes, mistakenly as it turns out, that 'il lui serait impossible de tromper son mari s'il la voyait en présence de Raymon' (it would be impossible for her to deceive her husband if he were to see her in Raymon's presence) (p. 118). The narrator, however, calls Delmare a man 'sans esprit, sans tact et sans éducation' (devoid of wit, tact and education) (p. 132), and gently mocks his misinterpretation of Rayon's motivations in visiting his sickbed. Delmare's mind-reading skills are, at best, adequate, as are his personal outcomes in the storyworld of the novel.

Noun, surely the least powerful character of *Indiana*, is a poor reader of other characters' motivations. She mistakenly decides, on the basis of Raymon's prompt response to a letter from her, that he still loves her, and subsequently fails to infer the reason for his particular interest in discussing Indiana with her.[28] In conversation with Raymon, she may be alert to her lover's 'air froid et mécontent' (cold and discontented air), but she misunderstands an allusion he makes to Indiana (p. 102). The poverty of Noun's mind-reading skills is compounded by her general lack of education: she can barely write intelligibly, and is ignorant about the world.[29] Her naivety permits her manipulation by Raymon, and therefore plays a contributing role in her early suicide.

Indiana too has less than excellent mind-reading skills. As already seen, she rarely thinks to question Raymon's account of his own motivations, including the reason why he was intruding on the grounds of Lagny, upon first entering her life. Later, we read that Noun's secret pregnancy 'devenait impossible à cacher' (was becoming impossible to hide), and yet Indiana manages to remain oblivious to the cause of her maid's suffering: 'madame Delmare s'apercevait de cet état maladif sans en pénétrer la cause' (Madame Delmare noticed this sickly state without detecting its cause) (p. 98). When she observes, on returning unannounced from a stay in Paris, that a fire is lit in her bedroom, she asks Noun how she knew to prepare it, but does not wait for an answer (she never suspects that her maid might have been entertaining someone in that room). In evoking Raymon's part in Noun's death, Indiana does not understand that his visible distress betrays the fact that he played a far greater role than she realises; she misinterprets the meaning of his tears, thinking them proof of his goodness rather than a sign of his guilt. After Ralph tells Indiana of Raymon's affair with Noun, the narrator explains the heroine's resentment towards the Englishman by reference to her inadequate understanding of either his feelings or those of his rival: 'Indiana ne pouvait pas lire au fond de son cœur, elle n'avait pu pénétrer celui de Raymon. Elle était injuste, non point par ingratitude, mais par ignorance' (Indiana could not read to the bottom of his heart, she had not been able to understand Raymon's. She was unjust, not from ingratitude, but from ignorance) (p. 189). The heroine fails, furthermore, to discern the disingenuousness of Raymon's pledge to love her platonically henceforth. For most of the novel, Indiana is in thrall to her feelings for Raymon, and at various points only narrowly avoids those feelings leading to her death: Ralph rescues her as she appears about to copy Noun's suicide, and then again later as she languishes in her hotel bedroom; later, he mysteriously falters just as he is about to leap to his death, with her in his arms.

Indiana does have some incisive intuitions, however, about other people's intentions and motivations: she is alert, for example, to Raymon's reasons for bringing his mother on a visit to Lagny. Despite her general ignorance, the narrator tells us that 'dans toutes les crises de sa vie, elle conservait une grande netteté de jugement, une grande force d'esprit' (in all the crises of her life, she preserved a great accuracy of judgement, a great strength of spirit) (p. 190). In the episode where she observes Raymon's reactions to a bundle of Noun's hair, which she pretends to have cut from her own head, 'un éclat pénétrant' (a perceptive gleam) shines from her eyes (p. 191). When she presents herself to Raymon, in his bedroom, having left Delmare, she suddenly sees him for what he is: 'Un rayon de lumière vint enfin éclairer Indiana et lui montrer à nu l'âme de Raymon' (A ray of light finally came to enlighten Indiana and lay bare for her Raymon's soul) (p. 222). At other moments of crisis, the heroine places her instinctual trust in Ralph, as for example when she breaks away from Raymon in her bedroom, or when he warns her that Delmare has returned unexpectedly to Lagny, or when he brings her home from the river's edge on the morning after she has run away from her husband.

Indiana's moments of insight tend, however, to be sporadic only. At the end of the novel, Ralph calls her an 'injuste et aveugle femme' (unjust and blind woman) (p. 325), because she did not recognise his efforts to protect her within her own home, and reproaches her for never having realised that the early death of his son continues to be a source of intense pain for him. Furthermore, until she acquires definitive understanding, thanks to external events, of the very different characters of the two male protagonists, the heroine is unable or unwilling to confront 'la sèche vérité' (the harsh truth) (p. 251) in any lasting way, and to take action accordingly. The decisions she makes, such as her attempts to avoid Raymon and her escape from Delmare in Paris, either lead nowhere or are dictated by others: even her dramatic flight from Île Bourbon is a programmed effect of Raymon's manipulations, while her final suicide attempt is suggested to her, and subsequently choreographed with great precision, by Ralph. Indiana's mind-reading skills may be sufficient to enable clear judgement in moments of crisis, but they are not sufficient to confer social power on her. As the narrator tells us, 'Indiana n'avait pas d'*usage*; elle ne possédait ni l'habileté ni la dissimulation nécessaires pour conserver l'avantage de sa position' (Indiana lacked *know-how*; she possessed neither the skilfulness nor the power of dissimulation necessary to maintain the advantage of her position) (p. 144).

Raymon, by contrast, is one of the most socially successful characters in the novel, and he is also one of the text's most gifted readers of other characters' thoughts and feelings. The reader of the novel is regularly privy to his readings of other people's facial expressions. For example, upon visiting the apartment of Indiana's aunt, he interprets the faces of the women who play cards: 'sur leurs traits rigides, Raymon croyait lire la secrète satisfaction de la vieillesse, qui se venge en réprimant les plai-sirs des autres' (on their rigid features, Raymon thought he could read the secret smugness of old age, which avenges itself by restricting the pleasures of others) (p. 87). When Noun reprimands him for unveiling and asking questions about a portrait that hangs in Indiana's bedroom, her tone may well be playful but her words are telling: 'ce n'est pas bien de vouloir pénétrer les secrets de ma maîtresse' (it is not good to want to find out my mistress's secrets) (p. 107). Later, in the company of Ralph and Indiana, 'Il éprouva un violent sentiment de dépit en voyant l'affection simple et confiante de ces gens-là' (He felt a violent sense of spite upon seeing the simple, trusting affection of those people) (p. 154).

Raymon is the only character who is explicitly presented as suspecting that there is more to Ralph than meets the eye. Noticing the 'nuance imperceptible de surprise et de plaisir' (imperceptible nuance of surprise and pleasure) on Ralph's face as he takes Indiana's pulse, and his subsequent attentiveness to the heroine, 'Raymon s'efforça vainement de chercher s'il y avait de la crainte ou de l'espoir dans ses pensées; Ralph fut impénétrable' (Raymon vainly tried to work out if there was fear or hope in his thoughts; but Ralph was impenetrable) (p. 151). Despite such occasional limits to his omniscience, Raymon is so astute a mind-reader that his perceptions are often indistinguishable from those of the narrator, as in the episode just cited, where internal focalisation and the perspective of the omniscient narrator appear to merge with one another. Similarly, Raymon's conclusions are often indistinguishable from those of the observant reader. For example, in the passage just referred to, the careful (or second-time) reader will deduce from the textual evidence, just as Raymon can be presumed to deduce (at least in part) from Ralph's physical manifestation of surprise and pleasure, that the latter has noticed an improvement in Indiana's usually poor health, and that while this improvement gives him considerable hope, he also fears the cause of this improvement. Raymon is certainly perspicacious enough to suspect, alongside the watchful, suspicious reader, that Ralph has feelings for Indiana, going on for example to observe his host's attempts to keep them apart, asking Indiana for her thoughts on the matter, and being the only character to note Ralph's dramatic response to the false rumour that Indiana has suffered a fatal accident at the hunt, and the reason for that response: 'Raymon, qui, dans cet instant de trouble et de délire, avait seul conservé assez de raison pour comprendre ce qu'il voyait, avait pu juger quelle était l'affection de Ralph pour sa cousine' (Raymon, who in that moment of confusion and delirium was alone in maintaining enough reason to understand what he saw, had been able to judge the nature of Ralph's affection for his cousin) (p. 164).

Raymon also regularly reads Indiana's body language accurately, understanding the extent of his power over her by the colour of her cheeks and the swelling of her chest. He even appears to intuit the fundamental facts about her life, telling her he knows her entire life story, speaking to her about Delmare's treatment of her, and even suggesting that he knows her future: 'je sais tous les secrets de votre destinée, et vous ne pouvez pas espérer vous cacher de moi' (I know all the secrets of your destiny, and you cannot hope to hide yourself from me) (p. 94). In addition, Raymon divines Indiana's former dream that a 'libérateur' (liberator) (p. 89) would one day come and rescue her from her cruel father; he tells her that when she dreamed of a friend and a saviour, she was in fact dreaming of him. Raymon goes so far as to claim retrospectively to have divined everything about Indiana during their first conversation: 'N'ai-je pas lu toute l'histoire de votre cœur dans le premier de vos regards qui vint tomber sur moi?' (Did I not read the entire history of your heart in the first of the looks that you let fall upon me?) (p. 148).

Raymon's skill at divining the thoughts and feelings of others means that he is also very capable of manipulating others. In his seduction of Indiana, he consistently appeals, for example, to her philanthropic sense, depicting her as his saviour: 'toi, mon bon ange, tu planais sur moi, et tes ailes m'ont protégé' (you, my good angel, you hovered over me, and your wings protected me) (p. 96). When she tells him that he has 'bien de l'esprit' (great wit), after an evening of conversation with Ralph's house guests, Raymon understands the reproach hidden in the compliment, and spends the entire next day paying attention to her. This ability to interpret others means that Raymon knows what to say to Noun, when he is surprised by the latter in Indiana's company in Paris, in order to maintain her trust. He even thinks himself capable of fooling both Indiana and Noun when the former discovers him in her bedroom; in the end, Indiana inadvertently reveals crucial information to Noun, so that he succeeds in deceiving only one of the two heroines as to his relationship with the other. When he sees Indiana alone for the first time after Noun's death, he quickly calculates, on the basis of her weakened appearance, the best approach to adopt in order to seduce her: he will affect and express sadness about her poor health in order to inspire first her fear and then her hope for a better future. The ruse has the desired effect, in that Indiana is caught off guard by encountering generous solicitude where she had expected to find a sense of guilt.

It is not just Raymon's love life that is facilitated by his highly developed mind-reading skills. The great power that the character knows how to wield on the social and political stage is also linked to his ability to read other people. As the Restoration enters its last days, Raymon realises that his fortune is likely to change imminently: he knows that people are on the point of rebelling against the government that he has heretofore supported. In order to ensure his own social survival and not become a politically blind 'dupe', he cultivates alliances with anti-monarchists to complement his existing monarchist alliances. Raymon's marriage to the noble-born adoptive daughter of a rich industrialist is calculated to ensure the continuation of his social power. Unfortunately for him, his new wife is an even more capable mind-reader than he, and knows how to use her 'regard pénétrant' (perceptive gaze) (p. 287), her 'bon sens' (common sense) and her 'connaissance du monde actuel' (knowledge of current society) (p. 290) to ensure her continuing power over him.

Laure's mind-reading skills give her a distinct tactical advantage over her husband, ensuring that she never falls under his sway: 'elle le connaissait trop pour l'aimer' (she knew him too well to love him) (p. 290). Laure is also, interestingly, presented as knowledgeable about fiction and art: when we first meet her, she categorises her future husband as a character from Samuel Richardson's *Clarissa*, as we have seen, and on her first interview with him she mocks the 'ridicules fictions' (ridiculous fictions) (p. 286) of eighteenth-century pastoral painting.

As Laure's interpretive superiority suggests, Raymon is not quite as omniscient as he sometimes appears. There are instances when Raymon needs to correct his own initial misreading of Indiana's character, feelings or intentions. For example, when he sees her on horseback he suddenly understands that she is possessed of a far more formidable character than he had initially realised; during a period of illness and reflection, he realises that her love for him was genuine: 'Je l'ai mal jugée, pensa-t-il' (I judged her poorly, he thought) (p. 264); and in one episode he misreads her so badly that she tricks him into revealing that he had an affair with Noun. However, these misreadings are merely provisional. More significantly and more profoundly, we are informed at various points in the text that Raymon never arrives at a full understanding of Indiana's character. After the would-be seducer interprets Indiana's resistance to his sexual designs as proof that she does not love him, and that 'son coeur est sec, son caractère hautain' (her heart is sterile, her character haughty), the narrator tells us that Raymon had never understood her (p. 200). Ralph confirms Raymon's misreading of Indiana in the course of his long dramatic monologue in the final chapter: 'Il ne vous a pas comprise' (He did not understand you) (p. 327).

As the accuracy of this intuition suggests, Ralph himself is presented as a highly expert mind-reader. Christopher Bains observes that the character 'demonstrates narrator-like omniscience and remains a master character interpreter as he mysteriously seems to know the motivations and actions of others'.[30] Interestingly, however, Ralph's mind-reading expertise does not result in his social success; indeed, it is arguably the result of his social deficiencies. The narrator tells us that Ralph is an astute reader of his own heart and mind, on account of his long social isolation, during which, the narrator tells us, 'il avait appris à se connaî- tre lui-même' (he had learned to know himself) (p. 177); later, the nar- rator observes that '[il] consultait jour par jour le livre de sa conscience' (he consulted day by day the book of his conscience) (p. 313). There are hints throughout the text that Ralph is also highly perceptive with regard to other characters. In the second chapter, he attempts to reassure Indiana about her husband's nature; when she asks who has told him that she has any misgivings on the subject, he responds by telling her that she has, 'sans le vouloir' (without wishing it), through her body language: her sadness, her sickliness and her perpetually red eyes (p. 57). Indiana responds by saying that she never gave him permission to 'savoir tant de choses' (know so many things) (p. 57). Ralph also very quickly deduces, in the course of the third chapter of the novel, the real reason for Raymon's clandestine entry into Lagny, piecing together clues such as Noun's presence in the garden when he had gone looking for help for Indiana, her damp hair and muddy shoes, her behaviour when he found her and her cry when she subsequently heard a shot being fired. The narrator tells us, later in the story, that Ralph is very alert to the various twists and turns in the relationship between Indiana and Raymon, knowing even when the latter has planned to return to her bedroom: 'C'était un homme à qui rien n'échappait, parce qu'il observait tout avec sang-froid' (He was a man from whom nothing escaped, because he observed everything with sang-froid) (p. 182). Ralph warns the two of Delmare's imminent arrival when they are about to be discovered, and not only guesses, later, that Indiana has gone to Raymon's home when she goes missing, but also that she has made her way from there to the river, in memory of Noun. Later, he manages to find her after she has gone missing once more, and is once again close to death, this time in a Paris hotel.

Indeed, from a very early stage in the relationship between Indiana and Raymon, Ralph appears to suspect their feelings for one another: this is suggested by the trace of fear that Raymon detects in Ralph's features, and by the latter's efforts to keep the would-be lovers apart at the hunt. It is in the midst of these covert efforts that Ralph intercepts, and apparently draws the correct meaning from, an exchange of glances between Raymon and Indiana. Ralph proceeds to purchase Raymon's horse, in an effort to prevent him from riding with Indiana. She misreads the gesture, but in the process alludes entirely fittingly to her cousin's perspicacity: 'Il semble que ce bon Ralph a deviné le présent qui pouvait m'être le plus précieux' (It seems that the good Ralph has guessed the present likely to be most precious to me) (p. 154).

Raymon attempts to portray the gift of his horse to Indiana as self-interested; he describes it as a means for Ralph simultaneously to please Indiana and humiliate him, but is convinced that he must have devised this scheme 'à son insu' (inadvertently), not being capable of such genius (p. 155). However, if Raymon uses his considerable mind-reading skills for personal gain, Ralph does not generally do so. For example, instead of adroitly using his intuitions about Indiana's marriage to win her for himself, he irritates her by speaking 'à bonne intention' (with good intentions) to her husband, and by discussing the latter's concerns with her (p. 57). Despite the Englishman's perspicacious reading of Raymon's character, the narrator tells us that Ralph is too compassionate a character to tell anyone of his 'soupçons' (suspicions) about the young noble's role in Noun's death (p. 125). When Ralph does finally tell Indiana about Raymon's affair with Noun, and therefore indirectly about his rival's role in the servant's death, he does so with the aim of helping Indiana to protect herself from her seducer, and not for self-interested reasons. Ralph, despite his reputed selfishness, does not in fact deploy his mind-reading skills for selfish purposes.

The opposition between selfishness and compassion is in fact a recurring theme in *Indiana*, not least because the denouement reveals the apparent selflessness of a character previously presented and even labelled as an *égoïste*. While the figure of Ralph represents a special case, to which we will return, the selfish–generous opposition broadly maps onto an antithesis, in this novel, between mind-reading skills and resistance to seduction on the one hand, and on the other hand, affective sharing and openness to seduction. At its most basic level, Sand's novel suggests that generous characters such as Indiana and Noun, endowed with poor mind-reading skills, are open to manipulation by others, while more selfish characters such as Raymon and Laure, with highly developed mind-reading skills, are more likely to manipulate others.

On account of their shared susceptibility to Raymon's charms, Indiana and Noun can be understood figuratively to embody the naively credulous reader who allows herself to be seduced and manipulated by a fiction. They are also, as it happens, represented in the text as empathetic and generous characters. We have already cited, in an earlier section, Indiana's memory of Noun's ability to detect her suffering and alleviate it, and Noun is also explicitly described by the narrator as 'généreuse' (generous) (p. 98); the same word is applied by the narrator to Indiana (p. 289), who is also represented as possessing a certain capacity for affective empathy; the narrator refers to her as 'cette âme impressionnable' (this impressionable soul) (p. 59). The narrator recounts Indiana's frustrated desire to help the slaves among whom she spent her childhood, and for whom she felt 'compassion', and evokes her resulting philanthropic ambition: 'Un jour viendra où [. . .] je ferai du bien aux autres' (A day will come when [. . .] I will do good for others) (p. 89). The pregnant Noun describes Indiana as 'bonne' (good): 'c'est la seule personne au monde qui prendra pitié de moi!' (she is the only person in the world who will feel pity for me!) (p. 111). The heroine cannot help but feel '[un] prompt mouvement de douceur et de générosité' (a swift movement of gentleness and generosity) towards Raymon, who

inspires in her a certain 'tendresse involontaire' (involuntary tenderness) (pp. 145–6). The narrator tells us, furthermore, that, despite her
ambivalent feelings towards her husband, Indiana is both 'profondément affectée du malheur de ce mari' (deeply affected by the misfortune
of that husband) (p. 164), and extremely generous towards him during
his convalescence after his hunting accident. Even as she prepares to
leave him for the last time, she feels an inconvenient compassion for
her husband. Raymon knows that Indiana would offer him 'le bonheur
d'une affection pure et généreuse' (the happiness of a pure and generous
affection) (p. 266), while Ralph, at least as perspicacious as Raymon,
describes her as 'toujours bonne et miséricordieuse' (always kind and
merciful) (p. 324) and as 'un être [. . .] généreux' (a generous [. . .]
being) (p. 325). The narrator tells us that Indiana feels 'une sympathie
invincible' (an invincible sympathy) for Noun (p. 308), and listening
to Ralph tell his life story she feels 'une ardente sympathie religieuse'
(a passionate and religious sympathy) (pp. 313–14) for him; her face is
'baigné de larmes' and full of 'pitié' for him (p. 327). Further suggestive
of both her empathetic disposition and her generous inclinations is the
fact that the heroine feels, like Ralph, an instinctive liking and admiration for Raymon's generous mother. The narrator refers to Indiana's
'besoin de s'attacher à quelqu'un' (need to become attached to someone)
and to the 'sorte de fascination de cœur' (sort of fascination of the heart)
(p. 141) that she feels for Raymon's mother; soon, 'Indiana s'attacha à
la mère de Raymon avec enthousiasme et passion' (Indiana became passionately and enthusiastically attached to Raymon's mother) (p. 165).
Indiana's readiness to open herself to Raymon's mother is associated
by the text with her generous sensibility, which is admirably responsive
to the generosity of another character; this same sensibility is, however,
also responsible for her openness to Raymon's seductions.

If Sand's text suggests analogies between a susceptibility to seduction
by illusions, or affective sharing, and an altruistic disposition, it also
hints that this susceptibility and this disposition are linked to weak
mind-reading skills. Does this mean that the text suggests that mind-
reading, presented as important for social survival, is incompatible with
affective empathy and generosity? Certainly, Laure de Nangy, one of
the shrewdest mind-readers of the novel, appears entirely devoid of
either quality. She is 'moins généreuse que madame Delmare, mais plus
adroite, froide et flatteuse, orgueilleuse et prévenante' (less generous
than Madame Delmare, but more adroit: cold yet flattering, proud yet
attentive) (p. 290). When Laure sees Indiana on her knees in her former
bedroom at Lagny, her mind-reading skills allow her immediately to
understand the situation, but she shows no empathy or generosity

towards her defeated rival. As the narrator puts it elsewhere, in connection with Raymon, 'Rien ne nous confirme dans l'égoïsme comme la réflexion' (Nothing so confirms us in our selfishness as much as reflection) (p. 262). Despite her perspicuity, then, the text does not present the dispassionate Laure, described as 'calme et philosophe' (calm and philosophical), as any kind of ideal reader. Her lack of sensibility is not presented as admirable but as a form of evasion, an avoidance of emotion: 'elle eût rougi d'une déception comme d'une sottise; elle faisait, en un mot, consister son héroïsme à échapper à l'amour, comme madame Delmare mettait le sien à s'y livrer' (she would have blushed at being deceived as at being stupid; she made, in a word, her heroism consist in eluding love, as Madame Delmare made hers consist of abandoning herself to love) (p. 290).

Raymon is gifted at reading others, and is even capable of a susceptibility to seduction and an affective responsiveness that occasionally seem to align him with generous characters such as Noun and Indiana. However, he is profoundly selfish. The narrator tells us that '[à] force de générosité, [sa mère] n'avait réussi qu'à former un coeur égoïste' (his mother's great generosity had enabled her merely to nurture a selfish heart) (p. 223). To the extent that Raymon has a capacity for empathy, both affective and cognitive, this is instrumental only, just as his openness to seduction is ultimately self-serving; the narrator suggests repeatedly that he is drawn to Indiana for purely selfish reasons: 'il se mit à penser à Indiana, et il la regretta sincèrement, car alors elle lui eût été nécessaire' (he began to think of Indiana, and he regretted her sincerely, as at that moment she would have been very useful to him) (p. 262). This most selfish of characters may be capable of great empathy, but ultimately his treatment of other people is selfish; similarly, as his relationships with both Noun and Indiana show, once he starts to tire of his love objects, he abandons them.

The examples of Noun and Indiana suggest that affective empathy and generosity are closely linked, while the examples of Laure and Raymon suggest a strong connection between well-developed mind-reading skills and selfishness, a connection that in Raymon's case can override his affective empathy. However, *Indiana* also complicates any easy binary between affective empathy and generosity on the one side, and supposedly selfish mind-reading on the other. It shows, in the person of Ralph, that a character can be both a mind-reader who is associated with selfishness, and capable of great affective empathy and generosity. When he tells Indiana of Raymon's affair with Noun, 'il ne songeait plus qu'au mal qu'il venait de faire à la personne qu'il aimait le mieux au monde; il sentit son coeur se briser' (he no longer thought of anything but the harm that he had just done to the person he loved most in the world; he felt his heart break) (p. 184); when he finds her distressed and hallucinating on the banks of the Seine, 'lui aussi sentait sa tête se briser et son cerveau se fendre' (he too felt as if his mind were broken and his brain torn apart) (p. 228); as he observes the difficult scene that ensues between Indiana and Delmare, he feels 'plus malheureux de leurs chagrins qu'elles-mêmes' (more miserable about their sorrows than they themselves) (p. 231). He speaks of how Indiana's suffering made him forget his own jealousy of Raymon: 'vos maux furent si grands, que j'oubliai les miens [. . .] [J]e fus si insensé, si misérable de vous voir souffrir' (your troubles were so great that I forgot my own [. . .] I was so distressed, so miserable to see you suffer) (p. 326).[31] Ralph is also susceptible to narrative empathy, as already suggested: he talks in his pre-suicide monologue of how he had 'frissonné de sympathie' (shivered with sympathy) when reading *Paul et Virginie* (p. 318).

Madame de Ramière, too, is an excellent mind-reader, capable even of recognising her son's flaws, while also being generous and vulnerable to being charmed by others: the narrator refers, for example, to 'la sensibilité profonde et vraie de son coeur' (the deep and true sensibility of her heart), which makes her open her arms to Indiana (p. 225). Indeed, two of the most generous characters of *Indiana*, Ralph and Raymon's mother, are arguably also its most expert mind-readers, as suggested by their immediate understanding of the other's good intentions:

> Quelques mots suffirent entre eux pour comprendre la part mutuelle d'intérêt sincère et pur qu'ils avaient dans cette affaire. [. . .] Ralph, qui se sentait plus à l'aise devant elle qu'il ne l'était vis-à-vis de personne, laissa paraître sur ses traits une altération profonde. (p. 236)

> (A few words sufficed between them to understand that they shared a sincere and selfless interest in this matter. [. . .] Ralph, who felt more comfortable with her than he had ever felt with anyone, let a profound change appear upon his face.)

The examples of Ralph and Madame de Ramière suggest, then, that high levels of affective empathy and generosity can coexist with well-developed mind-reading skills, though this coexistence is far from given, as the examples of Noun, Indiana, Raymon and Laure indicate.

Mind-reading skills and affective sharing are sometimes shown to work at cross-purposes in *Indiana*, and are sometimes presented as compatible. One of the two stances can be prioritised over the other, as the extreme examples of Noun and Laure suggest: Noun is utterly seduced by, and trusting of, the stranger figure that is Raymon, while Laure, as a perspicacious mind-reader, is not at all seduced by him. Mind-reading and affective sharing can also be combined in a thoroughly self-serving way, as exemplified by the character of Raymon, who is deeply empathetic but ultimately ungenerous. As suggested, however, by the alternative examples of Ralph and Madame de Ramière, and even Indiana herself, the two dimensions of empathy can also be combined in a way that reconciles selfishness and generosity, affording important protections to the self while nevertheless permitting openness to others. This combination may involve moral ambiguity, as the case of Ralph most obviously suggests, but it may also be the only viable way of reconciling social survival with moral imperatives, just as island life represents, for Ralph, an imperfect but necessary accommodation. I would argue that *Indiana*, like the previous two novels analysed, actively engages the reader's capacity for affective sharing as well as her mind-reading skills, her openness to seduction as well as her critical suspicion, encouraging her not to privilege one attitude over the other, but to bring the two into a creative and ethical dialogue with each other.

The Ambiguity of *Indiana*

Indiana, as many commentators have noted, can be interpreted either as upholding or as challenging a conservative order of ideas. While the novel has often been read, particularly in recent decades, as a story about self-emancipation from oppressively fixed, socially determined identities, it can also be read in the other direction, as a defence of the naturalness of gender and even racial hierarchies. While the novel explicitly subverts gender hierarchies and critiques the barbarity of a system that effectively makes wives the slaves of their husbands, Indiana nevertheless continues in the conclusion to defer to a male, appearing far less worthy of the narrator's interest than her male companion.[32] As Harkness points out, the reactionary dimension of the novel does not come out of the blue: the reader's 'acquiescence in an ideology of gender [is] constantly solicited' in the novel, through the male narrator's regular appeals to the complicity of a male narratee.[33] Similarly, *Indiana* can be understood to challenge racial hierarchies through its critique of literal and metaphorical slavery and, more subtly, through its construction of various parallels between Indiana and Noun (who is probably dark-skinned) and Indiana (who is white-skinned), for example by means of the ambiguous term 'créole' (creole) that is applied to both.[34] However, Indiana appears to have no difficulty in treating her 'sœur de lait' (milk sister) and alleged friend, Noun, as her inferior; and while Ralph makes a reference in the conclusion to how the 'serviteurs' (servants) employed by him and Indiana are also his 'amis' (friends), the narrator makes no reference to the presence of these individuals, presumably former slaves, in the 'chaumière indienne' (Indian cabin) (pp. 342, 344); why are they passed over in silence by the narrator, who after all spends over a week with his hosts, if not because they are seen by the author, and her delegate, as somehow unworthy of attention?[35] Much as Sand's prefaces alternate equivocally between assertions and denials of subversive intent – with the preface of 1842 even suggesting that she had tried, in her novel, to strike a difficult balance between conservatism and progress – the novel lends itself to diametrically opposed readings. It overtly challenges received wisdom about gender and race but it also bolsters conventional categories. The task of the reader, I would argue, and as suggested by the novel's own plot, is to resist acquiescing entirely in either interpretation and to recognise, if not 'the free play of value systems',[36] at least the manner in which different value systems pull against one another within the novel, each potentially drawing the reader uncritically along with it.

Kathrin Bonin suggests that the openness of Sand's novel to 'multiple, opposing readings' militates against reader's 'sympathy'. 'Sympathy and irony', for Bonin, 'are incompatible', because without 'narrative transparency' there can be no 'instant recognition of indisputable truths'.[37] However, this is to underestimate both sympathy and irony, as sympathy can be intensified by a sense of ironic complicity.[38] While the kind of ironic detachment embodied by the unsympathetic Laure de Nangy is certainly not held up by the novel as a model to which the reader should aspire, the novel does encourage suspicion on the part of the reader, whether that suspicion is directed at the character of Raymon, as its most obvious target, at the narrator or at the character of Ralph. These fictional entities also, however, solicit the reader's sympathy or complicity. Ultimately, this chapter has suggested that a degree of suspicion is presented as indispensable for the reader of *Indiana*; even the naive eponymous heroine, after all, manages to maintain a minimal critical distance from Raymon's political and amorous narratives. Malkin notes that the novel's various 'metanarrative intrusions, as well as each edition's preface, indicate that, while wishing to entertain, Sand also hoped to create the opportunity for readers to maintain a certain distance from the story', in order to 'allow them to actively engage with the issues' raised by the novel.[39] Whether or not Sand consciously intended to offer readers this opportunity, as Malkin suggests, these conclusions are entirely compatible with the argument of this chapter, namely that *Indiana* both thematises and dramatises the operation and intrication of seduction and suspicion, sympathy and irony, affective sharing and mind-reading.

This analysis of *Indiana* began by proposing that the novel warns us, mainly through the fiction-associated stranger figure that is Raymon, to suspect the seductive illusions of fiction, including the illusion of authority established by Sand's narrator, and therefore to resist uncritical narrative empathy or affective sharing. It went on to suggest that the novel encourages us, principally through the fiction-associated figure of Ralph, both to deploy our mind-reading skills and to acknowledge the limits of those skills. In its final section, this chapter argued that Sand's novel, while it clearly argues for the social and practical importance of suspicion as a means of resisting seduction, also reveals suspicion and seduction to be capable of coexisting; and to the extent that this combination of attitudes is sometimes associated with generosity, the novel even hints that it may have ethical ramifications. In conclusion, the novel problematises any fixed hierarchical opposition between naive and critical reading practices, suggesting that a combination of openness to seduction and suspicion militates against the potential dangers of the former and the potential odiousness of the latter.

Notes

1. Naomi Schor reads *Indiana* as a novel that bears the traces of 'the difficult emergence of Sandian idealism from the matrix of Balzacian realism', highlighting 'the controversial epilogue that so spectacularly exceeds the bounds of bourgeois realism' and the author's deletion, after the first edition of the novel, of numerous narratorial interventions that had been designed to signal the novel's adherence to the aesthetic that would become known as realism. *George Sand and Idealism*, p. 52. See also the analysis of *Indiana* in Prasad, 'Contesting Realism', and the first chapter of Mathias, *Vision* for a thoughtful examination of the place of realism in *Indiana*.
2. Indeed, Sand reported that when Henri de Latouche initially perused the novel, 'on every page he cried out: "Come on! This is a pastiche from the school of Balzac!" He changed his mind the next day, deciding instead that 'Balzac and Mérimée are buried by *Indiana*.' Cited by Béatrice Didier in her notes to Sand, *Indiana*, p. 358. This edition will be cited, alongside my translations, henceforth in this chapter.
3. See Prasad, 'Intimate Strangers', pp. 7–12.
4. See Chapter 3, note 61.
5. Indiana is repeatedly associated with variants of the word 'naïf' (pp. 174, 178), 'ingénu' (ingenuous) (pp. 71, 174, 181, 195) and 'ignorant' (pp. 83, 90, 174, 218, 273, 337). Noun too is associated with variants of the word 'naïf' (pp. 99, 126), and her mind is described by the narrator as 'ignorant et vierge' (ignorant and virginal) (p. 103).
6. Waller, 'Ending with *Indiana*', p. 192.
7. For further references to Raymon's desire to possess Indiana, see also pp. 154, 194, 197, 220, 221.

8. Malkin, 'Performing Sand's Pedagogical Project in *Indiana*', p. 176.
9. Harkness, *Men of Their Words*, p. 34. Harkness notes that Ralph's 'inaptitude', which eventually reveals itself to extend to his native language, is characteristic of a number of Sand's male anglophone 'outsiders', '"foreign bodies" [who] represent the "outside" of hegemonic masculinity' (pp. 34, 35).
10. Stivale, 'One or Several Ralphs', p. 118.
11. On fairy-tale elements in *Indiana* more generally, see Vest, 'Dreams'. This kind of transformation is typical, too, of twentieth-century romance fiction. Radway refers to 'the hole in the romance's explanatory logic with respect to the hero's transformation from the heroine's distant, insensitive, and cold superior into her tender, expressive intimate'. *Reading the Romance*, p. 216.
12. Prasad writes about the performance of mimesis within *Indiana*, but interestingly does not consider Ralph's masquerade nor its self-reflexive possibilities. 'Contesting Realism'. And in Harkness's exploration of unreadability in *Indiana*, it is the female, rather than male, body that is associated with the *illisible* in the novel. 'Performance, représentation et (il)lisibilité'. However, Mathias refers to Ralph's 'troubling strangeness', and the implicit challenge he poses for Sand's 'supposed realist framework of coherence and legibility' (*Vision*, p. 34).
13. See Barthes, *S/Z*, p. 21.
14. See Zunshine, 'Theory of Mind and Fictions of Embodied Transparency', p. 72.
15. 'The exertion toward significant form in realistic fiction serves the cause of significant, coherently structured character. [. . .] Personality is as rigorously structured in the realistic novel as it is in Racinian tragedy.' See Bersani, *A Future for Astyanax*, p. 55.
16. In a survey essay on the subject of empathy, Amy I. Nathanson observes that individuals very low in 'emotional expressiveness [. . .] should have difficulty experiencing empathy'; 'the individual has difficulty engaging in emotional situations and therefore can neither identify nor express the emotions of others'. 'Rethinking Empathy', p. 113.
17. Dayan, 'Owning People'.
18. Boutin, 'Indiana between Men', p. 107.
19. Ralph himself counters an accusation of hypocrisy by claiming that there is no contradiction between selfishness and philanthropy: 'l'égoïsme bien entendu nous conduit à faire du bien aux hommes pour les empêcher de nous faire du mal' (selfishness in the true sense leads us to do good for other men to prevent them from doing harm to us) (p. 123).
20. On the ambiguous treatment of race in *Indiana*, see for example Machelidon, 'Teaching Race, Class, and Slavery in *Indiana*'.
21. Charles Stivale refers to the narrator's 'myopic – not to say unreliable – point of view'. 'One or Several Ralphs', p. 111.
22. This fact problematises Peter Dayan's nevertheless compelling argument that Ralph is essentially the quasi-omniscient and somewhat incoherent (both honest and dishonest) narrator whose sexist worldview shapes the novel. 'Who is the Narrator in *Indiana*?'
23. Schor, *George Sand and Idealism*, p. 106.

24. See for example ibid. p. 106.
25. A similar 'undecidability' hangs over Indiana's relationship with Delmare. See Schor, Introduction to Sand, *Indiana*, p. xiv.
26. The references to '[le] *front* de ce monument *étrange*' (the façade ('*front*') of this *strange* monument), to 'une *main* immortelle' (an immortal *hand*), and to 'des *impressions* hiéroglyphiques' (hieroglyphic *imprints*) anticipate 'le héros de tant de contes *étranges*' (the hero of so many *strange* tales), 'ses *mains* étaient purs comme son *front*' (his *hands* were as pure as his brow ('*front*'), while 'une *cristallisation* basaltique' (a basalt *crystallisation*) prepares 'la transparence *cristalline*' (*crystalline* transparency), and the use of phrases such as 'puérile prétention' (childish aspiration) and 'inutiles recherches' (useless quests) in connection with the narrator's study of the rocks anticipate the 'sentiment d'oisive curiosité' (feeling of idle curiosity) he claims to have felt in relation to Ralph (pp. 332–3, 336, my emphasis).
27. Pinzka, 'Teaching Historical Myth and Memory in *Indiana*', p. 26.
28. 'Il m'aime encore, se disait-elle, il ne veut pas m'abandonner' (He loves me still, she told herself, he does not want to abandon me) (p. 99); 'Raymon l'écoutait avec un intérêt dont elle ne se méfiait pas' (Raymon listened to her with an interest that did not arouse her suspicion) (p. 109).
29. Noun's ignorance of the world is frequently evoked in the novel. See for example pp. 102, 104, 106.
30. Bains, 'Character Study', p. 160.
31. There are other evocations, too, of Ralph's empathetic disposition: Indiana tells him that she knows her sufferings find an echo in his heart, and he says that seeing her suffering is beyond his capabilities (p. 305), while the narrator remarks that even in the depths of his own suffering he feels sadder for Indiana than for himself (p. 327).
32. On the role of 'the phallic order' at the end of the novel, see Petrey, 'George and Georgina Sand', p. 146.
33. Harkness, *Men of Their Words*, p. 46. On the homosocial dynamics of the narratorial voice in the novel, see also Harkness, 'Masculinity and the Performance of Authority', pp. 119–25.
34. On this subject, see for example Kadish, 'Reading Race in *Indiana*'.
35. Waller notes of the conclusion that 'the freed slaves operate like shades in the novel, with no story, no voice of their own'. 'Ending with *Indiana*', p. 194.
36. Boutin, 'Indiana between Men', p. 109.
37. Bonin, '*Indiana* and the Literary Island', p. 131.
38. A similar argument is made in Shank, 'Irony as Cognitive Empathy'.
39. Malkin, 'Performing Sand's Pedagogical Project', p. 174.

Chapter 7

Towards an Empathetic Ethics of Fiction-Reading

This book set out to see whether a close reading of literary texts could yield insights into the question of how, and possibly why, fiction engages affective sharing and mind-reading skills. On the basis of recent work in psychology and cognitive studies, the first chapter proposed an idea that, to my knowledge, has not been explored in those fields but that is likely to find fairly ready acceptance among literary scholars, at least once the terms of the argument are shifted from affective sharing and mind-reading to seduction and suspicion. This new but not new idea is that the closely connected skills of affective sharing and mind-reading are regularly brought into creative conflict by fictional texts, both at the thematic level and at the level of reception. In order to make its case, this book proposed, in its third chapter, that literary texts can thematise their own reception in the representation of responses inspired by a stranger figure who is closely associated with fiction. Close readings of three novels were subsequently proposed by way of illustration. This concluding chapter will outline a couple of general conclusions about the fiction–empathy relationship that might tentatively but plausibly be drawn from this book's close readings of fictional responses to fictional stranger figures. It will also ask, in closing, what specific contributions this study might be considered to make to the wider cross-disciplinary conversation on the subject of the relationship between fiction and empathy.

The Limits of Mind-Reading

As discussed in the chapter on *La Fille aux yeux d'or*, the realist novel appears to promise total legibility of character, and of the social world more generally.[1] However, the more or less realist fictions selected for study here show us on an explicit, thematic level that characters, and by extension people, can be other than they seem, and resistant to mind-reading. Whether or not Henri finally succeeds in deciphering the truth of Paquita's desire is a moot point. Julien's motivations for shooting Madame de Rênal remain opaque at the end of *Le Rouge et le Noir*, not least to himself. Even the generous nature of Ralph's intentions towards Indiana is at least partially thrown into doubt by elements in his self-presentation. For Greiner, the reluctance to offer total access to the thoughts and feelings of a character, a tendency she describes as 'sympathetic detachment', is a feature characteristic of the Victorian realist novel (which slightly post-dates the French novels discussed in this book), and a feature that differentiates it from the more empathetic, fusional modernist novel that follows it.[2] Rebecca N. Mitchell, in a similar vein and acknowledging a debt to the work of the philosopher Emmanuel Levinas, suggests that Victorian realist novels and paintings 'depict the *unknowability* of the human other', revealing the 'radical, inalterable alterity' of other people.[3] It is possible, however, that the insistence on the unknowable qualities of others is a more common feature of fiction than these arguments suggest. As Cave notes, 'many fictions, indeed, [. . .] seem designed to show that knowing other people is tragically impossible'.[4] Indeed, one cognitive scholar has gone so far as to say that the unknowability of other human beings is 'a cliché of literary studies'.[5] Certainly, the communication of a sense of the limits of our knowledge can be closely associated with the kind of fiction that presents itself as, and that is received as, literature. It has even been argued that the creation of an 'effect of uncertainty' can serve as a 'marker of the literary text', an index of artistry.[6] It is possible that the texts selected for study in this book point to the limitations of mind-reading because they are early examples of a particular narrative genre (realism) or because they have literary ambitions. However, given that the novels in question are early examples of a genre that characteristically offers privileged access to the fictional minds of its characters, and that tends to straddle the popular and the literary, it is also possible that what these texts say about mind-reading is paradigmatic of what narrative fiction more generally says about mind-reading.

While the confrontation orchestrated by our selected texts, and arguably narrative fiction more generally, with the limits of our knowledge about ourselves and others can be understood pessimistically, the discovery of the limits of interpersonal understanding does not need to be framed in negative terms. These limitations are arguably the very condition of story-making and story-reading. As noted by Iser, a key reference for Theory of Mind approaches to literature, 'it is the very lack of ascertainability and defined intention that brings about the text-reader interaction', just as interpersonal relations arise from 'the fact that people cannot experience how others experience them'.[7] No engagement with narrative fiction, whether as reader or writer, can bypass the blindspots implicit in the self–other encounter. The novelist Patrick Modiano has suggested that an insight into the mysteriousness of other people is attributable to the 'hyper-lucidity' of the writer, and that the cultivation of this mystery is one of the purposes of fiction and poetry:

> I have always thought that poets and novelists are able to impart mystery to individuals who are seemingly overwhelmed by day-to-day life, and to things which are ostensibly banal – and the reason they can do this [is] that they have observed them time and again with sustained attention, almost hypnotically. Under their gaze, everyday life ends up being enshrouded in mystery and taking on a kind of glow-in-the-dark quality which it did not have at first sight but which was hidden deep down. It is the role of the poet and the novelist, and also the painter, to reveal the mystery and the glow-in-the-dark quality which exist in the depths of every individual.[8]

Curiosity about other people, as noted in the third chapter, is one of the key factors that motivate fiction-reading; and yet, as the novels studied in this book suggest, fiction also frustrates curiosity, even while nurturing it. To make this observation is not to essentialise opacity, or mystery, but it is to suggest that a desire to understand others plays an important structural role in the reception of narrative fiction.

This book has argued, therefore, in line with psychological and cognitive approaches to the question, that narrative fiction appeals to our mind-reading skills; but it has also argued that narrative fiction, even in its most apparently transparent, realist modes,[9] reminds us of the limits of such skills. It is certainly true that many fictions offer far more rational, readable portraits of other people's minds than we have access to in real life, as thinkers from Proust to Nussbaum have suggested.[10] However, my readings have suggested that fictions *also* remind us of the unreadability of other people, and by extension of our own persons, an unreadability that can often be forgotten in everyday life. As Denis Diderot observes in his *Éloge de Richardson*, novels can show the reader all that is hidden and secret in the emotional outbursts so often witnessed, but so rarely understood, in real life.[11] According to Dorrit Cohn, it is precisely this access that fiction offers to other people's minds that distinguishes it from reality; but importantly, it also reminds us, according to Cohn, that other people have a 'hidden side', minds that are normally unreadable to us:

> If the real world becomes fiction only by revealing the hidden side of the human beings who inhabit it, the reverse is equally true: the most real, the

'roundest' characters of fiction are those we know most intimately, precisely in ways we could never know people in real life.[12]

Even in offering us unusual access to the minds of others, in other words, fiction reminds us how little we can know of real others. In the real world, as suggested by the term 'theory' in the formula 'Theory of Mind', certain knowledge of the inner worlds of others, as of ourselves, is impossible.[13] Fiction reminds us, nowhere more directly than in its depiction of strangers, of this simple fact, namely that people in the real world are often, like Sir Ralph Brown (though not usually, thankfully, to the same extent), other than we think; less easy to pigeon-hole, and more (or less)[14] complex.

In its insistence on the intriguing and ultimately irreducible opacity of other minds, my study aligns itself in an approximate way with philosophical perspectives (sometimes characterised as ethical, Levinasian or post-structuralist)[15] from which cognitive and empirical scholars tend to distance themselves. I have taken the position that, insofar as fiction teaches us something about other people, it does more than simply help us to understand them better (though this would in itself be a considerable achievement); it also unsettles our understanding of other people, rescuing that understanding from reification. It may be, then, that something similar to what Derrida says of the stranger can be said of narrative fiction: 'The stranger shakes the threatening dogmatism of the paternal logos.'[16] This unsettling of certainties would make of fiction-reading an ethical practice, beyond any benefits that it might be understood to bring to our social understanding: reading narrative fiction reminds us of the limits of our knowledge, notably with regard to other people. This is what I understand by Attridge's assertion that, 'in a sense, the "literary" is the ethical'.[17]

One of the key arguments of this book has been that fiction can teach us about the limits of our knowledge of other people: the close readings presented here have suggested that fiction can both hone our mind-reading skills and point to the limits of those skills, both appeal to our curiosity about others and frustrate that curiosity. In each novel studied in this book, a stranger figure appears to reveal the secret of his or her desire: Paquita supposedly lets slip the true object of her love, Julien discovers his apparently enduring love for Madame de Rênal and Ralph confesses his feelings for Indiana. However, the revelation is ambiguous in each case, posing its own problem for interpretation: does Paquita's exclamation really mean what Henri thinks it means? If Julien has always loved only Madame de Rênal, as he claims, why does he shoot her, and why does he appear, before that, to love Mathilde so intensely? Are Ralph's feelings as innocent as he claims? The invitation to decipher motivations, a principal source of fiction's appeal according to cognitivists, can lead to the discovery of an irreducible resistance to definitive decryption, a resistance that is also literature's secret, its appeal to the reader and arguably its point of departure.[18] One of the purposes of this book has been to insist that fiction does more than just train our mind-reading capabilities and hone our social skills (though the available evidence suggests that it may well do these things) – it also highlights the limits of those skills, and herein, many literary scholars would argue, lies a significant part of its ethical role.

The Antagonistic Dynamics of Fiction-Reading

I have referred just now to the appeal of fiction to the reader. Fiction, to the extent that it involves and interests us, arguably engages both mind-reading skills and affective sharing. As discussed in the first chapter of this study, the interaction of reflection and affect in the engagement with narrative fiction has been associated by psychologists with self-change, largely through the operation of either narrative transportation or estrangement. What the close readings presented in this book have repeatedly suggested is that mind-reading (which we associated with suspicion) and affective sharing (which we linked to seduction) can work not just with but also against one another in the reception of fiction. This idea has not, to my knowledge, been explicitly addressed to date by psychologists or by cognitive and empirical literary scholars, despite the fact that literary theory, as we shall see, regularly pits two readerly attitudes against one another. According to Booth, for example, there are three possible ways of engaging with a fictional story:

> We can surrender uncritically to whatever appeals to us, scurrying from one narrative to the next without pause for reflection [. . .] Second, we can attempt an 'anaesthetic' reading and listening, preserving a distance that will protect us from character change. [. . .] Or, finally, we can pursue a two-stage kind of reading, surrendering as fully as possible on every occasion, but then deliberately supplementing, correcting, or refining our experience with the most powerful ethical or ideological criticism we can manage.[19]

Booth's 'two-stage kind of reading' is thematised in all of the texts studied in this book, in the responses of fictional characters to fictional strangers. In *La Fille aux yeux d'or*, Henri's eventual decryption (however bogus) of Paquita's desire undoes the charm to which he had provisionally surrendered. In *Le Rouge et le Noir*, Mathilde's interpretations of Julien's motivations sometimes intensify her feelings for him, but they can also often correct and modify those feelings. At key junctures in Sand's narrative, Indiana's interpretations of Raymon's intentions release her, at least temporarily, from his seductive hold. Madame de Ramière, similarly, corrects her initially favourable reading of Ralph when she notes the violence of his feelings towards her son. Such depictions of relations to a fiction-associated stranger figure remind us that our relationship to fiction tends to be dynamic, moving between seduction and suspicion, affective sharing and mind-reading. The novel's spell is always eventually broken, even if only because narratives always come to an end. The spell can also be broken if elements within the narrative jar. For example, events or alternating perspectives within a fictional narrative may lead a reader to take a distance from a character to whom she had previously felt close; or an attentive reader may note inconsistencies in the presentation of a character that lead her to question the narrator's presentation of events.[20] I would argue, in fact, after Stendhal, that novels cultivate suspicion, or a resistance to seduction, even as they seduce us. This hypothesis is supported by those empirical investigations that have suggested that readers of fiction are obliged to work to disbelieve what they are reading and to counteract their own credulity.[21]

I have argued, thus, that the fictions studied in this book repeatedly draw attention, by way of their representations of seductive strangers, to the need to resist narrative seduction by nurturing critical reading habits. But this is only part of the truth, because these fictions also nurture an openness to seduction. So, although psychologists and cognitive scholars argue that fictional narratives develop mind-reading skills, or ToM, stories also encourage readers to suspend their disbelief, or let their cognitive guard down. Citing recent empirical research into the ethical benefits of immersive reading, Keen suggests that 'we ought to revise our prejudice against immersion in fantasy worlds and escapism as prominent effects of fiction reading'.[22] To the extent that fiction has an ethical role to play, at least some of this role may hinge upon its successful seduction of readers. In our own study, characters repeatedly choose to be seduced rather than heed their own misgivings about the stranger figure: Paquita understands that Henri's temperament could lead him to kill her, but she surrenders to him anyway; Madame de Rênal worries about the permanence of Julien's love for her, but sacrifices everything for him nonetheless; Mathilde has qualms about the consequences of giving Julien power over her, but decides to fall for him regardless, certain that her sense of self will survive the relationship; and Indiana continues to love Raymon even as her understanding of his unworthiness improves. Just as the characters mentioned above choose to lay their misgivings to one side and embark on an emotional adventure, readers can choose to lay aside their critical skills in their engagement with fiction. This means that, despite the various textual clues offered by Sand's narrator, for example, it is possible for readers who are fixated on the main seduction plot of *Indiana* to remain unaware of the nature of Ralph's feelings for the heroine until he confesses them at the end of the novel. It also means that the identity of Paquita's lover can remain a mystery for casual readers of Balzac's text, despite the fact that it is virtually given away towards the beginning of the story. And it means that readers of *Le Rouge et le Noir* believe the hero, against all the evidence of the text, when he tells Madame de Rênal that he has, all this time, loved her alone. In 'readerly' fictional texts such as those analysed in this book, our interpretations of character will inevitably be shaped by our identificatory investments and empathic projections, such that no entirely dispassionate reading, no continually suspicious reading, is possible.

The tension between what this book has characterised as seduction and suspicion, in fiction-reading, has been evoked by various literary scholars. For example, Iser writes of fiction that

> the reader is caught up in ineluctable doubleness: he or she is involved in an illusion, and is simultaneously aware that it is an illusion. It is through the incessant hovering between the closed and the punctured illusion that the transformation effected by the play of the text makes itself felt to the reader.[23]

Jouve, similarly, writes that reading fiction involves 'a complex experience wherein sensation and reflection are inextricably combined', and that 'the relation to the narrative depends for a large part on the dialectic between distance and participation'.[24] The same theorist suggests that fiction-reading resembles daydreaming, insofar as it prohibits the 'complete surrender' that characterises nocturnal dreaming, and oscillates 'between the hallucinatory strength of imaginary representations and the distancing imposed by the part of the "I" that remains conscious': 'The reader, far from being a stable and unified subject, alternates ceaselessly between one reading position and the other.'[25] The writer and literary critic Michel Picard, similarly, evokes an alternation, on the part of the reading subject, between 'playing' and 'game', or between 'surrender to the fantasy' and 'lucid, informed, indeed erudite reflection'.[26] David Hayman contends that all fiction sets up an interplay of distance and involvement, and that high modernist fiction, in particular, intensifies this antithetical play.[27] Felski argues persuasively against any opposition between what she calls suspicious reading and gullible reading, any 'stultifying division between naïve, emotional reading and rigorous, critical reading'; she presents reading as an activity that involves an intertwining of interpretation and affect, 'rapprochement and distancing, relaxation and suspense, movement and hesitation', and that takes the form of 'a cocreation between actors that leaves neither party unchanged': 'Critical reason [. . .] is often infused with moments of enchantment, and suspicion turns out to be not so very far removed from love.'[28] With more specific reference to narrative empathy, Patrizia Lombardo associates fiction-reading with 'a cognitive distance that coexists with emotional participation', while Robson refers to the discomfort of the reader of a narrative of suffering, who must 'avoid on the one hand maintaining a fixed distance between self and other, and on the other hand seeking to erase or deny the reality of that gap'.[29]

In fact, the interaction of immersion and separation in the reception of art has long been a theme in aesthetic theory. Jauss points to the interaction of 'the immediacy of identification' and 'critical reflection', or pleasure and instruction, in the reception of seventeenth-century French theatre, and notes that 'the shift from identification to reflection becomes, in the eighteenth century, a condition of enlightened reading'.[30] According to Diderot, writing in the 1770s, the gifted actor is 'double', capable of maintaining an internal distance from the role he is playing, however emotionally intense that role is.[31] The phenomenon of Romantic irony, closely associated with the German thinker Friedrich Schlegel, is that alternation between illusion and detachment that is often understood to characterise self-reflexive works of prose fiction. Wilhelm Worringer's *Abstraktion und Einfühlung*, published in 1908, contends that all aesthetic activity proceeds from a dialectical interaction between fusional empathy and abstraction.[32]

What is the point, though, of the peculiar dynamic that artistic production, and notably narrative fiction, sets in play? What wider purpose, if any, can be served by the practice of combining two attitudes in fiction-reading, one of which is more or less credulous, affective and immersive, and one of which is more or less sceptical and distanced? The most obvious answer is similar to that proposed by cognitive and empirical scholars of literature in the first chapter, and to that gestured at by more mainstream literary theorists in the second: self-modification. The idea that the interplay between participation and separation can lead to self-renewal has been a theme in aesthetic thought since the work of Aristotle, who countered Plato's negative evaluation of drama by attributing cleansing potential to the release from emotion, or *catharsis*, that is permitted by the ending of a tragedy. Aristotle's therapeutic notion of art was reframed in the twentieth century by the French psychoanalyst

Jacques Lacan. The latter maintains, in seminars presented in 1959–60 and 1964 respectively, that by engaging the viewing subject's desires and drives, art invites a salutary and provisional surrender of the ego, a surrender that enables self-renewal.[33] Through engagement with art, the subject is exposed to the non-self, the strange, and change is enabled. The psychoanalytic literary theorist Norman N. Holland, similarly, though wary of suggesting that 'literature' has any 'long-term moral effect', argues that by permitting a temporary 'fusion of self and object in aesthetic experience', it 'may open for us some flexibility of mind so that growth from it and other kinds of experience remains possible'.[34] Encounters with art, including narrative fiction, have the potential, in other words, to be transformative.

So the argument goes; and it would certainly be hard to deny that Paquita and Henri, Mathilde and Madame de Rênal, Indiana and Noun are all changed in some way by their relationship with a seductive stranger. However, while any opening up of the reading subject to the possibility of self-change would surely represent a significant achievement on the part of art or fiction, perhaps the interplay of adhesion and separation, participation and detachment, seduction and suspicion – or affective sharing and mind-reading – does something else too. This book has suggested that, as well as opening readers up to the experience of others, the activity of reading trains us to be suspicious of the stories we are told. The ability to resist seduction has been associated in my readings with social power but also with personal freedom. According to Felski, readers are trained by unreliable narrators and other such modern literary devices to 'discount or delve behind obvious meanings'.[35] Rabaté suggests something similar when he notes that fiction-reading is threatening to totalitarian perspectives because it enables what he calls 'the faculty of disengagement (a disengagement that is the intrinsic condition of every free engagement)'.[36] Narrative fiction may encourage readers to adhere to certain perspectives, for example to identify with particular characters in a text, but it also trains the subject to dis-identify. It frees readers from the danger of belonging too fixedly to any one position, and has 'the power to change our habits of conceiving what is real'.[37] Dufays notes that the naive reader is trapped in his passive relation to the text: 'Fascinated by the stereotype's illusory power, the reader is in a sense trapped.'[38] But perhaps the reader of fiction is never really as passive as such formulations suggest. It seems plausible that all forms of fictional engagement, and not just literary reading, involve to varying degrees what Marielle Macé calls a 'struggle against other forms that gives us shape'; perhaps all narrative fictions are, at least potentially, productive of what Wilson calls a 'queer reader', one who, by confronting unknowability in the text, 'is led to recognise the traumatic instabilities of identification and desire'.[39] In other words, while texts that belong to the (disputed) category of literary fiction may be particularly likely to encourage suspicion or critical reflection, all narrative fiction must surely encourage it to some degree.

To open oneself to the strangeness or alterity of narrative fiction is arguably to train one's mind to be receptive to the otherness of the people we meet in our everyday lives: it is to acquire, in other words, an attitude of naivety.[40] However, the encounter with fiction may also train our critical faculties, imparting a habit of suspicion, or at least reflection, that complements this first attitude. This practice of detachment, developed through fiction-reading, may play a part in equipping an individual to make considered, ethical decisions. Amanda Anderson, in her study of the role of cosmopolitan impartiality in the work of Victorian thinkers and writers, mounts a strong defence of 'the critical, dialogical, and even emancipatory potential of cultivated detachment'.[41] By the same token, the habit of affective sharing, again cultivated by narrative fiction, can militate against tendencies to objectify and even dehumanise other people. The interruption and postponement of objectification is part of what Spivak considers to be the purpose of a literary or humanities education: 'the ethical interrupts and postpones the epistemological – the undertaking to construct the other as object of knowledge, an undertaking never to be given up'.[42]

Recent neuroscientific models of empathy propose that individuals 'flexibly deploy multiple, interactive processes' in the experience of empathy.[43] This book has placed its focus on the mechanics of this interaction as they play out both within the storyworlds of fictional narratives and as part of their reception by readers. What has not yet been addressed adequately by experimental means, to our knowledge, is the way in which fiction-reading encourages the reader flexibly to negotiate between different attitudes, whether these are characterised as seduction and suspicion, or as affective sharing and mentalising, or simply as alternative perspectives. It is easy enough to conceive of psychological experiments that could test this mental mobility or flexibility. For example, scientific studies have already suggested that fiction-reading renders individuals more empathetic; but are novel-readers any more capable than others of resisting manipulation of their empathic tendencies by advertisements, 'fake news' or propaganda? In the words of the philosopher Greg Currie, it is all very well to suggest that fiction makes us more empathetic, but does it make us 'more usefully discriminating empathisers'?[44] Conversely, despite their apparently superior mind-reading abilities, are readers of fiction more likely to postpone their conclusions about a person in real life, less inclined than non-readers to jump to firm conclusions about a person's intentions? This book has suggested, tentatively, that both of these questions might be answered in the affirmative, to the extent that a fiction-reader, and perhaps particularly a student of 'literary' fiction, learns to temper her own affective responses with her critical interpretations, and vice versa.

Final Conclusions

One literary scholar who read an early draft of this study commented that its close readings were not quite complex enough and its conclusions disappointingly unadventurous. A more scientifically oriented scholar, responding to the same version of the book, noted that the conclusions were far-fetched, and would only be capable of carrying any water if they were supported by empirical investigation, rather than by intricate close readings. The conundrum is probably familiar to many who have attempted to work in new ways between disciplines: the received wisdom and methodologies of one field can appear absurd in another, the approaches of one out of place in the other. It is true that the key argument of this book is likely to be considered unsurprising by many literary specialists, trained to resist narrative empathy, or seduction, and to maintain, or at least regularly return to, a critical, analytical or suspicious attitude. So obvious is this point, from a traditional literary studies perspective, that it could be argued that there is little point in writing about it. However, while it is true that scepticism is understood to be the characteristic attitude of the literary scholar, the idea that narrative fiction sets in play, within the reader, a dynamic of participation and separation is not as often highlighted by scholars as this concluding chapter might have suggested. In addition, in a context where psychologists, cognitive scholars and others are exploring the idea that engagement with fiction develops interpersonal skills, it seems worthwhile to relate these skills to the practical knowledge that comes with the study of literature, in the hope of giving scholars of other disciplines an alternative and potentially useful perspective on the debate and in the hope of giving literary scholars a new way of framing and valuing the work that they do. Finally, by proposing that fictional inscriptions of responses to a stranger figure, within a narrative text, might be understood to describe, reflexively, the dynamics experienced by the reader of that fiction, this book has offered a model of close reading that could be taken further by literary scholars interested in the mechanisms of reader response.

This book has attempted to nuance the emphasis placed by psychologists and cognitive scholars on how fiction engages our ability to read other people's body language and gestures. The close readings presented in this study have highlighted instead the fact that novels can remind us of all that we do not and cannot know about other people, and about ourselves. Three early works of French realism were privileged at least partly because this mode of writing attempts to present the social world as entirely assimilable to understanding. It was argued that the implied motivations of fictional characters are sometimes ambiguous, even in novels that appear to obey a demystificatory logic: the true object of Paquita's desire, Julien's motivations for shooting Madame de Rênal and his renewed love for her, the explanation for Ralph's transformation and the nature of his feelings for Indiana, all remain shadowy. Even those works, then, that seem most likely to support the argument that engagement with narrative fiction helps us to read, in the real world, other people's desires, intentions and motivations appear to suggest that other people – and indeed, by extension, we ourselves – are ultimately at least partly unreadable.[45]

Various thinkers, from across a range of disciplines, have suggested that fiction-reading is intrinsically morally improving, to the extent that it helps us to conceive of other people's realities and reality, and become more capable of empathy with real-world others. The historian Lynn Hunt, for example, has argued that novel-reading acted upon the brains of eighteenth-century Americans and Europeans to bring them to a point where the equal human rights of all people seemed self-evident rather than preposterous.[46] Without at all rejecting such ideas, this book has argued that there is also ethical value to be found in the resistance to narrative empathy. After all, to the extent that stories appeal to our emotions, they can be morally harmful; some, as Keen points out, have even offered 'a rationale for genocide'.[47] But if fiction appeals to our capacity for affective sharing, it also elicits scepticism, and does so by definition insofar as the illusion that fiction presents is a provisional and playful one, on the model of trompe-l'œil rather than counterfeit. Insofar as stories are presented as fiction, and not as fact, they arguably play an ethical role not only by nurturing our capacity for affective sharing but also by cultivating a countervailing scepticism (and vice versa). It is quite possible that some fictions (for example, novels received as literary, or realist novels, or modernist novels) are better than others at training readers to be alternately credulous and vigilant, open and guarded; but I would argue that all fictional stories perform this function to some degree. Our study of fictional responses to a number of fictional strangers has suggested that narrative fiction helps readers to be open to others, but that it also trains readers to maintain a certain critical

Empathy and the Strangeness of Fiction

distance from other people's stories, and from the stories that we tell ourselves. I would contend that this flexibility, and this uncertainty, are inherently ethical.

Narrative fiction has no one easily definable social role. The close readings performed in this book suggest that stories, in seducing us, encourage an openness to and curiosity about other people. This in itself offers a strong argument for the social value of fiction. However, this book has also argued that, beyond nurturing a habit of openness to counteract our detachment from other people, narrative fiction encourages us to maintain a habit of at least intermittent detachment to counteract our openness. In other words, narrative fiction develops an attitude of uncertainty, with regard to other people, to combat our certainties about them. This book has argued, in sum, that fiction does two things that can be forgotten in scientific studies of how it engages empathy and social understanding: it gives us a direct experience of the limits, along with the necessity, of mind-reading and of the risks, along with the importance, of affective sharing.

Notes

1. According to Jouve, the realist narrative always pretends to offer entirely readable characters, 'without mystery or obscurity'. *L'Effet-personnage*, p. 180.
2. Greiner, *Sympathetic Realism*, p. 139. Greiner differentiates sympathy from empathy insofar as the former relies upon (metonymic) detachment and the latter upon (metaphorical) fusion. See *Sympathetic Realism*, pp. 157–61. Timothy Vincent, similarly, associates empathy with modernism, and contrasts it with the sympathy characteristic of both realist and romantic literature. 'From Sympathy to Empathy'. Kirsty Martin takes a different approach by arguing that modernist novels allude to a form of sympathy that is bodily and intuitive rather than rational. *Modernism and the Rhythms of Sympathy*.
3. Mitchell, *Victorian Lessons in Empathy and Difference*, p. x. However, citing E. M. Forster's claim that 'in the novel we can know people perfectly' (p. xi), and even while acknowledging the limits of what is knowable and representable within the realist text, Mitchell argues that characters in realist fiction are transparent to readers, if not to each other.
4. Cave, *Thinking with Literature*, p. 28. The 'unknowable otherness' of particular characters, and of writing itself, is a recurring theme in Attridge, *J. M. Coetzee* (p. 29). On the insurmountable division between self and other as both a literary theme and a feature of literary reading, see Robson, 'The Limits of Empathy and Compassion'.
5. Palmer, *Social Minds in the Novel*, p. 2. However, the same author acknowledges, in an earlier work, that 'we should feel a little uncomfortable with

the assertion that we can easily determine facts about our own minds and other minds'. *Fictional Minds*, p. 199.

6. Chambers, *Story and Situation*, p. 169.
7. Iser, 'Interaction between Text and Reader', p. 109.
8. Modiano, Nobel Lecture.
9. Greiner too has suggested that realist fiction preserves the 'otherness' of other people, following a logic that she associates with Adam Smith's notion of sympathy. See 'Sympathy Time', pp. 28–9. Greiner develops this argument in *Sympathetic Realism*.
10. See Proust, *À la recherche du temps perdu*, vol. 1, p. 119 and Nussbaum, *Love's Knowledge*, p. 162.
11. Diderot, *Éloge de Richardson*, p. 8.
12. Cohn, *Transparent Minds*, p. 5.
13. The philosopher Dan Zahavi notes that the notion of Theory of Mind itself implies 'the fundamental opacity or invisibility of other minds': 'It is precisely because of the alleged absence of an experiential access to the minds of others that we need to rely on and employ either theoretical inferences or internal simulations.' 'Empathy, Embodiment and Interpersonal Understanding', p. 286. See also Rylance, *Literature and the Public Good*, p. 180.
14. See Figlerowicz, *Flat Protagonists*.
15. No synonymy is being proposed between the three terms in question.
16. Derrida, *De l'hospitalité*, p. 13.
17. Attridge, *J. M. Coetzee*, p. 111.
18. As Rick Rylance puts it, 'structured ambiguity has long been recognized as a defining property of the literary use of language, and it is well established that exploratory openness of meaning is a key property of literature'. *Literature and the Public Good*, p. 164. It has been argued that this defining indeterminacy of literary language is related to the fact that it tends to lend itself both to referential and figural/rhetorical readings. See for example Culler, 'Prolegomena to a Theory of Reading'.
19. Booth, *The Company We Keep*, pp. 280–1.
20. As various commentators have pointed out, and as my own close readings have suggested, when we read a novel or watch a film our sympathies can shift among different subject positions, experiences or characters, rather than being directed at just one character. See for example M. Smith, *Engaging Characters*, pp. 77–8, 230, and '*Engaging Characters*', pp. 250, 254.
21. This idea was discussed in the second chapter. A recent psychological study has attempted to show by empirical means that perspectives, in fiction-reading, are 'dynamic rather than consistent, effortful rather than automatic, and reactive, in the sense that they are a function of the reader's online processing as it interacts with narrative technique', and proposes that such dynamism is particularly characteristic of what it calls 'good literature' or 'writerly' texts than of popular fiction. The same study also suggests that 'if writerly texts inhibit facile perspective taking, they may also inhibit empathy'. Bortolussi et al., 'Putting Perspective Taking in Perspective', pp. 178, 185.
22. Keen, 'Novel Readers', p. 25.

23. Iser, 'The Play of the Text', p. 336.
24. Jouve, *Poétique du roman*, pp. 198, 156.
25. Jouve, *L'Effet personnage*, pp. 80, 81.
26. Picard, *Nodier, la Fée aux miettes*, p. 5.
27. Hayman, *Re-Forming the Narrative*.
28. Felski, *The Limits of Critique*, pp. 180, 176, 84, 113.
29. Lombardo, 'Empathie et simulation', p. 24; Robson, *I Suffer, Therefore I Am*, p. 125.
30. Jauss, 'Levels of Identification', pp. 311, 312.
31. Diderot, *Paradoxe sur le comédien*, p. 13.
32. On this point, see Nowak, 'The Complicated History of *Einfühlung*', p. 313.
33. Lacan, *Le Séminaire: Livre VII* and *Le Séminaire: Livre XI*.
34. Holland, *The Dynamics of Literary Response*, p. 340. Interestingly, the 'joke' that Holland offers as exemplary of the 'trick' that fiction habitually plays features what he calls a 'quite repulsively seductive' female stranger (p. 9).
35. Felski, *The Limits of Critique*, p. 43.
36. Rabaté, 'Identification du lecteur', p. 236.
37. Bruner, *Making Stories*, p. 94. In a similar vein, Yves Citton refers playfully to the 'witty suspicion of all beliefs' as an effect of fiction-reading. *Lire, Interpréter, Actualiser*, p. 353. Kristeva writes of the dangers of too fixed a sense of belonging, citing the example of the Nazis. *Étrangers à nous-mêmes*, p. 228.
38. Dufays, *Stéréotype et lecture*, p. 182.
39. Macé, 'Ways of Reading', p. 221. Wilson, *Sexuality*, p. 59. Macé is interested less in reading as an 'active task of deciphering' than in 'all the concealed passive facets of reading, which activate forms of behavior in relation to an object that both affects and constrains the reader' (p. 224).
40. Baudelaire claims, in his *Exposition universelle* essay of 1855, to have adopted 'impeccable naivety' as a means of appreciating the art of foreign cultures. *Œuvres complètes*, vol. 2, p. 578.
41. Anderson, *The Powers of Distance*, p. 177.
42. Spivak, 'Ethics and Politics', p. 17.
43. See Zaki and Ochsner, 'The Neuroscience of Empathy', p. 678.
44. Currie, 'Does Fiction Make Us Less Empathetic?', p. 51.
45. Hamon notes that there are very few partially illegible characters in Zola, by contrast with Balzac and Stendhal. *Le Personnel du roman*, p. 38. However, Hamon does highlight the often enigmatic qualities of Zola's female characters, and more generally the opacity of desire in Zola's novels (pp. 299–307). I would add that, if Zola's characters are legible to the reader, they are often opaque to one another and to themselves.
46. Hunt, *Inventing Human Rights*.
47. Keen, *Empathy and the Novel*, p. 25. The examples given by Keen (the story of the supremacy of the Aryan race or of the danger embodied by Jews) are, however, fictions that masquerade as fact.

Bibliography

Ahmed, Sara, *Strange Encounters: Embodied Others in Post-Coloniality* (London: Routledge, 2000).

Alcorn, Marshall W., Jr and Mark Bracher, 'Literature, Psychoanalysis, and the Re-Formation of the Self: A New Direction for Reader-Response Theory', *PMLA*, 100.3 (1985), pp. 342–54.

Alsup, Janet, *A Case for Teaching Literature in the Secondary School: Why Reading Fiction Matters in an Age of Scientific Objectivity and Standardization* (New York: Routledge, 2015).

Anderson, Amanda, *The Powers of Distance: Cosmopolitanism and the Cultivation of Detachment* (Princeton: Princeton University Press, 2001).

Ansel, Yves and Lola Kheyar Stibler, *Stendhal: Le Rouge et le Noir* (Neuilly: Atlande, 2013).

Attridge, Derek, *J. M. Coetzee and the Ethics of Reading: Literature in the Event* (Chicago: University of Chicago Press, 2004).

Attridge, Derek, *The Singularity of Literature* (London: Routledge, 2004).

Auyoung, Elaine, *When Fiction Feels Real: Representation and the Reading Mind* (New York: Oxford University Press, 2018).

Bains, Christopher, 'Character Study: The Art of the Literary Portrait in *Indiana*', in David A. Powell and Pratima Prasad (eds), *Approaches to Teaching Sand's* Indiana (New York: Modern Language Association of America, 2015), pp. 157–65.

Bal, P. Matthijs and Martijn Veltkamp, 'How Does Fiction Reading Influence Empathy? An Experimental Investigation on the Role of Emotional Transportation', *PloS One*, 8.1 (2013), e55341, pp. 1–12.

Balzac, Honoré de, *Histoire des Treize*, ed. Pierre-Georges Castex (Paris: Garnier Frères, 1966).

Balzac, Honoré de, *La Comédie humaine*, ed. Pierre-Georges Castex and others, 12 vols (Paris: Gallimard, Pléiade, 1976–81).

Barnes, Jennifer L., 'Imaginary Engagement, Real-World Effects: Fiction, Emotion, and Social Cognition', *Review of General Psychology*, 22.2 (2018), pp. 125–34.

Barthes, Roland, *S/Z* (Paris: Seuil, 1970).

Barthes, Roland, *Le Plaisir du texte* (Paris: Seuil, 1973).

Baudelaire, Charles, *Œuvres complètes*, ed. Claude Pichois, 2 vols (Paris: Gallimard, Pléiade, 1975–6).

Beauvoir, Simone de, Yves Berger, Jean-Pierre Faye, Jean-Ricardou, Jean-Paul Sartre and Jorge Semprun, *Que peut la littérature?*, ed. Yves Buin (Paris: Union générale d'éditions, 1965).

Béguin, Albert, *Balzac lu et relu* (Paris: Seuil, 1981).

Benjamin, Walter, 'The Storyteller: Reflections on the Work of Nikolai Leskov', in Dorothy J. Hale (ed.), *The Novel: An Anthology of Criticism and Theory 1900-2000* (Oxford: Blackwell, 2006), pp. 361–78.

Bennett, Jill, *Empathic Vision: Affect, Trauma, and Contemporary Art* (Stanford: Stanford University Press, 2006).

Bersani, Leo, *A Future for Astyanax: Character and Desire in Literature* (Boston, Toronto: Little, Brown and Company, 1976).

Billington, Josie, '"Reading for Life": Prison Reading Groups in Practice and Theory', *Critical Survey*, 23 (2011), pp. 67–85.

Biran, Maine de, *Œuvres philosophiques de Maine de Biran*, vol. 1 (Paris: Ladrange, 1841).

Black, Jessica E. and Jennifer L. Barnes, 'The Effects of Reading Material on Social and Non-Social Cognition', *Poetics*, 52 (2015), pp. 32–43.

Black, Jessica E. and Jennifer L. Barnes, 'Fiction and Social Cognition: The Effect of Viewing Award-Winning Television Dramas on Theory of Mind', *Psychology of Aesthetics, Creativity, and the Arts*, 9.4 (2015), pp. 423–9.

Bloom, Paul, 'Empathy and its Discontents', *Trends in Cognitive Sciences*, 21.1 (2017), pp. 24–31.

Bonard, Olivier, *La Peinture dans la création balzacienne: Invention et vision pictures de* La Maison du chat-qui-pelote *au* Père Goriot (Geneva: Droz, 1969).

Bonin, Kathrin, '*Indiana* and the Literary Island: Enlightenment Ideals, Nineteenth-Century Ironies', in David A. Powell and Pratima Prasad (eds), *Approaches to Teaching Sand's* Indiana (New York: Modern Language Association of America, 2015), pp. 128–34.

Booth, Wayne C., *The Company We Keep: An Ethics of Fiction* (Berkeley: University of California Press, 1988).

Bordwell, David, *Poetics of Cinema* (London: Routledge, 2007).

Boutin, Aimée, 'Indiana between Men: Narration and Desire in George Sand's Novel', in David A. Powell and Pratima Prasad (eds), *Approaches to Teaching Sand's* Indiana (New York: Modern Language Association of America, 2015), pp. 104–10.

Breithaupt, Fritz, 'A Three-Person Model of Empathy', *Emotion Review*, 4.1 (2012), pp. 84–91.

Breithaupt, Fritz, 'Empathic Sadism: How Readers get Implicated', in Lisa Zunshine (ed.), *The Oxford Handbook of Cognitive Literary Studies* (New York: Oxford University Press, 2015), pp. 440–60.

Breithaupt, Fritz, *The Dark Sides of Empathy*, trans. Andrew B. B. Hamilton (Ithaca: Cornell University Press, 2019).

Brooks, Peter, *Body Work: Objects of Desire in Modern Narrative* (Cambridge, MA: Harvard University Press, 1993).

Bruner, Jerome, *Making Stories: Law, Literature, Life* (Cambridge, MA: Harvard University Press, 2002).

Carroll, Joseph, 'Minds and Meaning in Fictional Narratives: An Evolutionary Perspective', *Review of General Psychology*, 22.2 (2018), pp. 135–46.

Carroll, Noël, 'On Some Affective Relations between Audiences and the Characters in Popular Fictions', in Peter Goldie and Amy Coplan (eds), *Empathy: Philosophical and Psychological Perspectives* (New York: Oxford University Press, 2011), pp. 162–84.

Carroll, Noël, 'Theatre and the Emotions', in Lisa Zunshine (ed.), *The Oxford Handbook of Cognitive Literary Studies* (New York: Oxford University Press, 2015), pp. 313–26.

Cave, Terence, *Thinking with Literature: Towards a Cognitive Literature* (Oxford and New York: Oxford University Press, 2016).

Chambers, Ross, *Story and Situation: Narrative Seduction and the Power of Fiction* (Manchester: Manchester University Press, 1984).

Citton, Yves, *Lire, interpréter, actualiser: Pourquoi les études littéraires?* (Paris: Éditions Amsterdam, 2007).

Clanchy, Kate, 'The Very Quiet Foreign Girls Poetry Group', *The Guardian*, 14 July 2016, <https://www.theguardian.com/society/2016/jul/14/very-quiet-for eign-girls-poetry-foyle-young-poets-kate-clanchy> (last accessed 19 October 2019).

Cohen, Ted, *Thinking of Others: On the Talent for Metaphor* (Princeton: Princeton University Press, 2008).

Cohn, Dorrit, *Transparent Minds: Narrative Modes for Presenting Consciousness in Fiction* (Princeton: Princeton University Press, 1978).

Compagnon, Antoine, *La littérature, pour quoi faire?* (Paris: Collège de France, 2007) <http://books.openedition.org/cdf/524> (last accessed 19 October 2019).

Coplan, Amy, 'Empathic Engagement with Narrative Fictions', *The Journal of Aesthetics and Art Criticism*, 62 (2004), pp. 141–52.

Coplan, Amy, 'Understanding Empathy: Its Features and Effects', in Peter Goldie and Amy Coplan (eds), *Empathy: Philosophical and Psychological Perspectives* (New York: Oxford University Press, 2011), pp. 3–18.

Couégnas, Daniel, *Introduction à la paralittérature* (Paris: Seuil, 1992).

Culler, Jonathan, 'Prolegomena to a Theory of Reading', in Susan R. Suleiman and Inge Crosman (eds), *The Reader in the Text: Essays on Audience and Interpretation* (Princeton: Princeton University Press, 1980), pp. 46–66.

Culler, Jonathan, 'Omniscience', *Narrative*, 12.1 (2004), pp. 22–34.

Currie, Gregory, 'Let's Pretend', *Times Literary Supplement*, 2 September 2011, pp. 14–15.

Currie, Greg(ory), 'Does Fiction Make Us Less Empathetic?', *Teorema*, 35.3 (2016), pp. 47–68.

Czyba, Lucette, 'Misogynie et gynophobie dans *La Fille aux yeux d'or*', in *La Femme au XIXe siècle: Littérature et idéologie* (Lyon: Presses Universitaires de Lyon, 1979), pp. 139–49.

Dällenbach, Lucien, *The Mirror in the Text*, trans. Jeremy Whiteley with Emma Hughes (Cambridge: Polity Press, 1989).

Davis, Kimberley Chabot, 'Oprah's Book Club and the Politics of Cross-Racial Empathy', *International Journal of Cultural Studies*, 7.4 (2004), pp. 399–419.

Davis, Mark H., 'Measuring Individual Differences in Empathy: Evidence for a Multidimensional Approach', *Journal of Personality and Social Psychology*, 44.1 (1983), pp. 113–26.

Davis, Philip, *Reading and the Reader* (Oxford: Oxford University Press, 2013).

Dayan, Peter, 'Owning People: Human Property in *Indiana*', in David A. Powell and Pratima Prasad (eds), *Approaches to Teaching Sand's* Indiana (New York: Modern Language Association of America, 2015), pp. 55–66.

de Waal, Frans B. M. and Stephanie D. Preston, 'Empathy: Its Ultimate and Proximate Bases', *Behavioral and Brain Sciences*, 25.1 (2002), pp. 1–20.

Decety, Jean and Philip L. Jackson, 'A Social-Neuroscience Perspective on Empathy', *Current Directions in Psychological Science*, 15.2 (2006), pp. 54–8.

Delattre, Geneviève, 'De *Séraphita* à *La Fille aux yeux d'or*', *L'Année balzacienne* (1970), pp. 183–226.

Denby, David, 'Lire le monde intérieur: la représentation du geste chez Hugo et Flaubert', *Irish Journal of French Studies*, 3 (2003), pp. 21–40.

Derrida, Jacques, *L'Écriture et la différence* (Paris: Éditions du Seuil, 1967).

Derrida, Jacques, *Mémoires d'aveugle: l'Autoportrait et autres ruines* (Paris: Réunion des Musées Nationaux, 1991).

Derrida, Jacques, *De l'hospitalité: Anne Dufourmantelle invite Jacques Derrida à répondre* (Paris: Calmann-Lévy, 1997).

Diderot, Denis, *Éloge de Richardson*, in Samuel Richardson, *Clarisse Harlove*, trans. Abbé Prévost, 2 vols (Paris: Publications du journal l'Estafette, 1845), vol. 1, pp. 5–13.

Diderot, Denis, *Paradoxe sur le comédien*, ed. Ernest Dupuy (Paris: Société française d'imprimerie et de librairie, 1902).

Djikic, Maja and Keith Oatley, 'The Art in Fiction: From Indirect Communication to Changes of the Self', *Psychology of Aesthetics, Creativity, and the Arts*, 8.4 (2014), pp. 498–505.

Djikic, Maja, Keith Oatley and Mihnea C. Moldoveanu, 'Opening the Closed Mind: The Effect of Exposure to Literature on the Need for Closure', *Creativity Research Journal*, 25.2 (2013), pp. 149–54.

Djikic, Maja, Keith Oatley and Mihnea C. Moldoveanu, 'Reading Other Minds: Effects of Literature on Empathy', *Scientific Study of Literature*, 3.1 (2013), pp. 28–47.

Djikic, Maja, Keith Oatley, Sara Zoeterman and Jordan B. Peterson, 'On Being Moved by Art: How Reading Fiction Transforms the Self', *Creativity Research Journal*, 21.1 (2009), pp. 24–9.

Dubois, Jacques, *Les Romanciers du réel: De Balzac à Simenon* (Paris: Éditions du Seuil, 2000).

Dufays, Jean-Louis, *Stéréotype et lecture* (Liège: Mardaga, 1994).

Eagleton, Terry, *Trouble with Strangers: A Study of Ethics* (Oxford: Wiley-Blackwell, 2009).

Eliot, George, 'The Natural History of German Life', *The Westminster Review*, 10 (1856), pp. 51–79.

Eliot, George, *Middlemarch* (Oxford: Oxford University Press, 1998).

Felman, Shoshana, 'Women and Madness: The Critical Phallacy', *Diacritics*, 5.4 (1975), pp. 2–10.

Felman, Shoshana, 'Rereading Femininity', *Yale French Studies*, 62 (1981), pp. 19–44.

Felski, Rita, *Uses of Literature* (Oxford: Wiley-Blackwell, 2008).

Felski, Rita, *The Limits of Critique* (Chicago: University of Chicago Press, 2015).

Figlerowicz, Marta, *Flat Protagonists: A Theory of Novel Character* (Oxford and New York: Oxford University Press, 2016).

Flaubert, Gustave, *Madame Bovary* ([Paris]: Gallimard, 1988).

Fong, Katrina, Justin B. Mullin and Raymond A. Mar, 'What You Read Matters: The Role of Fiction Genres in Predicting Interpersonal Sensitivity', *Psychology of Aesthetics, Creativity, and the Arts*, 7 (2013), pp. 370–6.

Forster, E. M., *Aspects of the Novel* (London: Edward Arnold, 1974).

Freud, Sigmund, 'The "Uncanny"' (1919) <http://web.mit.edu/allanmc/www/freud1.pdf> (last accessed 19 October 2019).

Gabriel, Shira and Ariana F. Young, 'Becoming a Vampire Without Being Bitten: The Narrative Collective-Assimilation Hypothesis', *Psychological Science*, 22 (2011), pp. 990–4.

Gaubert, Serge, '*La Fille aux yeux d'or*: un texte-charade', *La Femme au XIXᵉ siècle: Littérature et idéologie* (Lyon: Presses Universitaires de Lyon, 1979), pp. 167–77.

Gefen, Alexandre, 'Le Projet thérapeutique de la littérature contemporaine française', *Contemporary French and Francophone Studies*, 20.3 (2016), pp. 420–7.

Gefen, Alexandre, *Réparer le monde. La littérature française face au XXIᵉ siècle* (Paris: Corti, 2017).

Gerrig, Richard J., *Experiencing Narrative Worlds: On the Psychological Activities of Reading*, 2nd edn (Boulder: Westview Press, 1998).

Gerrig, Richard J., Jessica Love and Gail McKoon, 'Waiting for Brandon: How Readers Respond to Small Mysteries', *Journal of Memory and Language*, 60.1 (2009), pp. 144–53.

Gerrig, Richard and David N. Rapp, 'Psychological Processes Underlying Literary Impact', *Poetics Today*, 25.2 (2004), pp. 265–81.

Gerwin, Elisabeth, 'Power in the City: Balzac's *Flâneur* in *La Fille aux yeux d'or*', in David Evans and Kate Griffiths (eds), *Institutions and Power in Nineteenth-Century French Literature and Culture* (Amsterdam: Rodopi, 2011), pp. 101–14.

Goldman, Alvin I., *Simulating Minds: The Philosophy, Psychology, and Neuroscience of Mindreading* (New York: Oxford University Press, 2006).

Gormley, Lane, '"Mon roman est fini": Fabricateurs de romans et fiction intra-textuelle dans *Le Rouge et le Noir*', *Stendhal Club*, 21 (1979), pp. 129–38.

Green, Melanie C. and Timothy C. Brock, 'In the Mind's Eye: Transportation-Imagery Model of Narrative Persuasion', in Melanie C. Green, Jeffrey J. Strange, and Timothy C. Brock (eds), *Narrative Impact: Social and Cognitive Foundations* (Mahwah, NJ: Lawrence Erlbaum, 2002), pp. 315–41.

Greiner, Rae, 'Sympathy Time: Adam Smith, George Eliot, and the Realist Novel', *Narrative*, 17.3 (2009), pp. 291–311.

Greiner, Rae, *Sympathetic Realism in Nineteenth-Century British Fiction* (Baltimore: Johns Hopkins University Press, 2012).

Hakemulder, Frank, *The Moral Laboratory: Experiments Examining the Effects of Reading Literature on Social Perception and Moral Self-Concept* (Amsterdam: John Benjamins, 2000).

Hammond, Meghan Marie, *Empathy and the Psychology of Literary Modernism* (Edinburgh: Edinburgh University Press, 2014).

Hammond, Meghan Marie and Sue J. Kim (eds), *Rethinking Empathy through Literature* (London: Routledge, 2014).

Hamon, Philippe, *Le Personnel du roman: Le Système des personnages dans les Rougon-Macquart d'Émile Zola* (Geneva: Droz, 1998).

Harkness, Nigel, *Men of Their Words: The Poetics of Masculinity in George Sand's Fiction* (Oxford: Legenda, 2007).

Harkness, Nigel, 'Performance, représentation et (il)lisibilité du genre dans la fiction sandienne des années 1830', *Dix-Neuf*, 13.1 (2009), pp. 1–21.

Harkness, Nigel, 'Masculinity and the Performance of Authority', in David A. Powell and Pratima Prasad (eds), *Approaches to Teaching Sand's* Indiana (New York: Modern Language Association of America, 2015), pp. 119–25.

Hart, Kathleen R., 'Strangers to Ourselves: Animality and Theory of Mind in Honoré de Balzac's "A Passion in the Desert"', *Style*, 46.3–4 (2012), pp. 399–419.

Hatfield, Gary, 'The *Passions of the soul* and Descartes's Machine Psychology', *Studies in History and Philosophy of Science*, 38.1 (2007), pp. 1–35.

Hayman, David, *Re-Forming the Narrative: Towards a Mechanics of Modernist Fiction* (Ithaca: Cornell University Press, 1987).

Heathcote, Owen N., 'The Engendering of Violence and the Violation of Gender in Honoré de Balzac's *La Fille aux yeux d'or*', *Romance Studies*, 22 (1993), pp. 99–112.

Hemmings, Clare, 'Affective Solidarity: Feminist Reflexivity and Political Transformation', *Feminist Theory*, 13.2 (2012), pp. 147–61.

Hogan, Patrick Colm, 'Characters and their Plots', in Jens Eder, Fotis Jannidis and Ralf Schneider (eds), *Characters in Fictional Worlds: Understanding Imaginary Beings in Literature, Film, and Other Media* (Berlin: De Gruyter, 2010), pp. 134–54.

Hogan, Patrick Colm, 'Fictions and Feelings: On the Place of Literature in the Study of Emotion', *Emotion Review*, 2.2 (2010), pp. 184–95.

Holland, Norman N., *The Dynamics of Literary Response* (New York: W. W. Norton & Company, 1975).

Hunt, Lynn, *Inventing Human Rights: A History* (New York: W. W. Norton & Company, 2007).

Iacoboni, Marco, 'Within Each Other: Neural Mechanisms for Empathy in the Primate Brain', in Peter Goldie and Amy Coplan (eds), *Empathy: Philosophical and Psychological Perspectives* (New York: Oxford University Press, 2011), pp. 45–57.

Iser, Wolfgang, *The Act of Reading: A Theory of Aesthetic Response* (London: Routledge & Kegan Paul, 1978).

Iser, Wolfgang, 'Interaction between Text and Reader', in Susan R. Suleiman and Inge Crosman (eds), *The Reader in the Text: Essays on Audience and Interpretation* (Princeton University Press, 1980), pp. 106–19.

Iser, Wolfgang, 'The Play of the Text', in Sanford Budick and Wolfgang Iser (eds), *Languages of the Unsayable: The Play of Negativity in Literature and Literary Theory* (New York: Columbia University Press, 1989), pp. 325–39.

Jaffe, Audrey, *Scenes of Sympathy: Identity and Representation in Victorian Fiction* (Ithaca: Cornell University Press, 2000).

Jauss, Hans Robert, 'Levels of Identification of Hero and Audience', *New Literary History*, 5.2 (1974), pp. 283–317.

Jefferson, Ann, *Reading Realism in Stendhal* (Cambridge: Cambridge University Press, 1988).

Jefferson, Ann, 'Stendhal (1783–1842): Romantic Irony', in Michael Bell (ed), *The Cambridge Companion to European Novelists* (Cambridge: Cambridge University Press, 2012), pp. 159–75.

Johnson, Dan R., 'Transportation into a Story Increases Empathy, Prosocial Behaviour, and Perceptual Bias toward Fearful Expressions', *Personality and Individual Differences*, 52.2 (2012), pp. 150–5.

Johnson, Dan R., 'Transportation into Literary Fiction Reduces Prejudice against, and Increases Empathy for Arab Muslims', *Scientific Study of Literature*, 3.1 (2013), pp. 77–92.

Johnson, Dan R., Grace K. Cushman, Lauren A. Borden and Madison S. McCune, 'Potentiating Empathic Growth: Generating Imagery while Reading Fiction Increases Empathy and Prosocial Behavior', *Psychology of Aesthetics, Creativity, and the Arts*, 7.3 (2013), pp. 306–12.

Johnson, Dan R., Brandie L. Huffman and Danny M. Jasper, 'Changing Race Boundary Perception by Reading Narrative Fiction', *Basic and Applied Social Psychology*, 36.1 (2014), pp. 83–90.

Joly, Henri, *Études platoniciennes: la Question des étrangers* (Paris: J. Vrin, 1992).

Jouve, Vincent, *L'Effet-personnage dans le roman* (Paris: Presses Universitaires de France, 1992).

Jouve, Vincent, 'Lecture littéraire et lecture engagée', in Isabelle Poulin and Jérôme Roger (eds), *Le Lecteur engagé: Critique – enseignement – politique*, Modernités 26 (Bordeaux: Presses Universitaires de Bordeaux, 2007), pp. 221–8.

Jouve, Vincent (ed.), *La Valeur littéraire en question* (Paris: Éditions L'improviste, 2010).

Jouve, Vincent, *Poétique du roman* (Paris: Armand Colin, 2014).

Jurecic, Ann, 'Empathy and the Critic', *College English*, 74.1 (2011), pp. 10–27.

Kadish, Doris Y., 'Hybrids in Balzac's *La Fille aux yeux d'or*', *Nineteenth-Century French Studies*, 16.3–4 (1988), pp. 270–8.

Kadish, Doris, 'Reading Race in *Indiana*', in David A. Powell and Pratima Prasad (eds), *Approaches to Teaching Sand's* Indiana (New York: Modern Language Association of America, 2015), pp. 68–75.

Kaufman, Geoff F. and Lisa K. Libby, 'Changing Beliefs and Behavior through Experience-Taking', *Journal of Personality and Social Psychology*, 103 (2012), pp. 1–19.

Kearney, Richard, 'What is Carnal Hermeneutics?', *New Literary History*, 46.1 (2015), pp. 99–122.

Kearney, Richard and Kascha Semonovitch, 'At the Threshold: Foreigners, Strangers, Others', in Richard Kearney and Kascha Semonovitch (eds), *Phenomenologies of the Stranger* (New York: Fordham University Press, 2011), pp. 3–29.

Keen, Suzanne, 'A Theory of Narrative Empathy', *Narrative*, 14.3 (2006), pp. 207–36.

Keen, Suzanne, *Empathy and the Novel* (New York: Oxford University Press, 2007).

Keen, Suzanne, 'Narrative Empathy', in Peter Hühn et al. (eds), *The Living Handbook of Narratology* (Hamburg: Hamburg University Press, 2011).

Keen, Suzanne, 'Readers' Temperaments and Fictional Character', *New Literary History*, 42 (2011), pp. 295–314.

Keen, Suzanne, 'Novel Readers and the Empathetic Angel of Our Nature', in Meghan Marie Hammond and Sue J. Kim (eds), *Rethinking Empathy through Literature* (London: Routledge, 2014), pp. 21–33.

Kidd, David Comer and Emanuele Castano, 'Reading Literary Fiction Improves Theory of Mind', *Science*, 342.6156 (2013), pp. 377–80.

Kidd, David Comer and Emanuele Castano, 'Different Stories: How Levels of Familiarity With Literary and Genre Fiction Relate to Mentalizing', *Psychology of Aesthetics, Creativity, and the Arts*, 11.4 (2017), pp. 474–86.

Kidd, David Comer and Emanuele Castano, 'Panero et al. (2016): Failure to Replicate Methods Caused the Failure to Replicate Results', *Journal of Personality and Social Psychology*, 112.3 (2017), e1–e4.

Kidd, David, Martino Ongis and Emanuele Castano, 'On Literary Fiction and its Effects on Theory of Mind', *Scientific Study of Literature*, 6 (2016), pp. 42–58.

Koopman, Eva Maria, 'Empathic Reactions after Reading: The Role of Genre, Personal Factors and Affective Responses', *Poetics*, 50 (2015), pp. 62–79.

Koopman, Eva Maria, 'How Texts about Suffering Trigger Reflection: Genre, Personal Factors, and Affective Responses', *Psychology of Aesthetics, Creativity, and the Arts*, 9.4 (2015), pp. 430–1.

Koopman, Eva Maria, 'Effects of "Literariness" on Emotions and on Empathy and Reflection after Reading', *Psychology of Aesthetics, Creativity, and the Arts*, 10.1 (2016), pp. 82–98.

Koopman, Eva Maria, 'Does Originality Evoke Understanding? The Relation between Literary Reading and Empathy', *Review of General Psychology*, 22.2 (2018), pp. 169–77.

Koopman, Eva Maria and Frank Hakemulder, 'Effects of Literature on Empathy and Self-Reflection: A Theoretical-Empirical Framework', *Journal of Literary Theory*, 9.1 (2015), pp. 79–111.

Korthals Altes, Liesbeth, *Ethos and Narrative Interpretation: The Negotiation of Values in Fiction* (Lincoln: University of Nebraska Press, 2014).

Kristeva, Julia, *La Révolution du langage poétique* (Paris: Seuil, 1974).

Kristeva, Julia, *Histoires d'amour* (Paris: Denoël, 1983).

Kristeva, Julia, *Étrangers à nous-mêmes* (Paris: Gallimard, 1988).

Kuiken, Don, David S. Miall and Shelley Sikora, 'Forms of Self-Implication in Literary Reading', *Poetics Today*, 25.2 (2004), pp. 171–203.

Kuiken, Don, Leah Phillips, Michelle Gregus, David S. Miall, Mark Verbitsky and Anna Tonkonogy, 'Locating Self-Modifying Feelings within Literary Reading', *Discourse Processes*, 38.2 (2004), pp. 267–86.

Kulbaga, Theresa A., 'Pleasurable Pedagogies: Reading *Lolita* in Tehran and the Rhetoric of Empathy', *College English*, 70.5 (2008), pp. 506–21.

Lacan, Jacques, *Le Séminaire: Livre XI: Les Quatre Concepts fondamentaux de la psychanalyse* (Paris: Seuil, 1973).

Lacan, Jacques, *Le Séminaire: Livre II (1954–1955): Le Moi dans la théorie de Freud et dans la technique de la psychanalyse* (Paris: Seuil, 1978).

Lacan, Jacques, *Le Séminaire: Livre VII: L'Éthique de la psychanalyse* (Paris: Seuil, 1986).

LaCapra, Dominick, *Writing History, Writing Trauma* (Baltimore: Johns Hopkins University Press, 2001).

Lang, Luc, *Délit de fiction. La Littérature, pourquoi?* (Paris: Gallimard, 2011).

Lanzoni, Susan, *Empathy: A History* (New Haven, CT: Yale University Press, 2018).

Leverage, Paula, Howard Mancing and Richard Schweickert (eds), *Theory of Mind and Literature* (West Lafayette: Purdue University Press, 2011).

Levinas, Emmanuel, *Totality and Infinity: An Essay on Exteriority*, trans. Alphonso Lingis (Pittsburgh: Duquesne University Press, 1969).

Liu, Buyun, Guifeng Xu, Zhelan Huang and Yu Jin, 'Altruistic Sharing Behavior in Children: Role of Theory of Mind and Inhibitory Control', *Journal of Experimental Child Psychology*, 141 (2016), pp. 222–8.

Lombardo, Patrizia, 'De fête en fête: le Bonheur de la critique', *Critique*, 5.672 (2003), pp. 360–70.

Lombardo, Patrizia, 'L'Esthétique de la tendresse chez Stendhal', *Cahiers de l'Association internationale des études francaises*, 62.1 (2010), pp. 173–88.

Lombardo, Patrizia, 'Empathie et simulation', in Alexandre Gefen and Bernard Vouilloux (eds), *Empathie et esthétique* (Paris: Hermann, 2013), pp. 15–33.

Lowe, Brigid, *Victorian Fiction and the Insights of Sympathy: An Alternative to the Hermeneutics of Suspicion* (London: Anthem Press, 2007).

Macé, Marielle, 'Ways of Reading, Modes of Being', *New Literary History*, 44.2 (2013), pp. 213–29.

Machelidon, Véronique, 'Teaching Race, Class, and Slavery in *Indiana*', in David A. Powell and Pratima Prasad (eds), *Approaches to Teaching Sand's Indiana* (New York: Modern Language Association of America, 2015), pp. 67–74.

Majewski, Henry F., 'Painting as Intertext in Balzac's *La Fille aux yeux d'or*', *Symposium*, 45.1 (1991), pp. 370–84.

Malkin, Shira, 'Performing Sand's Pedagogical Project in *Indiana*', in David A. Powell and Pratima Prasad (eds), *Approaches to Teaching Sand's Indiana* (New York: Modern Language Association of America, 2015), pp. 174–81.

Mangen, Anne, Anne Charlotte Begnum, Anežka Kuzmičová, Kersti Nilsson, Mette Steenberg and Hildegunn Støle, 'Empathy and Literary Style: A Theoretical and Methodological Exploration', *Orbis Litterarum*, 73.6 (2018), pp. 471–86.

Manzini, Francesco, 'Reading Julien Sorel in the Age of Terror', *Dix-Neuf*, 19.1 (2015), pp. 49–66.

Mar, Raymond A., 'The Neural Bases of Social Cognition and Story Comprehension', *Annual Review of Psychology*, 62 (2011), pp. 103–34.

Mar, Raymond A., Jacob B. Hirsh, Keith Oatley and Jennifer dela Paz, 'Bookworms Versus Nerds: Exposure to Fiction Versus Non-Fiction, Divergent Associations with Social Ability, and the Simulation of Fictional Social Worlds', *Journal of Research in Personality*, 40.5 (2006), pp. 694–712.

Mar, Raymond A. and Keith Oatley, 'The Function of Fiction is the Abstraction and Simulation of Social Experience', *Perspectives on Psychological Science*, 3.3 (2008), pp. 173–92.

Mar, Raymond, Keith Oatley and Jordan B. Peterson, 'Exploring the Link between Reading Fiction and Empathy: Ruling out Individual Differences and Examining Outcomes', *Communications*, 34 (2009), pp. 407–28.

Mar, Raymond A., Jennifer L. Tackett and Chris Moore, 'Exposure to Media and Theory-of-Mind Development in Preschoolers', *Cognitive Development*, 25 (2010), pp. 69–78.

Marshall, David, *The Surprising Effects of Sympathy: Marivaux, Diderot, Rousseau, and Mary Shelley* (Chicago: University of Chicago Press, 1988).

Martin, Kirsty, *Modernism and the Rhythms of Sympathy: Vernon Lee, Virginia Woolf, and D. H. Lawrence* (Oxford: Oxford University Press, 2013).

Mathias, Manon, *Vision in the Novels of George Sand* (Oxford and New York: Oxford University Press, 2016).

McFee, Graham, 'Empathy: Interpersonal vs Artistic?' in Peter Goldie and Amy Coplan (eds), *Empathy: Philosophical and Psychological Perspectives* (New York: Oxford University Press, 2011), pp. 185–208.

McLellan, Faith and Anne Hudson Jones, 'Why Literature and Medicine?', *The Lancet*, 348.9020 (1996), pp. 109–11.

McWeeny, Gage, *The Comfort of Strangers: Social Life and Literary Form* (New York: Oxford University Press, 2016).

Mellmann, Katja, 'Objects of "Empathy": Characters (and Other Such Things) as Psycho-Poetic Effects', in Jens Eder, Fotis Jannidis and Ralf Schneider (eds), *Characters in Fictional Worlds: Understanding Imaginary Beings in Literature, Film, and Other Media* (Berlin: De Gruyter, 2010), pp. 416–41.

Miall, David S. and Don Kuiken, 'Beyond Text Theory: Understanding Literary Response', *Discourse Processes*, 17.3 (1994), pp. 337–52.

Miall, David S. and Don Kuiken, 'Foregrounding, Defamiliarization, and Affect: Response to Literary Stories', *Poetics*, 22.5 (1994), pp. 389–407.

Miall, David S. and Don Kuiken, 'A Feeling for Fiction: Becoming What We Behold', *Poetics*, 30.4 (2002), pp. 221–41.

Mitchell, Rebecca N., *Victorian Lessons in Empathy and Difference* (Columbus: Ohio State University Press, 2011).

Modiano, Patrick, Nobel Lecture, 7 December 2014 <https://www.nobelprize.org/nobel_prizes/literature/laureates/2014/modiano-lecture_en.html> (last accessed 19 October 2019).

Modleski, Tania, *Loving with a Vengeance: Mass-Produced Fantasies for Women*, 2nd edn (London: Routledge, 2008).

Moi, Toril, 'The Adventure of Reading: Literature and Philosophy, Cavell and Beauvoir', *Literature and Theology*, 25.2 (2011), pp. 125–40.

Mozet, Nicole, 'Les Prolétaires dans *La Fille aux yeux d'or*', *L'Année balzacienne* (1974), pp. 91–119.

Mumper, Micah L. and Richard J. Gerrig, 'Leisure Reading and Social Cognition', *Psychology of Aesthetics, Creativity, and the Arts*, 11.1 (2017), pp. 109–20.

Murdoch, Iris, *Existentialists and Mystics: Writings on Philosophy and Literature* (London: Chatto & Windus, 1997).

Nathanson, Amy I., 'Rethinking Empathy', in Jennings Bryant, David Roskos-Ewoldsen and Joanne Cantor (eds), *Communication and Emotion – Essays in Honor of Dolf Zillmann* (New York: Routledge, 2003), pp. 107–30.

Nell, Victor, *Lost in a Book: The Psychology of Reading for Pleasure* (New Haven, CT: Yale University Press, 1988).

Nowak, Magdalena, 'The Complicated History of *Einfühlung*', *Argument*, 1.2 (2011), pp. 301–26.

Nussbaum, Martha C., *Love's Knowledge: Essays on Philosophy and Literature* (New York: Oxford University Press, 1990).

Nussbaum, Martha C., *Upheavals of Thought: The Intelligence of Emotions* (Cambridge: Cambridge University Press, 2003).

Nussbaum, Martha C., *Not for Profit: Why Democracy Needs the Humanities* (Princeton: Princeton University Press, 2010).

Oatley, Keith, 'Emotions and the Story Worlds of Fiction', in Melanie C. Green, Jeffrey J. Strange and Timothy C. Brock (eds), *Narrative Impact: Social and Cognitive Foundations* (Mahwah, NJ: Lawrence Erlbaum, 2002), pp. 39–70.

Oatley, Keith and Maja Djikic, 'How Reading Transforms Us', *New York Times*, 19 December 2014, <https://www.nytimes.com/2014/12/21/opinion/sunday/how-writing-transforms-us.html> (last accessed 19 October 2019).

Oatley, Keith and Maja Djikic, 'Psychology of Narrative Art', *Review of General Psychology*, 22.2 (2018), pp. 161–8.

Oatley, Keith and Mitra Gholamain, 'Emotions and Identification: Connections between Readers and Fiction', in Mette Hjort and Sue Laver (eds), *Emotion and the Arts* (Oxford and New York: Oxford University Press, 1997), pp. 263–81.

Palmer, Alan, *Fictional Minds* (Lincoln: University of Nebraska Press, 2004).

Palmer, Alan, *Social Minds in the Novel* (Columbus: Ohio State University Press, 2010).

Panero, Maria Eugenia, Jessica Black, Deena Skolnick Weisberg and Thalia R. Goldstein, 'Does Reading a Single Passage of Literary Fiction Really Improve Theory of Mind? An Attempt at Replication', *Journal of Personality and Social Psychology*, 111.5 (2016), e46–e54.

Panero, Maria Eugenia, Jessica Black, Jennifer L. Barnes, Deena Skolnick Weisberg, Thalia R. Goldstein, Hiram Brownell and Ellen Winner, 'No Support for the Claim that Literary Fiction Uniquely and Immediately Improves Theory of Mind: A Reply to Kidd and Castano's Commentary on Panero et al. (2016)', *Journal of Personality and Social Psychology*, 112.3 (2017), e5–e8.

Pappas, Sara, 'Opening the Door: Reinterpreting Interior Space and Transpositions of Art in *La Fille aux yeux d'or* via Assia Djebar', *Symposium*, 64.3 (2010), pp. 169–86.

Paraschas, Sotirios, *The Realist Author and Sympathetic Imagination* (London: Routledge, 2013).

Pearson, Roger, *Stendhal's Violin: A Novelist and his Reader* (Oxford: Clarendon Press).

Pedwell, Carolyn, 'Affect at the Margins: Alternative Empathies in a Small Place', *Emotion, Space and Society*, 8 (2013), pp. 18–26.

Pedwell, Carolyn, *Affective Relations: The Transnational Politics of Empathy* (Houndmills: Palgrave, 2014).

Petrey, Sandy, 'George and Georgina Sand: Realist Gender in *Indiana*', in Judith Still and Michael Worton (eds), *Textuality and Sexuality: Reading*

Theories and Practices (Manchester: Manchester University Press, 1993), pp. 133–47.

Petrey, Sandy, *In the Court of the Pear King* (Ithaca: Cornell University Press, 2005).

Phillips, Adam and Barbara Taylor, *On Kindness* (London: Penguin, 2009).

Picard, Michel, *Nodier, la Fée aux miettes: Loup y es-tu?* (Paris: Presses Universitaires de France, 1992).

Pinker, Steven, *The Better Angels of Our Nature: The Decline of Violence in History and its Causes* (London: Penguin, 2011).

Pino, Maria Chiara and Monica Mazza, 'The Use of "Literary Fiction" to Promote Mentalizing Ability', *PLoS One*, 11 (2016), e0160254.

Pinzka, Lauren, 'Teaching Historical Myth and Memory in *Indiana*', in David A. Powell and Pratima Prasad (eds), *Approaches to Teaching Sand's Indiana* (New York: Modern Language Association of America, 2015), pp. 25–32.

Plantinga, Carl, 'Facing Others: Close-ups of Faces in Narrative Film and in *The Silence of the Lambs*', in Lisa Zunshine (ed.), *The Oxford Handbook of Cognitive Literary Studies* (New York: Oxford University Press, 2015), pp. 291–312.

Poulet, Georges, 'Phenomenology of Reading', *New Literary History*, 1.1 (1969), pp. 53–68.

Poulet, Georges and Jean Ricardou (eds), *Les Chemins actuels de la critique* (Paris: Plon, 1967).

Prasad, Pratima, 'Contesting Realism: Mimesis and Performance in George Sand's Novels', *Dix-Neuf*, 3.1 (2004), pp. 34–54.

Prasad, Pratima, 'Intimate Strangers: Interracial Encounters in Romantic Narratives of Slavery', *Esprit Créateur*, 47.4 (2007), pp. 1–15.

Prendergast, Christopher, *Balzac: Fiction and Melodrama* (London: Edward Arnold, 1978).

Prinz, Jesse J., 'Is Empathy Necessary for Morality?', in Peter Goldie and Amy Coplan (eds), *Empathy: Philosophical and Psychological Perspectives* (New York: Oxford University Press, 2011), pp. 211–29.

Proust, Marcel, *À la recherche du temps perdu*, vol. 1 (*Du côté de chez Swann*) (Paris: Nrf Gallimard, 1919).

Proust, Marcel, *À la recherche du temps perdu*, vol. 15 (*Le Temps retrouvé*) (Paris: Nrf Gallimard, 1927).

Proust, Marcel, *Contre Sainte-Beuve* (Paris: Gallimard, 1954).

Rabaté, Dominique, 'Identification du lecteur', in Isabelle Poulin and Jérôme Roger (eds), *Le Lecteur engagé: Critique – enseignement – politique*, Modernités 26 (Bordeaux: Presses Universitaires de Bordeaux, 2007), pp. 229–37.

Rabaté, Dominique, 'Comprendre le pire: Réflexions sur les limites de l'empathie', in Alexandre Gefen and Bernard Vouilloux (eds), *Empathie et esthétique* (Paris: Hermann, 2013), pp. 267–78.

Rabinowitz, Peter J., *Before Reading: Narrative Conventions and the Politics of Interpretation* (Ithaca: Cornell University Press, 1987).

Radford, Colin, 'How Can We Be Moved by the Fate of Anna Karenina?', *Proceedings of the Aristotelian Society*, Supplementary Volumes, 49 (1975), pp. 67–80.

Radway, Janice A., *Reading the Romance* (Chapel Hill: University of North Carolina Press, 1989).

Ratcliffe, Sophie, *On Sympathy* (New York: Oxford University Press, 2008).

Richell, R. A., D. G. Mitchell, C. Newman, A. Leonard, S. Baron-Cohen and R. J. Blair, 'Theory of Mind and Psychopathy: Can Psychopathic Individuals Read the "Language of the Eyes"?', *Neuropsychologia*, 41.5 (2003), pp. 523–6.

Rifelj, Carol de Dobay, *Reading the Other: Novels and the Problem of Other Minds* (Ann Arbor: University of Michigan Press, 1992).

Robinson, Jenefer, 'The Art of Distancing: How Formal Devices Manage Our Emotional Responses to Literature', *Journal of Aesthetics and Art Criticism*, 62.2 (2004), pp. 153–62.

Robinson, Jenefer, *Deeper Than Reason: Emotion and Its Role in Literature, Music, and Art* (Oxford: Clarendon Press, 2005).

Robson, Kathryn, 'The Limits of Empathy and Compassion in Delphine de Vigan's *No et moi* and *Les Heures souterraines*', *Modern Language Review*, 110.3 (2015), pp. 677–93.

Robson, Kathryn, *I Suffer, Therefore I Am: Engaging with Empathy in Contemporary French Women's Writing* (Cambridge: Legenda, 2019).

Romanowski, Sylvie, *Through Strangers' Eyes: Fictional Foreigners in Old Regime France* (West Lafayette: Purdue University Press, 2005).

Rorty, Richard, *Contingency, Irony, and Solidarity* (Cambridge: Cambridge University Press, 1989, repr. 1993).

Rousseau, Jean-Jacques, *Émile ou de l'Éducation*, in *Œuvres complètes de J. J. Rousseau*, vol. 2 (Paris: Chez Furne, 1835).

Rousseau, Jean-Jacques, *Discours sur l'origine et les fondements de l'inégalité* (Paris: Gallimard, 1969).

Rye, Gill, *Reading for Change: Interactions between Text and Identity in Contemporary French Women's Writing (Baroche, Cixous, Constant)* (Oxford: Peter Lang, 2001).

Rylance, Rick, *Literature and the Public Good* (New York: Oxford University Press, 2016).

Sand, George, *Indiana* (Paris: Gallimard, 1984).

Sanyal, Debarati, *The Violence of Modernity: Baudelaire, Irony, and the Politics of Form* (Baltimore: Johns Hopkins University Press, 2006).

Sarraute, Nathalie, *L'Ère du soupçon* (Paris: Gallimard, 1956).

Sartre, Jean-Paul, *L'Etre et le néant: Essai d'ontologie phénoménologique* (Paris: Gallimard, 1943).

Schaeffer, Jean-Marie, *Pourquoi la fiction?* (Paris: Seuil, 1999).

Schor, Naomi, 'Fiction as Interpretation/Interpretation as Fiction', in Susan R. Suleiman and Inge Crosman (eds), *The Reader in the Text: Essays on Audience and Interpretation* (Princeton: Princeton University Press, 1980), pp. 165–82.

Schor, Naomi, *George Sand and Idealism* (New York: Columbia University Press, 1993).

Schor, Naomi, 'Introduction to George Sand', in *Indiana*, trans. Sylvia Raphael (Oxford and New York: Oxford University Press, 2008), pp. vii–xxii.

Scott, Maria C., '*Le Rouge et le Noir* et la partialité de la perception', in Xavier

Bourdenet (ed.), *Lectures du 'Rouge et le Noir'* (Rennes: Presses Universitaires de Rennes, 2013), pp. 237–48.

Scott, Maria C., *Stendhal's Less-Loved Heroines: Fiction, Freedom, and the Female* (Oxford: Legenda, 2013).

Sestir, Marc and Melanie C. Green, 'You Are Who You Watch: Identification and Transportation Effects on Temporary Self-Concept', *Social Influence*, 5.4 (2010), pp. 272–88.

Shamay-Tsoory, Simone G., Judith Aharon-Peretz and Daniella Perry, 'Two Systems for Empathy: A Double Dissociation between Emotional and Cognitive Empathy in Inferior Frontal Gyrus Versus Ventromedial Prefrontal Lesions', *Brain*, 132.3 (2009), pp. 617–27.

Shank, Nathan, 'Irony as Cognitive Empathy: Mind-Reading *Tom Jones*'s Narrator', in Meghan Marie Hammond and Sue J. Kim (eds), *Rethinking Empathy through Literature* (London: Routledge, 2014), pp. 202–12.

Sharpley-Whiting, Denean T., '"The Other Woman": Reading a Body of Differences in Balzac's *La Fille aux yeux d'or*', *Symposium*, 51.1 (1997), pp. 43–50.

Shaw, Harry, *Narrating Reality: Austen, Scott, Eliot* (Ithaca: Cornell University Press, 1999).

Siegel, Lee, 'Should Literature Be Useful?', *The New Yorker*, 6 November 2013, <https://www.newyorker.com/books/page-turner/should-literature-be-useful> (last accessed 19 October 2019).

Simmel, Géorg, 'The Stranger' (1908), in *On Individuality and Social Forms: Selected Writings*, ed. and intro. Donald N. Levine (Chicago: University of Chicago Press, 1971), pp. 143–9.

Sklar, Howard, *The Art of Sympathy in Fiction: Forms of Ethical and Emotional Persuasion* (Amsterdam: John Benjamins Publishing, 2013).

Smith, Adam, *The Theory of Moral Sentiments*, 2nd edn (London: A. Millar, 1761).

Smith, Murray, *Engaging Characters: Fiction, Emotion, and the Cinema* (New York: Oxford University Press, 1995, repr. 2004).

Smith, Murray, '*Engaging Characters*: Further Reflections', in Jens Eder, Fotis Jannidis and Ralf Schneider (eds), *Characters in Fictional Worlds: Understanding Imaginary Beings in Literature, Film, and Other Media* (Berlin: De Gruyter, 2010), pp. 232–58.

Smith, Murray, 'Empathy, Expansionism, and the Extended Mind', in Peter Goldie and Amy Coplan (eds), *Empathy: Philosophical and Psychological Perspectives* (New York: Oxford University Press, 2011), pp. 99–117.

Soelberg, Nils, 'La Narration de *La Fille aux yeux d'or*: Une omniscience encombrante', *Revue Romane*, 25.2 (1990), pp. 454–65.

Speer, Nicole K., Jeremy R. Reynolds, Khena M. Swallow and Jeffrey M. Zacks, 'Reading Stories Activates Neural Representations of Visual and Motor Experiences', *Psychological Science*, 20.8 (2009), pp. 989–99.

Spivak, Gayatri Chakravorty, 'Ethics and Politics in Tagore, Coetzee, and Certain Scenes of Teaching', *Diacritics*, 32.3–4 (2002), pp. 17–31.

Spivak, Gayatri Chakravorty, *An Aesthetic Education in the Era of Globalization* (Cambridge, MA: Harvard University Press, 2012).

Stamelman, Richard, 'The Strangeness of the Other and the Otherness of the Stranger: Edmond Jabès', *Yale French Studies*, 82.1 (1993), pp. 118–34.

Stansfield, John and Louise Bunce, 'The Relationship Between Empathy and Reading Fiction: Separate Roles for Cognitive and Affective Components', *Journal of European Psychology Students*, 5.3 (2014), pp. 9–18.

Stein, Edith, *On the Problem of Empathy*, trans. Waltraut Stein (The Hague: Martinus Nijhoff, 1964).

Stendhal, *Racine et Shakspeare* (Paris: Michel Lévy, 1854).

Stendhal, *Chroniques italiennes* (Paris: Michel Lévy frères, 1855).

Stendhal, *Promenades dans Rome*, 2 vols (Paris: Michel Lévy frères, 1858).

Stendhal, *Molière, Shakspeare, la comédie et le rire* (Paris: Le Divan, 1930).

Stendhal, *Correspondance*, ed. Victor Del Litto and Henri Martineau, 3 vols (Paris: Gallimard, Pléiade, 1962–8).

Stendhal, *Œuvres intimes*, ed. Victor Del Litto, 2 vols (Paris: Gallimard, Pléiade, 1981–2).

Stendhal, *Histoire de la peinture* (Paris: Gallimard, 1996).

Stendhal, *Le Rouge et le Noir: Chronique de 1830* (Paris: Librairie Générale Française, 1997).

Stendhal, *Œuvres romanesques complètes*, 3 vols, ed. Yves Ansel and others (Paris: Gallimard, 2005–14).

Stendhal, *Journaux et papiers: Volume I: 1797–1804*, ed. Cécile Meynard, Hélène de Jacquelot and Marie-Rose Corredor (Grenoble: Editions littéraires et linguistique de l'université de Grenoble, 2013).

Stendhal, *De l'Amour* (Paris: Flammarion, 2014).

Stendhal, *Manuscrits de Stendhal* <http://stendhal.msh-alpes.fr/manuscrits/index.php> (last accessed 19 October 2019).

Sternberg, Meir, 'Telling in Time (II): Chronology, Teleology, Narrativity', *Poetics Today*, 13.3 (1992), pp. 463–541.

Sternberg, Meir, 'Omniscience in Narrative Construction: Old Challenges and New', *Poetics Today*, 28.4 (2007), pp. 683–794.

Stivale, Charles J., 'One or Several Ralphs: Multiplicity and Masculinity in *Indiana*', in David A. Powell and Pratima Prasad (eds), *Approaches to Teaching Sand's* Indiana (New York: Modern Language Association of America, 2015), pp. 111–18.

Sugden, Rebecca, 'Terre(ur): Reading the Landscape of Conspiracy in Balzac's *Une ténébreuse affaire*', *Nineteenth-Century French Studies*, 47.1–2 (2018–19), pp. 48–65.

Tamir, Diana I., Andrew B. Bricker, David Dodell-Feder and Jason P. Mitchell, 'Reading Fiction and Reading Minds: The Role of Simulation in the Default Network', *Social Cognitive and Affective Neuroscience*, 11.2 (2016), pp. 215–24.

Titchener, Edward Bradford, *A Beginner's Psychology* (New York: The Macmillan Company, 1915).

Tremblay, Victor-Laurent, 'Démasquer *La Fille aux yeux d'or*', *Nineteenth-Century French Studies*, 19.1 (1990), pp. 72–82.

Tremblay, Victor-Laurent, 'Qui es-tu, Paquita?', *Modern Language Studies*, 22.1 (1992), pp. 57–64.

van Lissa, Caspar J., Marco Caracciolo, Thom van Duuren and Bram van Leuveren, 'Difficult Empathy: The Effect of Narrative Perspective on Readers' Engagement with a First-Person Narrator', *Diegesis*, 5.1 (2016), pp. 43–63.

Vest, James M., 'Dreams and the Romance Tradition in George Sand's *Indiana*', *French Forum*, 3.1 (1978), pp. 35–47.

Vignemont, Frédérique de and Tania Singer, 'The Empathic Brain', *Trends in Cognitive Sciences*, 10.10 (2006), pp. 435–41.

Vincent, Timothy C., 'From Sympathy to Empathy: Baudelaire, Vischer, and Early Modernism', *Mosaic*, 45.1 (2012), pp. 1–15.

Waller, Margaret, 'Ending with *Indiana*: Romance, Romanticism, the Novel', in David A. Powell and Pratima Prasad (eds), *Approaches to Teaching Sand's Indiana* (New York: Modern Language Association of America, 2015), pp. 189–95.

Warner, Marina, *Stranger Magic: Charmed States and the Arabian Nights* (Cambridge, MA: Harvard University Press, 2011).

Whitehead, Anne, 'Reading with Empathy: Sindiwe Mogana's *Mother to Mother*', *Feminist Theory*, 13.2 (2012), pp. 181–95.

Wilson, Emma, *Sexuality and the Reading Encounter: Identity and Desire in Proust, Duras, Tournier, and Cixous* (Oxford: Clarendon Press, 1996).

Wimmer, Heinz and Josef Perner, 'Beliefs about Beliefs: Representation and Constraining Function of Wrong Beliefs in Young Children's Understanding of Deception', *Cognition*, 13.1 (1983), pp. 103–28.

Wimsatt, William Kurtz and Monroe C. Beardsley, 'The Affective Fallacy', *The Sewanee Review*, 57.1 (1949), pp. 31–55.

Wing, Nathaniel, *Between Genders: Narrating Difference in Early French Modernism* (London: Associated University Presses, 2004).

Wispé, Lauren, 'History of the Concept of Empathy', in Nancy Eisenberg and Janet Strayer (eds), *Empathy and its Development* (Cambridge: Cambridge University Press), pp. 17–37.

Wood, Margaret Mary, *The Stranger: A Study in Social Relationships* (New York: Columbia University Press, 1934).

Yanal, Robert J., *Paradoxes of Emotion and Fiction* (University Park: Pennsylvania State University Press, 1999).

Zahavi, Dan, 'Empathy, Embodiment and Interpersonal Understanding: From Lipps to Schutz', *Inquiry*, 53.3 (2010), pp. 285–306.

Zahavi, Dan, *Self and Other: Exploring Subjectivity, Empathy, and Shame* (New York: Oxford University Press, 2014).

Zaki, Jamil and Daniel Ochsner, 'The Neuroscience of Empathy: Progress, Pitfalls, and Promise', *Nature Neuroscience*, 15.5 (2012), pp. 675–9.

Zunshine, Lisa, 'Theory of Mind and Experimental Representations of Fictional Consciousness', *Narrative*, 11.3 (2003), pp. 270–91.

Zunshine, Lisa, *Why We Read Fiction: Theory of Mind and the Novel* (Columbus: Ohio State University Press, 2006).

Zunshine, Lisa, *Strange Concepts and the Stories They Make Possible* (Baltimore: Johns Hopkins University Press, 2008).

Zunshine, Lisa, 'Theory of Mind and Fictions of Embodied Transparency', *Narrative*, 16.1 (2008), pp. 65–92.

Zunshine, Lisa, 'From the Social to the Literary: Approaching Cao Xueqin's *The Story of the Stone* from a Cognitive Perspective', in Lisa Zunshine (ed.), *The Oxford Handbook of Cognitive Literary Studies* (New York: Oxford University Press, 2015), pp. 176–96.

Zunshine, Lisa, 'The Secret Life of Fiction', *PMLA*, 130.3 (2015), pp. 724–31.
Zunshine, Lisa, 'The Commotion of Souls', *SubStance*, 45.2 (2016), pp. 118–42.
Zunshine, Lisa, 'What Mary Poppins Knew: Theory of Mind, Children's Literature, History', *Narrative*, 27.1 (2019), pp. 1–29.

Index

CPSIA information can be obtained
at www.ICGtesting.com
Printed in the USA
BVHW041103180620
581805BV00010B/97